25-Jun 93

TW - 548 - 4425

N N
2

MAC ARTHUR'S HEALTH = P 37)

# REFIGHTING
# THE LAST WAR

# REFIGHTING THE LAST WAR

## Command and Crisis in Korea
## 1950–1953

## D. Clayton James

### With Anne Sharp Wells

**THE FREE PRESS**
*A Division of Macmillan, Inc.*
NEW YORK

Maxwell Macmillan Canada
TORONTO

Maxwell Macmillan International
NEW YORK   OXFORD   SINGAPORE   SYDNEY

THE FREE PRESS
*A Division of Macmillan, Inc.*
866 Third Avenue, New York, N. Y. 10022

Maxwell Macmillan Canada, Inc.
1200 Eglinton Avenue East
Suite 200
Don Mills, Ontario M3C 3N1

Macmillan, Inc. is part of the
Maxwell Communication Group of Companies.

*Printed in the United States of America*

printing number
1  2  3  4  5  6  7  8  9  10

We thank the copyright-holders of the following sources for permission
to include quotations from their work within this volume.

Excerpts in Chapter 4 from *The Sea War in Korea* by Malcolm W. Cagle
and Frank A. Manson. Copyright © 1957, U.S. Naval Institute,
Annapolis, Maryland.

Excerpts in Chapter 5 from *From the Danube to the Yalu* by Mark W. Clark.
Copyright 1955 by Mark W. Clark. Reprinted by permission of HarperCollins
Publishers.

**Library of Congress Cataloging-in-Publication Data**

James, D. Clayton.
Refighting the last war: command and crisis in Korea, 1950–1953/
D. Clayton James, with Anne Sharp Wells.
p.  cm.
Includes index.
ISBN 0–02–916001–4
1. Korean War, 1950–1953—Campaigns.  2. Military art and science—
Decision making.  3. Korean War, 1950–1953—United States.
I. Wells, Anne Sharp.  II. Title.
DS918.J36  1993
951.904′2—dc20                    92–26986
CIP

To ERLENE

*An Invaluable Partner in This and All Ventures*

# Contents

# Abbreviations

| | |
|---|---|
| CBI | China-Burma-India Theater |
| CIA | Central Intelligence Agency |
| CCF | Chinese Communist Forces |
| CCS | Combined Chiefs of Staff |
| CINCFE | Commander in chief, Far East Command |
| CINCUNC | Commander in chief, United Nations Command |
| CINCPAC | Commander in chief, Pacific |
| CO | Commanding officer |
| EUSAK | Eighth United States Army, Korea |
| FDR | President Franklin D. Roosevelt |
| FEAF | Far East Air Forces |
| FECOM (FEC) | Far East Command |
| FRUS | Foreign Relations of the United States |
| G-1 | Personnel and administration section (or chief) |
| G-2 | Intelligence section (or chief) |
| G-3 | Operations and training section (or chief) |
| G-4 | Supply section (or chief) |
| G-5 | Military government and civil affairs section (or chief) |
| GHQ | General headquarters |
| JCS | Joint Chiefs of Staff |
| JSPOG | Joint Strategic Plans and Operations Group |
| KATUSA | Koreans Attached to United States Army (later Korean Augmentation to the United States Army) |
| LST | Landing ship, tank |
| NATO | North Atlantic Treaty Organization |
| NAVFE | United States Naval Forces, Far East |

| | |
|---|---|
| NSC | National Security Council |
| RCT | Regimental combat team |
| RG | Record group |
| ROK | Republic of Korea [South] |
| SAC | Strategic Air Command |
| SCAP | Supreme Commander for the Allied Powers, Japan |
| SHAPE | Supreme Headquarters, Allied Powers in Europe |
| UNC | United Nations Command |
| UNSC | United Nations Security Council |

# Preface

This is an introduction to the five principal high-level American commanders of the Korean War and to the six most crucial command decisions of that conflict that were primarily United States responsibilities. The choices were based on the author's research and reflections of many years on the high command of this strange war of 1950–1953. The commanders herein are limited to the commander in chief, the three theater commanders, and the officer who doubled as head of naval forces and of the armistice delegation. The command decisions are restricted to the ones that the author considers to be the key turning points in the military, not diplomatic, developments of the conflict.

The term "command decisions," interestingly, is not defined in the *Dictionary of Military and Associated Terms* of the Department of Defense (Joint Chiefs of Staff Publication no. 1, 1974). Thus, a stipulated definition will have to serve in lieu of a standard one: a decision, usually in the form of an order, by a commander to bring about a particular operation or series of related actions by military forces. In this book, the stipulated usage is further limited to decisions at the level of high command and usually involving large-scale operations. As stated, however, above these in the hierarchy of such decision-making were the shapers of policy, who, especially in the cases of the wars in Korea and Vietnam, included civilians without command authority but whose actions mightily affected military affairs, for better or worse.

Three characteristics of the Korean War will be stressed: First, the focus is on high command, but since command decisions evolved from policy formulations, the impact of the Department of State, especially of Dean G. Acheson and the Policy Planning Staff, has to be considered. Quite unlike the Second World War, Acheson and his lieutenants heavily influenced military policy, military strategy, and even their operational implementation by the armed forces.

Second, like most previous wars, the conflict of 1950–1953 was influenced by the previous major hostilities in which the United States was engaged. The Korean struggle had two distinct military phases, the first of which was the war against North Korea alone, June–October 1950, which tended toward becoming by that autumn a refighting of the Second World War, wherein American forces went for such extreme objectives as annihilation of the enemy army, total war, decisive victory, and unconditional capitulation.

Third, with the war's next phase, the entry of the Communist Chinese, however, the American military and civilian officials who assumed the chief responsibility of the United Nations', really the U.S.-dominated coalition's, strategy and operations in Korea changed to an endeavor to coordinate military and diplomatic efforts toward achieving their aims while also terminating the hostilities. Gradually there developed in both camps of belligerents unspoken and unwritten agreements, usually for wholly different reasons, to place significant restraints on their own conduct of ground, sea, and air operations.

Thus emerged the first limited war between the Cold War powers, both directly and by proxy. It was complicated by its dual nature in also being a civil war that mixed nationalism and communism in ways largely incomprehensible to either side. Yet somehow the remarkable understanding on self-imposed limits held long enough to achieve an armistice, which, however tenuous, kept the Korean peninsula and, indeed, the world from suffering the massive destruction that a refighting of the Second World War portended. The commanders and the tactics, as well as many of the troops and weapons, were largely from the global war of 1941–1945, but thanks mainly to some wise men on both sides who formulated the silent, implicit agreement on limits, the legacy of World War II was abandoned as the world was led uncertainly into a new era of limited and unconventional warfare.

Acknowledgment is extended with deep gratitude for the assistance given by the staffs of the following repositories: the MacArthur Memorial, Norfolk, Virginia; the George C. Marshall Research Library, Lexington, Virginia; the Seeley G. Mudd Library, Princeton University, Princeton, New Jersey; the Mitchell Memorial Library, Mississippi State University, Mississippi State, Mississippi; the Harry S. Truman Library, Independence, Missouri; the Dwight D. Eisenhower Library, Abilene, Kansas; the Herbert C. Hoover Presidential Library, West Ames, Iowa; the U.S. Army Military History Institute, Carlisle Barracks, Pennsylvania; the Air Force Historical Research Center, Maxwell Air Force Base, Alabama; the Office of Air Force History, Washington, D.C.; the Naval Historical Center, Washington, D.C.; the Marine Corps Historical Center, Washington, D.C.; and the National Archives, Washington, D.C. Most helpful in obtaining photographs were the George C. Marshall Research Library, the MacArthur Memorial, and the National Archives. Picture credits all are U.S. Army or U.S. Army Signal Corps. The Administration, Foundation, and Department of History and Politics of the Virginia Military Institute have been most helpful in the logistical assistance they have given.

Ms. Anne Sharp Wells has been indispensable in every step of the making of this book, ranging from basic research to final revisions. My wife, Erlene, has contributed generously and significantly to the project in proofreading, reorganizing, and other helpful ways. I am also appreciative of the strong support and sound counsel provided by Joyce Seltzer, my editor.

*Virginia Military Institute*　　　　　　　　　D. CLAYTON JAMES
*November 1991*

# REFIGHTING
# THE LAST WAR

# PROLOGUE

# *The Last War Revisited*

The differences between the Second World War and the Korean conflict are numerous. While World War II was the greatest global struggle in the annals of warfare, Korea was a war fought with a unique and complex set of restrictions that precluded its escalation into a general war. The Korean conflict incorporated, especially in its early stages, many similarities to the previous war, some actual and others assumed. Due to their training and experience, the civilian and military leadership of the United States was especially prone to see the Korean emergency from the perspective of the 1939–1945 ordeal.

The beginnings of the two wars offer some interesting parallels. The failure of American intelligence to recognize the noises and the signals of the impending Japanese attacks on Pearl Harbor and Clark Field is matched by the intelligence blunders that failed to warn of the North Korean invasion in June 1950 and the Communist Chinese intervention that autumn. America was caught off guard in other ways as well, in both wars. The American government and public in 1941 were alert to the probability of war with Germany, but U.S. entry into World War II was precipitated by unexpected action in the Pacific. Likewise, in 1950, American attention was focused mainly on the menace of a Red Army takeover of West Europe and certainly not on the little-known and strategically unimportant peninsula of Korea. In both cases, the United States was concentrating on Europe and neglecting signs from Asia. The highest strategic priority of the United States and its chief ally, the United Kingdom, was "Europe first."

The assumed motivation of North Korea in its aggression was that it was functioning as a satellite force representing the Soviet Union in its effort to spread communism and become globally dominant. It was easy for Washington leaders, civilian and military, to equate this with Nazi Germany's naked use of force to spread its ideology and become a world state. It was assumed in 1950 that yielding to such an aggressive global-minded power would incite the Kremlin-directed communist monolith to further aggression. The notion of appeasing the North Koreans was compared to the infamous Anglo-French appeasement at Munich in 1938 that did not satiate the Nazi appetite, despite the vastly different historical circumstances of the two situations.

It was not hard to understand the reasons for these analogies. From Washington to the American Far East Command, the officers from field-grade to flag-officer levels, as well as senior civilian officials, had seen extensive duty in World War II. The President and commander in chief in 1950 was the same man who had headed the nation's huge armed forces during the final stages of the defeat of Germany and Japan in 1945. Even at lower levels in the armed services, such as junior officers, noncommissioned officers, and enlisted men, there were many called into service for the Korean War because they still retained their reserve or National Guard positions after serving in the European or Pacific wars. Only five years had passed from the end of World War II to the eruption of conflict in Korea. It is not surprising that the large combat-experienced manpower reservoir created by the earlier war would lead and fight in the Korean conflict.

In addition to the men who had served in World War II, there were the materials. With the outstanding exceptions of helicopters and jet fighters, the weapons and equipment of the American forces in Korea were all of World War II vintage or modified versions of them. The early defensive and counteroffensive operations against the Soviet-supplied North Korean Army were made possible primarily because of the convenient proximity of large stocks of war matériel that had been stored in occupied Japan. In one of his more farsighted decisions during the late 1940s, Douglas MacArthur had inaugurated a massive roll-up program whereby weapons, vehicles, and all sorts of military equipment and non-perishable supplies at Pacific bases and battle sites were brought to Japan. There, these materials were renovated, largely under contracts with Japanese firms and employing mainly Japanese skilled workers. This process of roll-up, renovation, and storage in Japan and then shipment to Korea of World War II items continued throughout the Korean conflict. Japanese contractors and workers enjoyed a lucrative business of repairing weapons and equipment thereby giving a tremendous boost to their nation's economy. The impetus of this ongoing enterprise would help propel Japan to major-power status economically in the ensuing decade.

On the other hand, what benefited Japan may have retarded American and United Nations Command (UNC) tactical innovations at the front. With a large measure of the American-led forces made up of men and matériel from World War II, it is not surprising that the tactical doctrine and techniques employed against the North Koreans and Communist Chinese were conventional and quite typical of those used in operations of 1941–1945 by American infantry, artillery, armor, and land-based and carrier-based aviation, together with units involved in naval gunfire support and amphibious warfare.

In the important area of ground-air support, which had been neglected between 1945 and 1950, a fresh start had to be made. As in World War II, the Far East Air Forces (FEAF) had to relearn tactical air warfare—indeed, reinvent its tactical organization—and adapt to the unique characteristics of the Korean battleground. Necessary tactical techniques included close coordination with carrier air strikes and use of ground control operatives with American, ROK, and Allied ground units. As in the war against Japan, the most effective ground-air support was demonstrated by the Marines, whose ground and air units were accustomed to training together. It took a while, but gradually tactical air power became as vital to UNC ground operations as it had been to Allied armies by the latter half of World War II. In both wars, ground troops sometimes cursed the airmen for their mistakes in targeting, but more often the soldiers were relieved by their timely support.

The heavy American reliance in World War II on motorization and mechanization, especially mobile artillery and armored vehicles, was carried forward into the Korean operations. This put a premium on operations along the roads, especially in the valleys, leaving the high ground in the largely mountainous peninsula as the domain of the infantry. As in World War II, American infantry were often handicapped in rugged uncharted terrain which the enemy knew as familiar and populated by friendly inhabitants. Long American supply lines were susceptible to interdiction by infiltrating or enveloping forces, and the Chinese proved superb in exploiting the mountains, using tactics of rapid infiltration and bypassing. The seemingly enormous advantage of the UNC in mechanization and motorization was often offset by dependence upon the peninsula's roads, which at best were barely adequate and often were little more than trails. On a number of occasions the Chinese were able to ambush road-bound columns from higher ground and leave the columns highly vulnerable after blocking the road by putting the lead vehicles out of commission.

Douglas MacArthur's mindset about the Pacific war heavily influenced the strategic course during the first year of fighting in Korea, when battlefield conditions were still fluid. Accustomed to fighting in the Southwest Pacific, he perceived Korea as an island and was convinced that his air units could effectively seal it off from the mainland. During his Southwest Pacific offensives, he had been won over by General George C. Kenney to the miracles that his powerful Fifth Air Force could perform. MacArthur had become filled with such an uncritical admiration of air power that, five years later, he was persuaded that his FEAF and Seventh Fleet aircraft could isolate the Korean battleground from Communist Chinese penetration. Moreover, both MacArthur and his current air chief, George E. Stratemeyer, were convinced that strategic bombing could bring the enemy forces in North Korea to their knees, as well as destroy both the North Korean and Communist Chinese governments' will to continue the fight. As in World War II, such unbounding confidence in strategic bombing as a decisive element in defeating the enemy proved disappointing.

Fortunately for the UNC naval forces, the Soviets did not supply the North Koreans or the Communist Chinese with naval craft beyond the level of small coastal defense vessels, though they did provide a weapon that gave the UNC ships considerable difficulties. The American Navy and its Allied components, as in World War II, were indispensable in shore bombardment, carrier air raids, and transportation and support of troops and supplies in amphibious assault and evacuation operations. But since there was no significant enemy naval force, the UNC naval units, chiefly the U.S. Seventh Fleet, faced no surface engagements. Neither had the Soviets made submarines available to North Korea or Red China. Soviet-built mines, however, proved to be a continual problem. As in the Allied navies' coastal operations in the Mediterranean, North Sea, and Bay of Biscay in 1940–1945, along with several coastal actions in the Pacific war, the UNC naval forces were never supplied with an adequate number of minesweepers. In both wars, mine fields accounted for losses in men and ships beyond expectations, yet minesweeping was never given the priority such losses warranted. In view of the critical need for production of other types of ships, such as carriers, minesweepers were continually far down the list in construction during both conflicts.

As in the previous war, the enemy came to be characterized in terms of evil and alien. Advancing UNC forces found numerous cases of atrocities, committed mainly by North Korean troops on a scale of ruthlessness that equaled Japanese brutalities against captured soldiers in the previous war. In addition, the biases exhibited by both sides, based on ethnocentrism and racism, brought a high level of savagery to the Korean conflict—again, as had happened during the war in the Pacific. Many on the UN side, especially Americans, believed that they were fighting on the side of good and world peace against ruthless evil atheists who were bent on spreading their diabolical ideology by aggression. American anticommunism had reached a fever pitch at home. In the case of American fighting men in Korea, it did not take long for many of them to develop a deep hatred of the enemy and his alleged cause. The troops, like the American public, seldom bothered to distinguish between nationalism and communism.

The United States anointed itself as the leader of the coalition that took on the aggressors in 1950 and, as during the years 1941–1945, by virtue of its arsenal and force strength, the United States arrogated to itself the directorship of strategy-making, its allies being permitted a modicum of input on the direction of the war. Like World War II, however, the British, even before the wily Winston S. Churchill returned as prime minister in 1951, managed to exert more influence on American policy in the Korean conflict than their actual contribution in troops and war matériel warranted. The British influence pushed America toward moderation rather than acceleration of the combat operations, mainly for fear that America would deploy more military resources to Korea than to Europe. Likewise in World War II, Churchill and the British chiefs of staff had worked hard—and usually successfully—to keep the preponderance of American strength engaged against Germany rather than Japan.

Throughout the Second World War, the Anglo-American Combined Chiefs of Staff had been divided along national lines on the basic issue of whether to fight a war of attrition, as the British preferred, or to adopt the bloodier and more decisive American aim of annihilation. So too in the Korean conflict, it was the United States that eagerly spearheaded the UN response to North Korea's invasion. America also led the way in not only ousting the invaders from South Korea but in boldly trying to conquer all of North Korea and to reunite Korea forcibly under a noncommunist regime. During the Second World War it was America's allies, especially Britain, the Soviet Union, Nationalist China, and Australia, who throughout the hostilities focused on the shape of the postwar world and the fate of their national interests in it. The Americans, meanwhile, devoted primary attention to winning the war and put off until later the settling of political issues. In an interesting parallel, in 1950–1953, the United States at first appeared to want to fight a war of annihilation and then, with the Chinese intervention, endeavored to terminate the hostilities by a strictly military agreement, choosing again, as in 1945, to postpone efforts to settle major East Asian political differences. This second failure within a decade to link military and nonmilitary objectives is one of the key factors that would lead the United States into its tragic entanglement in Vietnam. Senior American officers had not been well schooled in the distinctions between military and national strategies before World War II. This failure of the curriculum and teaching of the top service schools was not corrected after 1945 and was reflected in the muddled strategy in Korea. (Astonishingly, the senior military colleges offered virtually nothing about the lessons of the Korean conflict and the confusion of military and national strategic objectives to prepare the upcoming senior leaders of America's forces in the Vietnam War.)

In spite of professing little prior strategic interest in Korea, the Truman administration plunged with haste and confidence into the war to drive the invaders out of South Korea. The communist leadership in Moscow, Pyongyang, and Peking had badly miscalculated the American response, however logically and lucidly the signals from Washington may have indicated no military reaction would be forthcoming. Having defeated the North Korean Army below the 38th parallel, the American-led coalition plunged into a crucial escalation of the war by trying to save what they perceived as an occupied North Korea from her communist oppressors. As MacArthur's forces began the "liberation" of North Korea, an aura of excited anticipation pervaded Tokyo and Washington that was reminiscent of the glorious days when France and the Lowlands were freed from Nazi rule. North Korea, however, was not like Holland, where people had longed for release from their Nazi occupiers. Instead, it proved to be a tightly controlled society and Soviet satellite that was utterly hostile toward the West and virtually impenetrable by Western intelligence means.

Despite well-meaning, if ineffective, efforts to communicate to Peking's leaders that the UNC advance across North Korea spelled no security threat to Red China, fear and rage engulfed the leaders and the people of the world's second most powerful communist nation. When the Korean War erupted, Red China had been regrouping its forces for a summer invasion of Formosa and the decimation of the remaining Nationalist Chinese forces that had fled there the previous autumn. By mid-1950, Communist China possessed an enormous army, which consisted of not only the victorious communist troops from the mainland civil war of 1945–1949 but also a surprisingly large number of veteran Nationalist troops who had defected as Chiang Kai-shek's regime retreated to Formosa. With the unexpected intervention of this nation that was so rich in manpower and so ready to expend its troops, UN (largely American) plans to save South Korea and then to seize the communist satellite above the 38th parallel quickly turned to ashes.

In the late autumn of 1951, when the war of maneuver ground to a halt and the front line was stalemated, American artillery and air firepower reached bombardment levels comparable to those of World War II. The last two years of the war were characterized on the front lines by both sides' heavy usage of trenches, bunkers, and tunnels, with frequent night-patrol skirmishes and intense artillery barrages. It began to look more like World War I. By then, however, with the enemy deeply dug in, the predominance of American and Allied firepower, ground and air, could not dislodge or destroy the bulk of the enemy. Regardless, UNC directives did not permit attempts at massive penetration of the few enemy positions that had been severely weakened by artillery and air bombardments. This situation was familiar to General Mark W. Clark, who had experienced many agonizing months of costly and indecisive static warfare along Field Marshal Albert Kesselring's brilliantly conceived Gustav, Gothic, and other German defensive lines in the mountains of Italy.

Suddenly it was no longer another scenario from World War II, and the American side could not overwhelm and defeat the enemy with greatly superior production and firepower. The most important numbers, troop strength, were in the enemy's favor, the alleged lower priority of the North Korean and Chinese opponents on human life boded ill, the enemy's unconventional style of warfare was well suited to the Korean situation, and the enemy peasant soldiers proved able to fight and endure under terrible conditions. So, the Chinese threw the UNC out of North Korea. Although the American, ROK, and Allied forces eventually pushed a short way into that country again, neither Tokyo nor Washington had any real hope of reaching the Yalu or conquering all of North Korea. The belligerents found themselves locked in a bloody stalemate which offered the awful prospect of becoming a microcosm of World War I, an indecisive killing ground without meaning.

For the two superpowers in Moscow and Washington, this depressing battlefield situation carried the possibility of exploding into another world war. To avert this global suicide, the warring sides had to begin talking about mutually acceptable terms for an armistice. Further, in order to avert a world explosion, the two sides had to work with their allies and satellites to make sure that the conflict stayed limited. In an unusual understanding that was implicit rather than explicit, the major powers agreed to limit ground, sea, and air operations. The most overt acknowledgment of this mutually self-imposed restraint was made in May 1951 at the Senate hearings on MacArthur's relief when Generals George C. Marshall and Omar N. Bradley clearly emphasized "a virtual commitment by the Truman administration to keep the war confined to the Korean peninsula so long as the Communists did likewise."[1] These much-publicized hearings were attentively followed by communist leaders in Moscow, Peking, and Pyongyang.

This unwritten understanding was more important in the long run than the much-debated legalistic document that the warring powers finally signed and called an armistice agreement. The Korean conflict is unique in the history of warfare because with little spoken or written communication, both belligerent camps worked out limitations that signaled to the other the parameters of risk-taking that they were willing to accept. This potentially disastrous process of limitations through silent understandings and unspoken assumptions somehow spared the world from destruction in this most dangerous East-West collision of the Cold War era.

# Part I

★

# THE SENIOR COMMANDERS

# CHAPTER

# 1

# *Truman: The Right Thing to Do*

## FROM CONTAINMENT TO CONQUEST

"By God, I'm going to let them have it!" exclaimed President Harry S. Truman to several top officials upon returning to the nation's capital after learning of the North Korean invasion across the 38th parallel. Secretary of State Dean G. Acheson, Secretary of Defense Louis A. Johnson, and Under Secretary of State James E. Webb, who were in the limousine with him from the airport to Blair House, had proposals ready regarding the U.S. response. Truman said that "of course" he would listen but warned that "you know how I feel."[1] They knew that after he gave vent to his feelings, he would consider their recommendations; and then he would make his decisions with speed and no later regrets. Actually, he knew little about the internal strife between the North and South Koreans, but he was acquainted with the tension-plagued relations between the Soviet and American occupation forces on the peninsula following World War II. He saw the North Korean action as Moscow-directed aggression that called for a strong American response. If communism was on the march, Truman responded as he would to the spread of some evil force; it must be stopped, for by its nature it could not be appeased. It was not long before the President was recalling how Hitler's expansionism could not be satiated in the 1930s.

"Help me to be, to think, to act what is right, because it is right; make me truthful, honest and honorable in all things; make me intellectually honest for the sake of right and honor and without thought of reward to me." Thus Truman recorded in his diary in August 1950 a prayer he had said "over & over all my life."[2] He had emerged from his farm and small-town beginnings in the Midwest with an image of himself as a simple person committed to doing right and working hard. He had developed a view of the world as an essentially moral battleground where individuals and nations played out their destinies according to such absolute principles as integrity and justice. But by the time he took the oath of office as President, a month before his sixty-first birthday, he was not a simple man and he had come to see the world as very complex. During his years in the White House, however, he would often act as if people and issues were as uncomplicated as they had seemed throughout his childhood and youth in Missouri.

As a banker, artilleryman, clothier, judge, and U.S. senator from 1935 to 1945, he had demonstrated traits of personality and leadership style that would characterize him as President. At most times he was highly principled, decisive, gutsy, unpretentious, and commonsensible. His "horse sense" became legendary not only in Missouri but also on Capitol Hill, particularly during his shrewd leadership of the Senate's investigation of the defense program in World War II. Nevertheless, he could be cocky, impetuous, and petty with certain persons and groups, and excessively deferential and compromising toward others. While believing sincerely in the moral absolutes on which he had been reared, Truman exhibited his brightest and darkest skills when playing the simultaneous roles of master politician, interest-group broker, and horse trader. Such a political creature, blending enormous power and judgmental morality behind a facade of folksy simplicity, was not to be underestimated, a fact some of his adversaries would learn too late.

Somewhere between his combat experience as a junior officer of field artillery in World War I and his Senate subcommittee's inquiry into the waste and mismanagement of the military-industrial complex in World War II, Truman cultivated an ambivalent attitude toward things military. He was intensely patriotic and believed in the citizen-soldier's obligation to defend his country. Indeed, he had served commendably in battle himself. He accepted the necessity to use force or the threat of force, becoming the only head of state ever to order atomic warfare and serving as commander in chief in two of America's major wars. Two of his three most influential advisers and confidants in foreign affairs were military: General of the Army George C. Marshall and Fleet Admiral William D. Leahy (the third being Secretary of State Acheson).

Nevertheless, Truman's strong propensity to fulfill the domestic reforms set forth in his Fair Deal program left him frequently at odds with the military establishment, whose annual budgets were slashed severely in the five years after the Second World War. He clashed with his service chiefs over strategic priorities and new weapons systems, particularly General of the Army Dwight D. Eisenhower and Admiral Louis E. Denfield, and he differed sharply with his military occupation commanders in Germany and Japan, especially General of the Army Douglas MacArthur. The President's relations with the first secretary of defense, James V. Forrestal, were sometimes less than harmonious and became volatile with his successor, Johnson. In fact, by the eve of the Korean War, most leaders of the armed services laid blame for the military's precipitous decline in strength and combat readiness on President Truman's apathy, even hostility, toward the defense hierarchy, and on his favored treatment of liberal programs expanding or extending President Franklin D. Roosevelt's New Deal.

Truman's dreams of civil rights measures, federal assistance to education, and other Fair Deal objectives could not be realized if the United States maintained its post-1945 armed forces on a large scale. Yet American troops in numbers unprecedented in peacetime were deployed in many areas of the globe after World War II either on occupation duty or at bases where they could be used to deter or halt aggression by the Soviet Union and its new communist satellites. If his domestic reforms were not to be hampered by the military burdens imposed by the new global threat of communist expansion, it was imperative that he find nonmilitary responses to Premier Joseph Stalin's perceived probes and incursions in the Cold War. As alternatives to increased military spending, Truman promoted economic assistance to endangered nations, such as the Greek-Turkish Aid Act, the European Recovery Program, and the Point Four Plan, and he organized collective-security arrangements, particularly the Rio Pact and the North Atlantic Treaty Organization (NATO).

His ideal was for the United States to assume only limited liability for the economic and military costs of containing Soviet and Communist Chinese expansionism. During the first five years of

his presidency, Truman became increasingly concerned that the
Anglo-American alliance be strengthened, that the whole North
Atlantic community of nations unite against communism's spread,
and that the United Nations serve as a reservoir for multilateral
economic and military efforts to combat global communism. Some
of the Truman administration's efforts in organizing collective opposition to Soviet menaces were successful, notably the Marshall
Plan and the Berlin air lift. Such successes, however, strengthened
the President's faith that Stalin's moves could be countered with
methods and means other than unilateral American military power.
But he was soon to learn that coalitions could be illusory and disappointing creations. By the eve of the Korean War, the effectiveness of the American military had been sacrificed in large part to
the President's priorities: promotion of the Fair Deal at home and
concentration on collective security and economic aid abroad. The
situation boded ill if a shift from a cold to hot war should occur.

That change did occur suddenly, on June 25, 1950, when powerful armor-led North Korean Army units crossed the 38th parallel,
which marked the boundary drawn in 1945 to separate Soviet and
American occupation zones. They rapidly advanced into South Korea against ineffective resistance by the small, poorly trained, and
inadequately armed defending troops. Within a week, President
Truman ordered into action first air and naval, then ground forces
of the United States in defense of the Republic of (South) Korea.
The standard historical perception of the President during those
first days of the emergency is that of a commander in chief acting
boldly, courageously, and decisively to do what was right to repel
blatant communist aggression and to save the weak, beleaguered
South Korean republic. The commitment was undertaken at the
executive level without consulting Congress, much less obtaining
a formal declaration of war. Not until months later, when American
involvement was still escalating and the tide of battle was turning
toward disaster or costly attrition did important opposition leaders
on Capitol Hill begin to criticize Truman for acting precipitously
and imperially and thereby severely limiting the opportunity for
bipartisan support of the war effort.

Truman himself regarded the intervention of the United States
in the Korean conflict as the "toughest decision" of his career,[3] but,
in truth, Secretary of State Acheson was the actual initiator of most
of the key early decisions. Truman was at his home in Indepen-

dence, Missouri, when he heard of the outbreak of war along the 38th parallel, and Acheson rapidly made the initial basic decisions in Washington. When Truman got back to the nation's capital on June 26, he concurred in Acheson's prompt action to obtain the United Nations Security Council's resolution calling for a cease-fire in Korea and the withdrawal of the North Korean invaders from South Korea. Although he liked the strategic recommendations his secretary of state put before him, he realized they pointed toward quick involvement of American troops. Acheson also understood the consequences. "It looked as though we must steel ourselves for the use of force," he later said of the conclusion he had reached even before Truman's return. Acheson admitted that before he went to Blair House on the night of June 26 to confer with the President and other key executive advisers, his own mind "was pretty clear on where the course we were about to recommend would lead and why it was necessary that we follow the course."[4]

In the next days of tense conferences between Truman and his top advisers, the President went along with virtually all the proposals put forth by Acheson, who, in turn, was framing the early strategic and diplomatic initiatives of the United States in the Korean War. Acheson, not Truman, was the most fervent proponent of committing American air, naval, and ground forces to the Korean action, and it was the secretary of state who was the instigator of the Security Council's resolution on June 27 calling upon member states to contribute men and matériel to the defense of South Korea. Moreover, Truman's bypassing of Congress was undertaken upon the persistent advice of Acheson. So strong was Acheson's influence on Truman that none of the foremost military officials who were involved in the Blair House sessions that final week of June, including boisterous Secretary of Defense Johnson and much-respected Chairman of the Joint Chiefs of Staff Omar Bradley, challenged the secretary of state's main ideas, even on military matters.

Truman surely deferred to Acheson's judgment in taking the United States into the Korean conflict, but the President made the ultimate decision himself and alone. He agreed with Acheson because he thought what he advocated was right, and both men viewed appeasement of North Korea's aggression as wrong and fraught with consequences as disastrous as the infamous appeasements of the 1930s. Truman later remarked, "It was my belief that if this aggression in Korea went unchallenged, as the aggression in Manchuria in 1931 and in Ethiopia in 1934 had gone unchallenged, the world was certain to be plunged into another world war."[5] The free world had failed to meet Adolf Hitler's challenge when he crossed the borders of Austria and Czechoslovakia, and World War II was the result. Now, the North Korean attack across a clear-cut territorial boundary recalled the totalitarian expansionism of the 1930s and carried a parallel threat.

Actually, the North and South Koreans had been engaged in bloody clashes for several years on an escalating scale of violence. The 38th parallel was accepted by neither as more than a temporary occupation border imposed by the United States and the Soviet Union. The Korean War originated in chaotic conditions marked by tensions not only of the global Cold War but also of the indigenous civil war. However, Truman's primary concern was to contain the great evil, communism, and he saw intervention as his only option. He tended to see choices in black and white and not to evaluate fully the gray areas in between. This precluded an assessment of alternative courses.

Truman's next decision of monumental significance in the Korean situation was to authorize General of the Army Douglas MacArthur, commander in chief of the United Nations Command (CINCUNC), to advance into North Korea, liberate it from communist control, and bring about the reunification of the Korean nation. Twelve days had passed since MacArthur's strategically brilliant amphibious assault at Inchon on September 15 that led to the rapid rout and disintegration of the North Korean Army operating below the 38th parallel. The Joint Chiefs of Staff, with Truman's enthusiastic endorsement, issued a new directive for MacArthur, proclaiming his aim now to be the "destruction of the North Korean Armed Forces." He was "authorized to conduct military operations north of the 38th Parallel in Korea, provided that at the time of such operations there has been no entry into North Korea by major Soviet or Chinese Communist forces."[6] On September 29, General of the Army George Marshall, who had succeeded Johnson as secretary of defense the previous week, sent a cordial, supportive cable to MacArthur, apparently with the President's sanction: "We want you to feel unhampered tactically and strategically to proceed north of the 38th Parallel."[7] MacArthur's self-assured response was a harbinger of things to come, proclaiming that he considered "all of Korea open for our military operations."[8]

South Korean troops marched into North Korea on October 1, and that day MacArthur broadcast an unconditional surrender ultimatum to North Korea. Truman concurred wholeheartedly as Acheson and the U.S. delegation at the United Nations drafted a resolution that, in essence, would give UN approval to MacArthur's forces liberating North Korea and reuniting the two Koreas as an independent, democratic state. The UN General Assembly adopted it on October 7 by a lopsided margin of forty-seven to five, with seven abstentions.[9]

With the President's vision of the Korean debacle as a Cold War issue and with Washington euphoric after the spectacular Inchon triumph, Truman and his military chiefs moved boldly, if prematurely, to launch the liberation of North Korea from communist control. Surprisingly little attention was paid to possible Communist Chinese reactions as official Washington focused on the Soviet Union's response and potential problems involved in the reunification and rehabilitation of the two Koreas. Truman and his advisers did not anticipate the withdrawal of Allied support in the face of an enormous escalation of fighting and the threat of World War III. The United Kingdom, the British Commonwealth nations, Turkey, and the other countries who had sent men and matériel to defend South Korea now might back away from involvement in a mounting conflict that Truman had initially characterized as a "police action."

In shifting America's objective from saving South Korea to rescuing North Korea, Truman also risked the chance of sacrificing the Fair Deal reforms at home, which were always more important to him personally than the outcome on the Korean peninsula. After the invasion of North Korea and the subsequent Chinese intervention, the media in America and in Allied countries frequently spoke of "Truman's War." Thus Truman found himself identified with a radically new and impossible objective, the liberation of North Korea, and an unpopular war which would become a bloody stalemate that he could neither win nor terminate. His hasty decisions had led him into an uncharted and undesired war that would ultimately lead to his political demise. The quixotic goal of seizing an entire state was the most absurd case in the Korean conflict of American leaders reveling in the vision of glorious triumphs as in the days of the Second World War.

## EUROPE'S PRIORITY AND JAPAN'S OPPORTUNITY

Besides the American entry into the Korean War and the abortive effort to liberate North Korea, Truman played an extremely important role in creating the post-1945 network of collective security arrangements of the United States. Like Acheson and W. Averell Harriman, one of the most trusted White House advisers, Truman believed it was crucial for the United States to exert its military strength in Korea under the cover of the United Nations Command. He extolled the peace-keeping function of the United Nations, particularly since the General Assembly and Security Council could usually be counted upon to vote the way America wished. The identification of American security interests with those of the United Nations seemed beneficial to Truman. It bolstered the image of the United States in world public opinion and made the machinations of Moscow, Peking, and Pyongyang appear to be beyond the pale of international legitimacy. Truman took full advantage of the UN Charter's section on collective security to create defense pacts with Japan, the Philippines, Australia and New Zealand, Latin America, and, most significantly, the nations of the North Atlantic Treaty Organization.

During the worst crisis of the Korean War, when Communist Chinese armies were expelling MacArthur's troops from North Korea in December 1950, Truman named General of the Army Dwight Eisenhower as the first supreme Allied commander of NATO military forces. He also announced that American troops in Europe would be strongly reinforced and would serve as the nucleus of the new NATO military arm. This was a serious disappointment to MacArthur, who had been asking for four additional Army divisions to stop the Chinese advance. Senator Kenneth S. Wherry of Nebraska, the Republican floor leader and an ardent supporter of MacArthur, introduced a resolution in early January 1951 stating that "it is the sense of the Senate that no ground forces of the United States should be assigned to duty in the European area for the purposes of the North Atlantic Treaty pending the formulation of a policy with respect thereto by the Congress."[10]

Wherry's resolution precipitated the Great Debate, a long, acrimonious argument in the Senate and in the national media that centered on the President's power to send troops to NATO without the approval of Congress and to set the strategic priority of the United States on West Europe rather than on the Korean struggle. With Senator Robert A. Taft of Ohio, the most prominent of Republican conservatives, endorsing the Wherry resolution, the Senate's Armed Services and Foreign Relations committees began joint hearings on the issues in late January. On Capitol Hill, Generals Marshall and Eisenhower, as well as Acheson and other administration leaders, came to the assistance of President Truman in support of building NATO's military strength against the contingency of a Soviet incursion into West Europe.

In spite of the news of increased fighting and soaring casualties in Korea, Secretary of Defense Marshall, with Truman's public support, announced in mid-February 1951 that four American Army divisions were being transferred to West Europe. That April, Eisenhower established the new supreme Allied headquarters of NATO outside Paris. Meanwhile, the Senate tabled the Wherry resolution and accepted another that supported Eisenhower's NATO appointment and the shipment of the four divisions to West Europe, although it added some rather weak provisions to restrict the American commitment to NATO, such as a caveat to the President to consult Congress before sending more American forces to Europe. The finale of the Great Debate was the Senate's passage of this resolution in early April. It delighted Truman, who would attain another of his much-desired objectives the next week when he replaced MacArthur with General Matthew B. Ridgway as head of the United Nations, United States Far East, and Japanese occupation commands.

The President had been steadfast and courageous in his advocacy of the strategic priority of West Europe in American global planning. His position was not new, for he had been zealously striving for an Atlantic alliance to contain Soviet expansionism throughout the crises of 1947–1949 that led to the Marshall Plan, the Berlin air lift, and the birth of NATO. There is no question that Truman, while often making ultimate judgments in favor of positions earlier developed by such close advisers as Marshall, Acheson, and Harriman, was the crucial decision-maker in holding to the European priority. He preserved this through a crucial, chaotic period of Asia-first excitement in America when the pressures of the Korean War, McCarthyism, and the China Lobby were at their zenith.

The President's judicious oversight of the occupation policies and administration in Japan since 1945 contributed to reshaping that nation and, if inadvertently, preparing it to serve as the invaluable base of operations for American and UN forces during the Korean conflict. Truman strongly supported the work of the State-War-Navy (and later Air Force) Coordinating Committee that formulated the basic policies for the American-dominated occupation of Japan. During the critical "reverse course" phase in policy shifts in 1947–1948, he was intensely interested in and committed to changing the occupation objectives from demilitarization and democratization to economic rehabilitation so that Japan could be molded into "the workshop of the Far East" and the economically strong ally of the West in the Cold War. The economic recovery of Japan had progressed slowly to 1950, so devastating had been the war's impact on the country. But the seeds of the incredible economic boom of the ensuing decades were planted during the Korean War, thanks to farsighted efforts of the Truman administration. Its influence on Japan's greatly improved business confidence and her new place in international trade was provided by the American-dominated formulation of the peace treaty with Japan that was signed at the San Francisco Conference in September 1951, over which Truman proudly presided.

On the advice of MacArthur as well as the Joint Chiefs, Truman approved major changes in occupation economic policy that unshackled Japanese big business from earlier restrictions. They allowed Japanese industry to provide many of the material needs of the huge buildup of United Nations Command personnel and facilities in the four main home islands. For the duration of the Korean hostilities, the Japanese economy was greatly boosted by eased loan credits, tax cuts, and other favorable policy alterations. Japan quickly became not only a powerful base of operations for the forces committed to the Korean peninsula but also the "arsenal of democracy" for the United Nations Command, reminiscent of the U.S. role toward Britain in 1940–1941. The huge influx of American special procurement orders for military materials and services, as well as loans and various forms of economic assistance from the United States, along with the personal spending of hundreds of thousands of American and Allied servicemen, brought a great surge in prosperity to Japan.

Prime Minister Shigeru Yoshida praised the Truman administration in an address to the Diet in early 1951 and noted that "the Korean War provided more stimulus for Japanese economic resurgence than did all the occupation efforts."[11] Many of the key American economic consultants sent to occupied Japan were men who had worked closely with Truman and were selected by him, one of whom was banking leader Joseph M. Dodge, who developed a vigorous program to stabilize Japan's post-1945 economy and prepare the foundations for Japanese business to take advantage of the opportunities that came with the Korean War. (Earlier, Truman had sent Dodge to West Germany, where he had formulated a successful currency reform program.) Researchers have not yet given Truman the credit he deserves for his appointees who tried to help Japan and West Germany toward economic recovery. Truman was not an authority on economics, but in many of these selections he proved to be an uncannily keen judge of men, especially those with horse sense.

## PROBLEMS OF WAR, NEGOTIATIONS, AND COMMANDERS

Though generally admiring Truman's pugnacious stand against communist expansionism, a number of high-ranking American military leaders deplored his decision to open truce negotiations in July 1951. Earlier that summer Communist Chinese troops were suffering heavy losses in combat, facing serious supply shortages because of increased air raids, surrendering in unprecedented numbers, and attempting futilely to check the slow but steady advance of the UN forces. General James A. Van Fleet, commander of the U.S. Eighth Army, was vehement in his criticism of the orders from Washington prohibiting large-scale offensive operations when the truce talks got under way.

Inflexible and uncompromising toward communists, Ridgway at first saw the negotiations as "not unwelcome," but he later became bellicose about the communists' negotiating tactics of distortion and obstructionism. In September 1951 he complained to Army

Chief of Staff J. Lawton Collins that the negotiations showed "the clear pattern of a consistent search for measures, whereby in one form or another, we accede to Communist demands. . . . There is only one language the Communists understand. Unfortunately we have yet to speak that language and conform our action to our words. We have yet to tell them 'Here we stand and here we stay,' and then to stay."[12] When Ridgway left Korea in 1952 to take command of NATO forces, he was not at all certain, to put it mildly, that the truce efforts were the wisest course.

Some maintain that Truman's plan to virtually cease hostilities and move to the truce table in mid-1951 was a blunder because it presented the enemy with an unexpected opportunity to regroup forces and strengthen positions. They argue persuasively that it was erroneous for America and its coalition to conclude that a limited war had to end in a draw. It was not out of the question to achieve a limited military triumph or a negotiated peace that was more favorable than the armistice of 1953. If the Anglo-American alliance of World War II attained total victory but dubious postwar political gains, perhaps it was expecting too much for their leaders to adjust so quickly to limited conflict that they could perceive strategic assets being derived from it.

Vice Admiral C. Turner Joy, commander of U.S. Naval Forces, Far East (NAVFE), 1949–1952, and head of the American delegation during the first half of the prolonged Korean negotiations, believed that "the greatest handicap under which we negotiated was the apparent reluctance or inability, in a number of instances, of Washington to give us firm and minimum positions which would be supported by national policy. In other words, positions which we could carry through to the breaking point of negotiations if necessary."[13] Truman understood his presidential position clearly when he said "the buck stops here." His roles in beginning the truce talks and inadequately supporting Joy and his successor on the overall American policy picture leave him quite vulnerable to criticism. His old Missouri standard of choosing the right thing was not all the counsel he needed in coordinating truce and combat moves and in dealing with communist negotiators.

Nevertheless, Truman's exercise of his sense of right could be impressive. U. Alexis Johnson, a longtime senior official of the State Department, recalled a session with the President and his top lieutenants in the summer of 1952 when the "tough, hard issue" of voluntary repatriation of prisoners of war in Korea was discussed long and heatedly. "Truman made, at the [end of the] meeting, a very clear, unequivocal decision that he expressed to everybody there, that we were going to stand for voluntary repatriation, because that was the moral and the right thing to do."[14] In a later statement Johnson elaborated further:

> With that clear-sighted sense of higher moral duty that guided him throughout his Presidency, Truman held out for the right of communist prisoners to refuse to be sent home to a life they hated and possibly to a firing squad. Had he taken the easy way out, I believe an armistice could have been signed well before the 1952 presidential election.[15]

Surely the President's most courageous decision during the Korean War was to relieve MacArthur of his commands over U.S. and UN forces in the conflict and over the Allied occupation of Japan. Despite the fame of the Truman-MacArthur controversy, it is still a surprisingly little-known fact that the two men met only once—for a few hours on Wake Island in mid-October 1950. By then each had largely accepted the stereotype of the other that his assistants had long described.

Whereas MacArthur's inner circle of generals at his Tokyo headquarters viewed Truman as a second-rate liberal politician with no knowledge of strategy or military affairs, they greatly underestimated Truman's intelligence, cunning, determination, toughness, and especially his deep dislike of arrogance and pretension. On the other hand, Truman's lieutenants who were most influential in his war-related decisions of 1950–1951—namely, Acheson, Harriman, Marshall, and Bradley—generally saw MacArthur as a vain, exhibitionistic, politically ambitious commander whose aggressiveness could trigger a third world war. Except for the dramatic triumph of the Inchon operation and the traditional respect among warriors for a senior and successful member of their clan that Marshall and Bradley still nourished, Truman's principal advisers found little to praise about "The Big General," as they and Truman sometimes called him. The President, echoing the sentiments of his confidants, also referred to the sometimes overbearing, presumptuous, and self-righteous officer as "The Right-Hand Man of God" and greatly oversimplified his removal of the Far East commander:

"MacArthur left me no choice—I could no longer tolerate his insubordination."[16] In truth, neither the President nor the general tried very hard to establish effective communications with the other.

Truman did send a good friend and able representative, Major General Frank E. Lowe, to serve as liaison between the White House and the high command in Tokyo. He yanked Lowe home, however, when he removed MacArthur from Korea, mainly because Lowe had become more sympathetic to MacArthur's views than to Truman's on the conduct of the war. Afterward, Lowe retained a strong esteem for both men and was convinced that Truman and MacArthur "actually saw things alike" on many matters, but "the two were deliberately pulled apart and pitted against each other by third parties" in the White House and General Headquarters, Tokyo.[17] In retrospect, the Truman-MacArthur collision was precipitated not only by differences over strategy and civil-military relations but also by an unfortunate breakdown in communications between the two men, as well as between MacArthur and the Joint Chiefs of Staff.

Ridgway succeeded MacArthur in April 1951 and, in turn, was followed by General Mark Clark in May 1952 as head of the United Nations Command, United States Far East Command, and United States Army Forces, Far East.[18] Truman had comparatively few problems in his dealings with Ridgway. The President observed later that Ridgway had done "a fine job of carrying out the administration's policy. General Ridgway did not always agree with policy or with the Joint Chiefs of Staff, but he was meticulous in carrying out directives." Truman particularly praised Ridgway's "firm and effective" leadership of the occupation in Japan and his relations with President Syngman Rhee and other ranking South Korean civil and military leaders.[19] Ironically, the next President, five-star General Eisenhower, would encounter great difficulties with Ridgway as Army chief of staff, and the latter would resign his post after two tempestuous years.

The third and final wartime head of the UN and Far East commands was General Mark Clark, for whom Truman had developed considerable respect during and since his dogged leadership of American forces in Italy in World War II. He named Clark as Ridgway's successor in Tokyo in May 1952; Clark retained the position until after the Korean armistice in July 1953. Truman seemed satisfied with Clark's performance, though it was a tense period of balancing truce moves with limited combat operations that was frustrating for Clark and his forces. Later, Clark commented, "In carrying out the instructions of my government, I gained the unenviable distinction of being the first United States Army commander in history to sign an armistice without victory. . . . I believe that the Armistice, by and large, was a fair one—considering that we lacked the determination to win the war."[20] By the time of the truce, of course, Clark was serving under a new commander in chief—Eisenhower.

Ridgway and Clark enjoyed harmonious relations, for the most part, with the Truman administration because of two factors lacking in the MacArthur-Truman relationship. First, they had served in high-level military positions in Washington and Europe during the early years of the Cold War and had been involved in or kept well informed on the formulation of America's postwar strategy, of which the centerpiece was containment in Europe. MacArthur, to the contrary, had not been on duty in the States since 1935, was not closely in touch with the Cold War strategists' thinking, and was identified with critics of the Truman administration's East Asian policy. Second, Ridgway and Clark had the good fortune, if serving during a stalemate can be so labeled, to hold the Far East theater command when American policy objectives in Korea had become fairly stabilized and consistent. On the other hand, the objectives of the United States in Korea changed at least four times between May 1950, the eve of war, and April 1951, when MacArthur left Tokyo. The American positions ranged from the prewar one of pronouncing Korea strategically useless to the later one of forcefully liberating North Korea from the communist sphere.

MacArthur may not have had a valid grievance when he charged that the Truman administration had no clear policy on Korea, but he had grounds for complaint that the policy shifts were too frequent and too abrupt, and that he was not kept fully informed. It may well be that neither Ridgway nor Clark could have survived the roller-coaster effect of American policy changes in Korea during the period when MacArthur presided over the first phase of U.S. and UN operations. As America's first modern limited war and the first armed clash between the Cold War opponents, the Korean War was a unique challenge to Truman and his officials; experimentation and flexible responses may have been necessary.

But there is little question that, with the flawed communications between MacArthur and official Washington, he was not kept as abreast of the intent of his superiors as were Ridgway and Clark. Demonstrating patience and understanding toward pompous, defiant generals was not Truman's forte.

## STEPS TOWARD DESEGREGATION

In ousting MacArthur, the President appeared to be acting on a potpourri of rational and emotional impulses, as well as noble and petty motives. In contrast to this equivocal decision-making, his longtime advocacy of civil rights led to firm and genuine progress in desegregating the armed forces of the United States during the Korean conflict. After World War II, the services had continued to be primarily segregated despite "an almost universal demand of the black community by 1948 for their integration."[21] In late July 1948, as the presidential campaign was mounting in fervor, Truman issued an executive order declaring a policy of "equality of treatment and opportunity for all persons in the armed services without regard to race."[22] By the same order, he created the President's Committee on Equality of Treatment and Opportunity in the Armed Services; it was charged with examining current practices and advising him of needed reforms. At a September meeting of the committee, Truman stated that he hoped they could work with the military in accomplishing desegregation "in such a way that it is not a publicity stunt."[23]

Truman's concern was real and unprecedented in presidential history. Nevertheless, as in many of his attempts to do the right thing, there seemed to be evidence of the master politician at work, too. The equal opportunity order significantly helped the President unite the nation's minorities behind his 1948 candidacy.

The President's advisory committee concentrated on desegregating the Army. By the time the Korean War began, some progress had been made, but many segregated units remained. Although Truman had emphasized in 1948 that his executive order was to be the beginning of the end of segregation in the armed forces, some commanders had thought that the somewhat vaguely worded text of the order would allow them to evade change. Indeed, it was disregarded rather widely until, according to a reliable source, "the Army, fighting in Korea, was forced by a direct threat to the efficiency of its operations to begin wide-scale mixing of the races."[24] Heavy combat forced the military to use all its manpower efficiently. In the Eighth Army headquarters, pragmatism prevailed as it "began assigning individual black soldiers just as it had been assigning individual Korean soldiers to understrength [white] units."[25]

A furor erupted, however, when thirty-nine black soldiers of the predominantly black 24th Infantry Regiment, which had been engaged in a number of fierce engagements, were convicted of "misconduct before the enemy" and sentenced to lengthy prison terms. A black engineer officer of that regiment later undertook a close study of the performance of many American regiments in the Korean fighting and concluded candidly: "24th Infantrymen, black and white, fought as well as other American regiments," though the 24th faced "serious deficiencies among senior COs as well as almost constant commitment to action under the most difficult conditions."[26] The 24th Infantry Regiment performed erratically in its Korean operations, sometimes poorly while satisfactorily on other occasions, which was true of a number of all-white units of the Eighth Army. Overall, its combat record demonstrated the need to terminate segregated units not only in the name of minority rights but also in the attainment of more effective fighting units.

Truman approved the dispatch of Thurgood Marshall, special counsel of the National Association for the Advancement of Colored People (NAACP), to investigate in Japan and Korea the circumstances and evidence related to the courts-martial. Thanks to Truman's pressure and Thurgood Marshall's "highly critical report," most of the convicted black soldiers got reversed judgments or reduced sentences.[27] MacArthur belatedly remarked about Marshall's findings, "I am willing to concede that these courts-martial may have been excessive."[28]

At the time of Marshall's visit to the Far East Command in early 1951, it was found that "almost 90 percent of black soldiers in the Army still served in segregated units."[29] Ridgway got behind the desegregation effort strongly, and by late 1951 all of the Eighth Army's units were integrated in Korea, although integration did not make much headway among American Army forces in Europe until the spring of 1952. Not until late 1954 did the Army, the service with the largest number of blacks by far, integrate its last all-black units. The Marine Corps and the Air Force dissolved their remaining all-black units by the end of 1952, while the Navy was considerably slower, with approximately half of its blacks serving as lowly stewards. Equal and fair condition for blacks in the armed services had not been achieved altogether by any standards, but definite progress had been made by the end of the Korean conflict. One of the most far-reaching consequences of that war had been the steps toward equality and fairness for minority personnel in the American military establishment. Truman's initiative and continuing pressure on the high command had been significant in this cause.

Civil rights had been a major plank in Truman's Fair Deal program from the start, and it was one of his few goals that bridged domestic and foreign affairs. It would be his fate as President to make his most significant decisions not in the realm of domestic reforms but in military and foreign crises of global dimensions, such as his decisions to use atomic warfare against Japan, to provide economic assistance to war-crippled or backward nations in the path of communism, and to commit the United States to war in Korea.

The thread that ran through nearly all of Truman's decision-making, whether on domestic or foreign issues, was his commitment to determine the right course to take. Harriman, who came as close as any of the President's confidants to understanding his manner of reaching decisions, observed that "one of his great qualities was that he never made a snap decision. He sometimes appeared to because he was very sharp in his words. . . . He was an avid reader. . . . But before he made his decisions he consulted everybody that he thought he should. . . . After he made up his mind, he said, 'Well, this is the best that I can do.' Then he went home, did some reading, and slept. He never had any second thoughts."[30] On another occasion Harriman commented, "Roosevelt, for whom I also had the privilege to work, tried to avoid crises and tried, if possible, to find ways to get around them, but President Truman met them head on—though always with the most extraordinary amount of care." He added, "He did act on his concepts of what was right and wrong. He never asked, 'What are the options?' but, 'What's the right thing to do?'"[31] As the American commander in chief confronting the unique and confusing struggle over Korea, Truman often used his simple criterion in deciding courses of action—a practice that would have its liabilities as well as assets.

# CHAPTER

# 2

# *MacArthur: The Flawed Military Genius*

## PREDICTABLE BUT NECESSARY

General of the Army Douglas MacArthur welcomed the opportunity to serve as theater commander in the Korean War for two main reasons: First, his long career was nearing its end, and since his personal leadership over the occupation of Japan had declined during its later stage as the State Department's influence had grown, he strongly desired to end his military service with the kind of overwhelming success that he had experienced in his offensives of the final two years of the war against Japan. Such success was touched by a flourish of glory that occupation administrative duties could not match. A great triumph in Korea would be the capstone that would ensure his place among the great captains. Second, in his mind there was no question of the grand stakes at issue in Korea: It was clearly the long-awaited collision between the forces of freedom, capitalism, and light on one side against the legions representing bondage, communism, and darkness on the other. He had railed against communism since Marxists had allegedly taken over the Bonus Army in 1932, and in occupied Japan he had done all in his power to curb the influence of the Soviet Union on occupation policy and to restrict severely the Japanese Communist Party. With the outbreak of the war in Korea he now was driven to repeat or even surpass his earlier triumphs on the battlefield and to lead the climactic fight against the global spread of communism. He was blessed suddenly with the opportunities that General George S. Patton, Jr., had longed for at the end of World War II. Unhappily, Patton died prematurely, and MacArthur would find his exercise of power restrained and finally terminated during the Korean conflict.

In the wake of the Second World War a number of contemporary authorities selected General MacArthur as the outstanding American commander of that conflict, the adulators included such British luminaries as Prime Minister Winston Churchill and Field Marshals Alan Brooke and Bernard L. Montgomery. It was not unusual for high-ranking officers of that era, whether favorably or unfavorably disposed toward him personally, to describe him as "brilliant" or "a strategic genius." They often noted that, among the various principles of war, surprise was the one he exploited most in his offensives in the war against Japan.

For a bright commander whose forte was launching unexpected assaults, his leadership style from 1941 to 1951 ironically followed a highly predictable pattern, which was characterized by thorough and shrewd planning, boldness of vision, aggressiveness in operational execution, keen sensitivity to his carefully molded hero image, and arrogant challenges of his superiors' directives that sometimes bordered on insubordination. As head of the occupation of Japan, he performed along lines amazingly similar to those he followed in the Southwest Pacific war, displaying administrative excellence, enlightened concepts of occupation reforms, an image of imperial aloofness that remarkably suited the Japanese, and continuing incidents of brazen impunity toward his superiors. During his command of the United Nations forces in the Korean War, his leadership traits were consistent with his behavior as occupation chief, such as generally masterful handling of four high-level commands simultaneously, imaginative envelopment and crushing of the North Korean Army, supreme self-confidence that led to initial defeat but later recovery of the momentum against the Chinese Communist Forces (CCF), and sharp differences with Washington that finally led him to tragic insubordination.

When he was relieved of his commands in 1951, it could not be claimed that during his confrontations with the Truman administration MacArthur had acted contrary to his well-known and highly consistent mode of conduct of the past decade. If there were mistakes made by the principals in the Truman-MacArthur collision of 1950–1951, the first might well have been Truman's. He chose as his top commander in the Korean struggle a general who had long displayed not only genius in leadership, fervent patriotism, and commitment to duty but also independence, vanity, arrogance, and mendacity.

In his communiqués during the war with Japan, MacArthur's frequent references to "my ships" or "my aircraft," his contrasts of others' costly operations with his economical conquests or envelopments, and his failures to give credit to his field commanders or specific units that had performed notably produced annoyance and snickers about his "egomania" among leaders and troops from the Pacific to Washington. In occupied Japan he continued to pour out press releases that made the achievements of the Allied occupation appear to be virtually all under his personal supervision. Such practices undoubtedly reflected his vanity and showmanship, but they also effectively projected an image that worked to his advantage during the occupation. He convinced a large majority of the American populace that he was the chief architect of the triumph over Japan and persuaded many Japanese that he was their nation's postwar shogun who wielded enormous power in Washington. This image projection was an asset in winning the cooperation of most of Japan's influential conservative political leaders and in obtaining the support of powerful right-wing Republicans in the American Congress, without whose help many of MacArthur's relief, recovery, and reform programs in Japan would not have gotten strong American backing.

He manipulated this image to gain political support for himself among influential conservatives in America during World War II and in postsurrender Japan. In 1944 and 1948, right-wing Republicans tried to have him nominated as the party's presidential candidate. More than any senior American military officer since Major General George B. McClellan in the Civil War, he seemed to move and speak in public with larger audiences in mind than the immediate occasion required, sustaining suspicions among his critics about his possible political aspirations.

At the high level of combined (Allied) and joint (interservice) commands that MacArthur held from 1941 to 1951, the President and the Joint and Combined Chiefs of Staff allowed him a great deal of latitude and did not closely delineate the supreme commander's parameters of authority. MacArthur used this practice of loose control over trusted, proven leaders at the high-command dimension to develop theater strategy and policy largely as he pleased. In the war against Japan he held several commands simultaneously. In its final stages, he commanded both the Allied theater in the Southwest Pacific and all American Army forces in the Pacific theaters. During the occupation of Japan he also wore multiple hats, serving as the supreme commander for the Allied powers in Japan; head of all ground, sea, and air forces in the United States Far East Command (FECOM); and commanding general of American Army forces in the Far East. Both in the Southwest Pacific and in Japan he took full advantage of his multiple roles, cleverly playing off his Allied and American superiors against each other or exploiting ambiguity or vagueness in his directives from above. In the war with Japan, for instance, he was forbidden by his Allied theater directive to command national forces of army-level strength. When he did not get an American to head ground operations in the Southwest Pacific theater, he simply designated his American Sixth Army as Task Force Alamo to keep it directly under his control and away from Australian General Thomas Blamey, the theater's commander of Allied ground forces.

He usually played his shell-and-pea game with consummate skill, claiming his authority for a certain action was derived from his Allied powers if challenged by his American superiors, or vice versa depending on the case. He normally could cover his decision or move with some shell of authority, a stratagem he would use through the Pacific conflict, the occupation of Japan, and the Korean War. He would also decide or act without express authorization from above in crises during all three periods if he felt "time was of the essence" (a much-used caveat of his) and it would take too long to get his superiors' approval.

His desire and ability to expand his authority beyond its intended limits was evident in the spring of 1945 when he sent his Eighth Army to reconquer the Philippines south of Luzon despite the Joint Chiefs' expressed wish to restrict operations in that archipelago to Leyte and Luzon. In April, the Joint Chiefs changed their minds and authorized the operations elsewhere in the Philippines. But by that time MacArthur's forces had already undertaken eight of his planned eleven principal amphibious operations in that region. Rear Admiral Samuel Eliot Morison, among others, was puzzled by the "mystery how and whence . . . MacArthur derived his authority to use United States forces to liberate one Philippine island after another" when he then "had no specific directive for anything subsequent to Luzon." In his distinguished history of American naval operations in the war, he finds that "the J.C.S. simply permitted MacArthur to do as he pleased, up to a point."[1]

In Tokyo, he often took action on Washington-originated directives without first gaining the approval of the Allied policy-making body, the Far Eastern Commission; he utilized loopholes in the wording of the Moscow Agreement of December 1945 regarding that commission's authority vis-à-vis the U.S. government and the Allied occupation chief. When it was to his advantage in carrying out his duties, as he interpreted them, he would exploit feuds and differences of opinion between key officials of the State and Defense departments.

He possessed such skill at role-taking to achieve his ends that he was often compared to the master politician himself, Franklin D. Roosevelt. MacArthur could appear as liberal or conservative, aggressive or cautious, independent or obsequious, idealistic or realistic, calm or alarmist, and a host of other seemingly contradictory attitudes or parts as it suited his purpose at a particular time and with a particular audience. Like Roosevelt, he has been described a hundred different ways by a hundred contemporaries. Some of the persons who were closest to him, again as with FDR's confidants, have admitted that it is doubtful that anyone knew which role personified the real man.

Major General John H. Chiles, who was a colonel and secretary of MacArthur's General Staff in Tokyo in June 1950, recalled the teleconferences between MacArthur and the Joint Chiefs regarding American military responses to the invasion of South Korea:

> Every time MacArthur would ask a question, they'd say, "Wait, and then we'll reconvene in three hours," which meant that they had to go to the Secretary of Defense, who went to the White House. In each case MacArthur put into effect what he asked for before he got permission, to my personal knowledge, including the introduction of that first battalion into Korea. . . . After the second one of these "wait-three-hours" business, he said, "This is an outrage. When I

was Chief of Staff, I could get Herbert Hoover off the can to talk to me. But here not just the Chief of Staff of the Army delays, but the Secretary of the Army and the Secretary of Defense. They've got so much lead in there that it's just inexcusable." So, as I say, he went ahead and did what he asked for, and each time it was approved. An amazing experience!²

William J. Sebald, the State Department's top official in Japan, 1947–1952, was a sharp observer of MacArthur's stratagems. He remembered a conversation with the general prior to his dismissal by Truman: "MacArthur told me, 'There's nothing they can do to me because they'll have to get together the thirteen countries of the Far Eastern Commission and they have to agree to fire me. If they don't agree but still want to replace me, there has to be an international agreement.'" Years later, Sebald remarked about MacArthur's relief that, unlike the general, he was "surprised it didn't come earlier."³

Despite the arrogance of his command, MacArthur held deep convictions about the course of American foreign policy. In the Southwest Pacific and later in Japan, he argued vociferously and repeatedly for American strategy-makers to place a higher priority on the Far East and Pacific, predicting that after 1945 American strategic and security interests would be at stake in East and Southeast Asia to a far greater degree than imagined by the war-time "Europe-firsters." MacArthur later expressed his views on global priorities:

> . . . Europe's very survival is dependent upon our gaining a de-
> cisive victory in Asia, where Communism has already thrown down
> the gage of battle. . . . Our first line of defense for Western Europe
> is not the Elbe, it is not the Rhine—it is the Yalu. Lose there and
> you render useless the effort to implement the North Atlantic Pact
> or any other plan for region defense. What gullibility to think the
> free world would fight for freedom in Europe after refusing to do so
> in Asia!⁴

No small measure of the general's political clout in the States came from leaders of the China Lobby, who generally supported not only Generalissimo Chiang Kai-shek's Kuomintang but also the ruling conservative regimes in South Korea, Japan, and the Philippines. MacArthur did not hesitate to advocate American assistance to these nations, and in turn, he had the strong backing and admiration of Chiang of Nationalist China, Yoshida of Japan, Rhee of South Korea, and the successive presidents of the Philippines, Manuel Roxas and Elpidio Quirino. If MacArthur had a limited but influential right-wing following in America, he commanded high-level and widespread support in these four Asian nations. His popular image had transformed him in the eyes of these leaders and their peoples into far more than an American general: He was the symbol of America's strategic stakes in their region of the globe.

Despite the negative aspects of his leadership in the period 1941–1950, there was a considerable array of positive factors that he carried into his command in the Korean War. During the Second World War he was outstanding in several areas. He utilized the minimal logistical support he received, in contrast to the higher-priority Central Pacific, Mediterranean, and European theaters, to achieve maximum offensive effectiveness. In this way, he developed the Southwest Pacific theater into a far more significant axis of advance than the Anglo-American Combined Chiefs of Staff had originally envisioned. While accepting the Joint Chiefs' prerogative in issuing directives on his theater's overall functions and missions for a given period, he implemented these directives in very imaginative ways. He became so innovative in this regard that he was actually leading at a strategic level of his own—the regional dimension as contrasted with the JCS planning of global strategy—while delegating theater tactical planning to his senior field commanders.

Among other achievements was his cooperation with the Labour government of Prime Minister John Curtin in making Australia into a magnificent base of operations, which became an unexpected bonus in determining the course of the war with Japan. In addition, he oversaw the development of the planning, forces, techniques, and cover to launch fifty-six amphibious assaults, all successful and employing largely American Army troops. They were transported by Vice Admiral Daniel E. Barbey's efficient if sometimes ramshackle amphibious force and supported by General George C. Kenney's powerful Fifth Air Force and Admiral Thomas C. Kinkaid's small Seventh Fleet. These unconventional attacks from the sea, involving little of the main strength of the Navy and Marines in the Pacific war, usually bypassed Japanese strongholds and depended upon finely polished coordination between ground, sea, and air units. In all this, he demonstrated an extraordinary talent in prodding, inspiring, or otherwise transforming rather ordinary senior staff and field officers into aggressive, productive leaders who deserve more accolades than they have gotten in histories of the war.

In the occupation of Japan he helped facilitate a bevy of political, economic, and other changes that turned Japan from a militaristic, supranationalistic state to one committed to its own forms of democratization, demilitarization, and economic revival. He personally and relentlessly pressured his headquarters staff and the Japanese government to inaugurate many of the legal and constitutional reforms before the Far Eastern Commission became operative and Soviet obstructionism became a hindrance. He was instrumental in inaugurating a program of relief for the Japanese people even though the original occupation directive did not provide for such aid. Largely because of MacArthur's persistent demands, a more humanitarian direction was taken, and by 1951 the United States had provided over $2 billion in goods and services in relief and welfare programs in war-devastated Japan. This gesture, according to many Japanese leaders of the time, did much to begin the strong friendship between Japan and America.

Perhaps most significantly, MacArthur's role was decisive in protecting Emperor Hirohito from trial as a war criminal. He thereby preserved one of the main instruments to secure Japanese cooperation during the occupation. In early 1946, when the U.S. government was seriously considering war crimes prosecution of the Emperor, MacArthur sent the Joint Chiefs (through Army Chief of Staff Eisenhower) a strongly worded telegram warning that the branding of Hirohito as a war criminal would severely disrupt Japanese society and compel the United States to send "a minimum of a million troops" and "several hundred thousand" civilian administrators to Japan, and the occupation would have to be maintained "for an indefinite number of years."[5] The Joint Chiefs, as well as high-ranking officials of the State Department, agreed with unusual dispatch and near unanimity that these consequences were too awful to contemplate and thence let the matter die quietly and quickly.

Whatever his personal faults, it is likely that MacArthur's accomplishments in brilliantly commanding the reconquest of the Southwest Pacific and in administering probably the most benevolent and successful military occupation in history will get ample attention in future chronicles. These achievements were certainly prominent in the minds of Truman and his top advisers when it came to selecting a commander for the United Nations forces in the Korean conflict.

The United Nations Security Council passed a resolution on July 7, 1950, two weeks after the Korean hostilities began, calling upon UN members to provide "military forces and other assistance" in the defense of South Korea. The UN military organization would be established as "a unified command under the United States," with President Truman to "designate the commander of such forces."[6] Truman thus became the executive agent for the Security Council in this matter; he then requested the Joint Chiefs of Staff to recommend an officer. Presumably he would be an Army general since the preponderance of American personnel likely to be committed would be ground troops, principally the Eighth Army, which had been on occupation duty in Japan since 1945. The executive agent for the JCS would then become the chief of staff of the U.S. Army, General Collins, in dealing with the commander in chief of the new United Nations Command. The Joint Chiefs responded quickly to the President's request on July 8, recommending MacArthur, whom Truman promptly approved. Neither the Joint Chiefs nor the President apparently considered any other officer for the post. Indeed, the official chronicle of the JCS states flatly, "There was only one conceivable choice."[7]

Oddly, MacArthur's age and health did not deter his selection. He had reached the American military establishment's statutory retirement age of sixty-four in January 1944, thus making him a half year away from his seventy-first birthday when he was appointed CINCUNC. Though mentally sharp, he was increasingly bothered by problems of aging, especially poor eyesight and Parkinson's syndrome. Truman and his military advisers might have considered the option of choosing a war commander while leaving MacArthur in charge of the occupation of Japan, especially since John Foster Dulles, with MacArthur's assistance, was beginning the planning and negotiations for a Japanese peace treaty.

Generals Lawton Collins, Matthew Ridgway, Maxwell D. Taylor, and Mark Clark were among a host of younger, extremely able commanders who had won distinction in World War II and would have been potential choices to command the Korean War effort. Moreover, such officers had come to know most of the key Pentagon officials and were up to date on recent Washington thinking about strategies for cold war, limited war, and coalition war. MacArthur, on the other hand, had not served in the United States for fifteen years and was not on close terms with any of the current Pentagon leaders or Joint Chiefs, his Southwest Pacific commanders having been almost entirely ignored in the rush to postwar power in the Pentagon by former officers in the war against Germany.

Truman publicly announced MacArthur's appointment on July 8, and a grateful MacArthur responded by radiogram to his earlier personal notification: "I recall so vividly and with such gratitude that this is the second time you have so signally honored me," referring to his SCAP (Supreme Commander for the Allied Powers, Japan) appointment in August 1945. MacArthur then affirmed, "I can only repeat the pledge of my complete personal loyalty to you as well as an absolute devotion to your monumental struggle for peace and good will throughout the world. I hope I will not fail you."[8] Truman responded in kind, "Your words confirm me, if any confirmation were needed, in my full belief in the wisdom of your selection."[9] On July 9, correspondent James Reston sounded a more realistic, if sour, note when he wrote in the *New York Times*, "Diplomacy and a vast concern for the opinions and sensitivities of others are the political qualities essential to his new assignment, and these are precisely the qualities General MacArthur has been accused of lacking in the past." He went on to remind readers of MacArthur's "old habit of doing things in his own way, without too much concern about waiting for orders from Washington." He pointed out that already, during the first days of the Korean War, the Far East commander had ordered his aircraft to bomb Pyongyang before presidential authorization had been given. Reston concluded that MacArthur was "a sovereign power in his own right, with stubborn confidence in his own judgment."[10] Unfortunately, in the months ahead, the mutual respect of MacArthur and Truman would be laid aside as each man strove to outdo the other in stubbornness and self-righteousness.

## TROUBLE UNDER STRESS

"General MacArthur was not a simple man. . . . He was above the clouds," observed a Japanese journalist of the early fifties.[11] Geniuses are not normally predictable, but MacArthur was both. On the other hand, he was a most complicated person, often manifesting utterly contradictory characteristics. Indeed, one aspect of his fascination to his colleagues was the predictable pattern of his contradictions.

While some persons, usually those who knew him slightly or through media accounts, called him conceited, arrogant, aloof, and pretentious, others who were close to him professionally or personally described him as self-sacrificing, humble, charming, and modest. Nearly all those who knew him well maintained that no one would ever probe fully the complex personality and character of Douglas MacArthur. Some of them added that he was so adept at playing roles that none of his inner circle, whether of the World War II, Japanese occupation, or Korean War vintage, knew for certain which was the real MacArthur.

His contradictory nature was never more vividly apparent than during the Korean conflict. On occasion, he would visit battle zones at considerable risk, uncalled for by a theater commander, but at other times he would refuse to go to combat areas for lengthy periods. He would demonstrate strategic brilliance at times, while displaying hesitancy or recklessness at others. He would accomplish remarkable results with meager means, while misusing his resources when they were more than ample later. He would exhibit sincere concern over keeping troop losses at a minimum, yet he would allow his troops to be ambushed even though his intelligence had signaled trouble ahead. He would possess an awesome breadth and depth of knowledge on a variety of subjects but would then expound ad nauseum on topics about which he knew little or nothing. He would remain unduly sensitive about his public image but would blunder often in dealing with the press. He would prove to be a gifted administrator who could plan, organize, and lead his several commands with tight efficiency, but at the same time he would coddle some inept, sycophantic staff leaders and allow his chief of staff (Edward M. Almond) to assume dual staff and field positions of great power. An outspoken advocate of the values of Christianity and Americanism, which he found amazingly alike, he would engage in audacious scheming that bewildered West Pointers and others who tried to fathom his interpretation of "duty, honor, and country," the motto of the United States Military Academy that he often quoted. He would demand the last farthing in uncritical devotion and loyalty from his staff and field commanders, but he would severely criticize the Joint Chiefs of Staff and the President on the direction of the war in Korea.

Philip LaFollette, who was on MacArthur's staff and later became governor of Wisconsin, found the general to be "endowed with a first-class mind, which he enriched with prodigious reading and study. And all was dominated by a will of iron. . . . Rarely was he put to his mettle by other mortals. And when he was—if in his own military field—he was superb, dazzling." LaFollette continued: "But there was a serious flaw in this otherwise almost perfect combination of human qualities. He had no humility and hence no saving grace of a sense of humor. He could never laugh at himself—never admit mistakes or defeats. When these occurred they were never admitted, and he resorted to tricks—sometimes sly, childlike attempts—to cover up." He concluded: "This petty but understandable trait of wanting to be perfect, to ignore his obvious warts—warts that were insignificant against his towering intellect, superb courage, and inflexible will—became important only because they were denied."[12] Admiral Barbey, who was his amphibious chief in World War II and later Seventh Fleet commander, remarked frankly that MacArthur "was never able to develop a feeling of warmth and comradeship with those about him. He had their respect but not their sympathetic understanding or their affection. He could not inspire the electrifying leadership [Admiral William F.] Halsey had. He was too aloof and too correct in manner, speech, and dress. He had no small talk, but when discussing military matters he was superb."[13]

MacArthur's personality was such a twisted mass of contradictions that a psychohistorian could exhaust his knowledge of oxymorons in describing him. The general's ability to survive and succeed depended upon his control of his environment and upon the vital ingredient of successful military leadership: luck. During the Korean War, however, MacArthur's carefully regulated life-style became stress-laden and upsetting, his contradictions in personality lost their charismatic appeal, and his luck in war and strategy ran out. The principal flaws that brought him to disaster had all been evident in previous years but somehow had not been exhibited before the Korean debacle in a situation wherein he lost his control as well as his luck. The cardinal defects that underlay his fall from power in 1950–1951 were egotism and two of its corollaries—isolation and hypersensitivity.

At least as early as his cadet days at West Point he had demonstrated superior qualities of intellect and leadership that were often likened to those of Robert E. Lee. Buttressed by numerous acts of bravery in World War I that gave him a heroic image unusual for a senior officer, his military career became meteoric: He rose to brigadier general in 1918, became one of the youngest chiefs of staff in the Army's annals, staged an aggressive comeback from initial defeat in World War II to achieve an unbroken string of victories, and established a record of leadership in Japan that was unusually enlightened for a military occupation. He had proven to be outstanding as a warrior and as an administrator. He was a widely respected, if not universally liked, professional of the first rank in the military world. By the time the Korean War erupted, he was blessed with great seniority as well as superiority in his military experience as compared to most officers in the Pentagon who advised the President on the direction of the new war. Though he could be gracious and charming toward some of his peers and superiors, he could also be condescending and contemptuous toward those whom he obviously viewed as lesser mortals.

Correspondent Turner Catledge and publisher A. H. Sulzberger of the *New York Times* visited MacArthur in 1944 and, according to Catledge, it was "one of the most fascinating talks with a public figure that either of us had ever experienced. . . . As he spoke, he was variously the military expert, the political figure, the man of destiny. Sulzberger and I later agreed that we had never met a more egotistical man, nor one more aware of his egotism and more able and determined to back it up with deeds."[14] As long as MacArthur's luck held and he continued to be victorious on the battlefield or correct in his strategic arguments with his superiors, his arrogant ways were tolerated. With the failure of his predictions, however, MacArthur's egotism made him an easy target for critics in the media and, more important, in the Pentagon.

MacArthur's ego required frequent massaging, so he surrounded himself with a sycophantic staff. There is no doubt that MacArthur possessed charisma that attracted and held some of the senior staff officers in his headquarters for long periods. Often critical of each other, they were devoted to him, and he returned their loyalty in full. The group that formed his inner circle of confidants had begun in World War II with the "Bataan Gang," some of his officers who had served under him in the Philippines and went on to Australia to form the nucleus of his Southwest Pacific theater headquarters. Others joined these close advisers and friends in the advance back to the Philippines; still others became members of the inner group in Japan as older officers were transferred or retired; and by the time of the Korean conflict his senior staff officers included still more new faces. Yet there was always a core of old-timers who sustained and continued the legend of MacArthur and kept it vital and active into the Korean War.

The inner circle in 1950–1951 consisted of twelve members of his GHQ staff, led by Major Generals Courtney Whitney, his alter ego and chief of the occupation's Government Section; Edward M. Almond, his chief of staff and subsequent X Corps commander; and Charles A. Willoughby, his intelligence chief (his G-2) since 1941; and Colonel Laurence E. Bunker, his principal aide and later vice president of the John Birch Society. The only commander of field forces who was considered a MacArthur confidant was Lieutenant General George E. Stratemeyer, head of the Far East Air Forces.

Conspicuously absent from the group that enjoyed close ties with MacArthur were his top Navy and Army commanders, Vice Admiral C. Turner Joy, who led U.S. Naval Forces, Far East, and Lieutenant General Walton H. Walker, commanding general of the Eighth Army. The professional ties between MacArthur and his naval and ground chiefs were satisfactory, but neither Joy nor Walker was personally or socially close to MacArthur and his inner circle of confidants. Indeed, Walker faced personality clashes with three key members of this GHQ group: Almond, Willoughby, and Whitney. The basis for such nonprofessional differences is buried in a mountain of hearsay.

MacArthur was shielded by his GHQ senior staff officers in unfortunate ways; this was part of the legacy of their adulation of him from World War II. When occupation controls in Japan began to be gradually withdrawn in 1949, large numbers of officers and men of the Eighth Army were relieved of military government duties and went back to their regular units. This meant, particularly with Walker's assumption of the army command that year, a more vigorous training program was inaugurated. But MacArthur's staff shielded the Far East commander from evidence suggesting the Eighth Army's progress toward combat readiness was not impressive, and he was quite shocked by the troops' poor performances early in the Korean War. Actually, as in the Philippine defense buildup in the late 1930s that he oversaw, MacArthur seldom visited or inspected military units and installations but relied instead on information fed to him by his trusted staff leaders. During his five and a half years in Japan, he rarely departed from his daily itinerary between his quarters at the U.S. Embassy and his office at the Dai Ichi Building.

MacArthur lived strangely isolated, apart from the activities of his Far East Command. Sadly, his trust in Willoughby was so deep by then that MacArthur's intelligence data came almost solely from his G-2, and Willoughby could be quite selective and sometimes erroneous in what he provided his commander. Neither MacArthur nor Willoughby had much faith in the intelligence provided by the Office of Strategic Services (OSS) during the Second World War or the Central Intelligence Agency (CIA) and State intelligence sources before and during the Korean War. It was as if MacArthur existed in Tokyo in a cocoon, perhaps of his own choosing but possibly created by his sycophantic staff section chiefs. The price he would pay for such insularity would be tragically high.

Just how vulnerable MacArthur could become as a result of his enormous ego and extreme insularity was apparent at the Wake Island Conference on October 15, 1950, when Truman and the general, along with about sixty advisers (mostly the President's) and correspondents, converged on the tiny spot of land in the West Pacific. Truman called the session in order to discuss strategic issues of the Korean War and American policy on other Far Eastern matters, as well as to improve communications with MacArthur. The North Korean Army had been routed, and there was increasing fear that Communist China and perhaps the USSR might intervene to save the People's Democratic Republic of (North) Korea. U.S. policy toward the Nationalist Chinese on Formosa was another unsettled issue, as were the strategic relations with Japan, the Ryukyus, and the Philippines, all of which involved Mac-

Arthur's Far East Command. Actually, the conferees discussed briefly a number of topics but no matters of strategy or policy in substance.

It may well be that Truman and his political advisers used the conference to set MacArthur up as the potential scapegoat if the recent invasion of North Korea precipitated the entry of the Chinese or the Soviets into the war. The Far East commander's delight in delivering monologues on politics, diplomacy, all things Asian, and other topics far beyond his expertise was well known, and he could be counted upon to assume all responsibility for achieving victory in battle.

The Washington delegation at Wake undoubtedly was confident that the right question could prompt MacArthur to deliver another injudicious monologue. All it took was a question from Truman: "What are the chances for Chinese or Soviet interference?" The general stated emphatically: "Very little. Had they interfered in the first or second months it would have been decisive. We are no longer fearful of their intervention." Indeed, he was convinced that his air force could prevent most Chinese forces from crossing the Yalu River from Manchuria into North Korea and even if the CCF did cross they would face "the greatest slaughter."[15] MacArthur added the qualification that his view was quite speculative because the issue was one of political intelligence and therefore in the realm of State Department intelligence and the CIA. His theater military intelligence was absorbed in collecting and interpreting data about North Korean forces, not about China, which was then a nonbelligerent nation. His opinions at Wake were about the same as those recently reported by the CIA. Amazingly, there was no follow-up question, challenge, or response to MacArthur's remarks.

Truman and his administration officials, along with Democratic politicians nationwide, took full advantage of the general's unwise prophecy when the Communist Chinese entered the war a few weeks later. At the Senate hearings in May and June 1951 on MacArthur's dismissal, nearly every one of the administration witnesses referred to his Wake comments. The great majority of writings since then have noted MacArthur's erroneous judgment about Communist China as the most important happening of the Wake Island Conference. The Senate witnesses against the general and these later works assumed that if MacArthur's prediction had been different, the course of the war might have been altered. Actually, Truman and the Joint Chiefs agreed with MacArthur's views on this issue, and they were committed to the liberation of North Korea— the key reason for China's entry into the Korean War. However, it was MacArthur's sense of self-importance and melodrama that led him into needless and boastful statements which others would have regretted. The general's ego was so monumental that he boasted for the rest of his life that at least he had been right in predicting that the Soviet Union would not intervene in 1950.

The Communist Chinese offensive that forced the United Nations Command out of North Korea, November 1950–January 1951, was a catastrophic defeat for MacArthur. The rout of the Eighth Army on the west and the near-entrapment of the X Corps on the east, the latter saved by heroic Marine Corps resistance and efficient evacuation by the Seventh Fleet, were shocking reversals to MacArthur and Washington leaders, who had been expecting to wrap up the conquest of North Korea by Christmas. Before the Chinese drive was halted, it had pushed well below the 38th parallel and Seoul was once again in communist hands. MacArthur became depressed and short-tempered at GHQ and often spent the nights suffering insomnia and pacing back and forth along the Embassy hallway. His moods would swing to extremes—from buoyant optimism about winning the war before Christmas 1950 to alarmist predictions later that his troops would be compelled to withdraw to Japan unless mightily reinforced. He became persuaded that he had enemies to his front and rear, the communists on the battlefield and a host of conspirators in the States, trying to undermine his leadership. He would brook no reevaluations of his questionable selection of Almond to head X Corps and of that corps' advance into North Korea with a broad gap between it and the Eighth Army to the west. He became irritable when his comments were ridiculed in the media for launching an "all-out offensive" or "massive compression envelopment" in late November 1950 and then recategorizing it as "a reconnaissance in force" when it was stopped dead by Chinese surprise attacks and became a near-rout on the Eighth Army's front.[16]

His fear of enemies in the States was not totally paranoic. In the spring of 1949, a scheme was busily being hatched in the State Department to separate the positions of occupation head and commander of American forces in the Far East, with an ambassador to succeed MacArthur in the former role and Major General Maxwell Taylor in the latter post. MacArthur learned in March of the plotting by middle-echelon planners of the State and Defense departments. He set to work contacting influential friends in Washington to counter the movement. When he broached one aspect of the intrigue in a message to Bradley, the JCS chairman remarked to a colleague that MacArthur had sent him "a scathing diatribe the like of which I have seldom read," and that he had not been conscious of "the deep distrust with which MacArthur viewed our State Department in general and Dean Acheson in particular. He must have viewed me as a traitor too, 'selling out' to State."[17] The plan to remove MacArthur subsequently died somewhere in the bowels of the State Department or the Pentagon for reasons never fully explained. It is doubtful that either Acheson or Bradley was completely innocent or ignorant of this scheme.

In the late autumn of 1950, Brigadier General Thomas J. Davis, a former aide to MacArthur and then to Eisenhower, was asked to advise the Joint Chiefs of Staff on what he knew about MacArthur's "nuttiness, especially his dealings with women" and other evidence of his "bizarre personal conduct" in the 1930s. Thus in the midst of a war the extremely important military body, the Joint Chiefs, took time to enjoy some spicy and highly dubious tales that were part of an obvious smear job. The justification seemed to be to try to find evidence to support the removal of MacArthur on grounds that his alleged instability after the Chinese entry had a prior basis of earlier strange behavior.[18]

Also in 1950, General Walter Bedell Smith, the new CIA director, asked Lieutenant General Pedro A. del Valle, a distinguished Marine in the war against Japan, to come to Washington for an important meeting. There the astonished Marine officer learned that Smith "wanted me to establish a C.I.A. intelligence office in Tokyo to pull the rug out from under MacArthur." At the end of Smith's pitch, del Valle told the CIA chief that he considered MacArthur "the greatest soldier-statesman this country had" and bluntly rejected the offer. On his way out of CIA headquarters, del Valle stated that he "met Allen Dulles, second in command of the CIA. He was all smiles and greeted me cordially, saying he was glad I was joining them. I disabused him of this erroneous conclusion and departed." Del Valle subsequently shared some parts of Smith's wild ploy with MacArthur and assured him of his "staunch support, admiration, and approval."[19]

It is clear that MacArthur had more than ample reason to be anxious about enemies to his rear. Although the general did show signs of paranoia when under extreme stress, the myth that he was unjustifiably anxious about plots against him needs to be laid to rest. He felt himself endangered by his own superiors and he was. The effects of this on his command were to make him defensive, highly sensitive to criticism, and overly obsessed with protecting his image as a great warrior.

## THE TWILIGHT OF A GREAT CAPTAIN

From the perspectives of theater strategy, leadership, and personality, MacArthur went through four distinct phases from the beginning of hostilities in Korea to his ouster nine months later. The first phase, June 25–September 14, 1950, involved delaying and then halting the North Korean offensive. He relied on a rapid buildup of men and matériel and devastating aerial interdiction of enemy lines of communication to do this. MacArthur's leadership was aggressive; he often intervened in the conduct of operations, and he was eagerly anticipatory, his concern ever on planning a counteroffensive. He was active, vigorous, and confident, and he was blessed with luck on the timing of his reinforcements. This period, when he was overseeing the Naktong River defensive operations and winning over his superiors to his Inchon plan, was his "finest hour" in the Korean War and determined the outcome of the North Korean stage, which was the enemy's ouster from South Korea and the UN Command's advance well above the 38th parallel.

The second phase, September 15–November 24, 1950, was highlighted by the highly successful attack from the sea of MacArthur's forces at Inchon, the port for the South Korean capital of Seoul; the breakout of Walker's army from the Naktong defensive perimeter in the southeast corner of South Korea and the linkup of those forces with the Inchon assault units; the mopping-up of scattered North Korean troops below the 38th parallel; and the separate drives of the Eighth Army and the X Corps through North Korea, with several small units reaching the Yalu River, the border between North Korea and Manchuria. MacArthur was basking in the glory of his Inchon triumph and recklessly underestimating the risks inherent in the divided command he sent on the drive to the Yalu. He was bursting with optimism and believed the end of the war was imminent despite rumblings from Peking and reports that he received in late October and early November (which he discounted) that Chinese units were savagely attacking his spearhead forces and disappearing just as quickly as they appeared.

During the third phase, November 25, 1950–January 14, 1951, the Communist Chinese armies struck both the Eighth Army and X Corps in massive surprise assaults, overrunning or enveloping units in fast moves southward except against the well-disciplined withdrawal of the 1st Marine Division on the east side of North Korea. He experienced panic and then paralysis in his decisions, messages, and pronouncements, reacting with defiance and later resignation toward his Washington superiors. In the final phase, January 15–April 11, 1951, he left the running of the war largely to Ridgway and focused his attention on his battle with Washington, staying on his collision course with Truman until he was fired. Toward the end he was fatalistic and seemed to aspire to martyrdom, going out in a blaze of melodrama. During the first period, when he was most like his best performances of the Second World War, he suddenly found himself unable to exploit his new international position vis-à-vis his national commands. His multi-hat maneuvering had been very advantageous in furthering his interests in the war against Japan and the subsequent occupation, but on July 12, 1950, less than a week after his appointment as commander in chief of the United Nations Command, the JCS effectively began to tie his hands. Later that month they told him to send reports on operations about every two weeks; these would ultimately be forwarded to the Security Council after editing (censoring, in effect) by the Defense and State departments. The JCS blocked all direct communications from MacArthur to the Security Council in order, states the Joint Chiefs' chronicle, "to prevent the United Nations from involvement in strategy or tactics."[20]

At the Senate hearings the next spring, MacArthur said that throughout his tenure as United Nations commander "the entire control of my command and everything I did came from our own Chiefs of Staff and my channel of communications was defined as the Army Chief of Staff. . . . I had no direct connection with the United Nations whatsoever."[21] He still might be able to play shell-and-pea games with his three American commands and his Allied occupation position, but he was thwarted early with regard to his UN role.

There would have been no Inchon envelopment if not for MacArthur's vision, careful planning, and courageous stand against many of his military peers and superiors. He surely deserves credit for giving birth to Operation Chromite (the Inchon assault), one of the most bold and successful amphibious attacks ever launched. But regardless of how much praise is heaped on MacArthur for his contribution, Inchon cannot be fairly evaluated out of context or without considering its consequences, which were largely negative.

The Eighth Army underwent chaos and confusion when the main Chinese assault began in late November. MacArthur reacted like the exhausted, emotionally drained seventy-year-old he was. At the end of December he proposed a four-point plan for the future direction of the war that the JCS rightly rejected as militarily impractical and unsound. The plan included the blockading and bombarding of China and the use of Formosa-based Nationalist Chinese troops in Korea or against the Chinese mainland. Later, MacArthur would amend his list of proposals several times, but despite modification, they were unacceptable to the Joint Chiefs for a host of reasons. MacArthur could be strategically perceptive, but he was not in this case on two basic counts. The Truman administration had repeatedly turned down Nationalist Chinese troop assistance for diplomatic and logistical reasons. The United States woefully lacked the wherewithal in naval and strategic air strength to punish Red China as MacArthur proposed.

These proposals by MacArthur were unrealistic, but he made two wise and far-reaching decisions during this same week of despair and gloomy headlines. With Walker's death in a road accident north of Seoul on December 23, MacArthur asked Collins to send Ridgway as the new head of the Eighth Army; Marshall and Truman quickly approved, and Ridgway promptly left his Pentagon post and flew to Tokyo. He had won fame in the war against Germany as an airborne and corps commander and at the time of his Eighth Army selection was the Army deputy chief of staff for administration and training. Ridgway met with MacArthur the morning after Christmas and left this account:

> . . . I had known MacArthur since my days as a West Point instructor but, like everyone who had ever dealt with him, I was again deeply impressed by the force of his personality. . . . His immedi-

ate instructions were to hold as far as possible "in the most advanced positions in which you can maintain yourself." . . .

His chief concern at this conference seemed to be the fact that we were then operating in a "mission vacuum," as he termed it, while diplomacy attempted to feel its way. "A military success," he said, "will strengthen our diplomacy."

He urged me especially not to underestimate the Chinese. "They constitute a dangerous foe," he warned me. . . . "The entire Chinese military establishment is in this fight."

As for his own goal, the maximum he had in mind, he said, was "inflicting a broadening defeat making possible the retention and security of South Korea."

"Form your own opinions," he told me in closing. "Use your own judgment. I will support you. You have my complete confidence." . . .

My final question was simply this: "If I find the situation to my liking, would you have any objections to my attacking?" And his answer encouraged and gratified me deeply:

"The Eighth Army is yours, Matt. Do what you think is best."[22]

Ridgway earned almost universal praise from contemporary and later authorities on the Korean War for his amazing transformation of the Eighth Army into an aggressive fighting force again and for his later leadership of the United Nations, Far East, and other commands he took over from MacArthur. It was MacArthur who selected Ridgway as Walker's successor and bestowed such generous latitude on him, a privilege that he had not given the much-beleaguered but very able Walker. Unfortunately, in allowing the new army commander such loose reins, MacArthur did not keep as closely abreast of events and suffered the severe penalty of having Ridgway move to the counteroffensive in mid-January while his Tokyo boss was still warning Washington that an evacuation of United Nations forces from the peninsula might soon become necessary.

MacArthur was also insightful in that he was one of the earliest American public figures to argue against the concept of the Kremlin-run global communist monolith. At the Senate hearings in May 1951 regarding his relief from duty, he commented that the Soviet Union's decision to go to war would be determined by its own "timetable" and not by what Communist China was doing. He maintained that Moscow was not "sufficiently associated" with Peking and Pyongyang in the Korean conflict to view its national interests so threatened that it would enter the war. In fact, he speculated that Soviet leaders might be anxious "if China became too powerful" and might not mind if "this new Frankenstein" suffered a defeat in Korea.[23]

MacArthur's many comments refuting the communist monolith theory demonstrate that the general, a darling of anticommunists in America, was quite farsighted regarding the Soviet Union. He saw that there was no world communist plan and proved himself a harbinger of the coming Sino-Soviet dispute in the later fifties.

Nevertheless, in 1950–1951, Truman and leaders of the Pentagon and State Department felt that MacArthur was behind the times and could not comprehend the complex nature of the Cold War. How old-fashioned, they thought, were his words before Congress in April 1951 following his relief, especially his claim of "no substitute for victory."[24] MacArthur had felt that when he was held back from achieving victory, a war of indecisive stalemate was futile and immoral. It was wrong to send American boys to die in such places if there were not clear-cut, consistent objectives. MacArthur almost seemed to glimpse what many Americans later learned about the conflict in Vietnam: A protracted limited war, especially for a democratic nation, produces war-weariness, then loss of morale, and finally such divisiveness that the war is not worth it. Again and again MacArthur hit hard on the point that if the U.S. government was not lucid in formulating its war aims, then it should not send young citizen-soldiers to sacrifice their lives in combat. MacArthur, a seasoned warrior of three great conflicts, knew firsthand about trying to implement policies that were altered several times within a few months, and he had seen much of war's horrors. In his eighties, he would repeat this counsel earnestly to two successive presidents, both of whom admired him greatly, John F. Kennedy and Lyndon B. Johnson: Do not send American soldiers to fight on the Asian mainland unless you are sure that the cause is worth it and the American people endorse it.

Ultimately, MacArthur had much in common with the man who dismissed him. Both the general and Truman displayed courage in standing up for their convictions. MacArthur said it was the virtue he esteemed the most. He expounded on this in a letter to an officer-student at the Army Command and Staff College at Fort Leavenworth, Kansas, in 1956:

> Moral courage—true leadership—is based upon a fundamental but simple philosophy—to do what you think is right as opposed to what you think is wrong irrespective of the popularity or unpopularity which may result, and always with the realization that being human you may be wrong in your decision. Do this and you will always be a little lonesome although it will render you immune to two of the greatest frauds in the world, triumph and disaster—the roar of the crowd either in the acclaim of victory or in the disapproval of defeat.[25]

Sadly, in view of the irreparable tear in their relationship, Truman could have written the above as easily as MacArthur. In their private moments and public utterances both protagonists were continually referring to similar virtues and ideals, such as courage, character, freedom, and democracy, which had characterized their versions of what America was fighting for during World War II. Both perceived the Korean War as a struggle between the forces of right and wrong, and neither ever admitted how simplistic such a view of that conflict was.

CHAPTER

# 3

# Ridgway: From Wolfhound to Koje-do

## Revitalizing the Eighth Army

When Ridgway took over the Eighth Army in late December 1950, the battlefront situation looked grim. The Chinese Communist Forces had cut through and around the United Nations right flanks time after time, forcing the Eighth Army units that were not surrounded or decimated to flee southward toward the 38th parallel. In Washington and Tokyo the alternatives appeared to be narrowed to two: either try to establish a firm holding line south of Seoul or, if that failed, evacuate all forces to Japan. Ridgway's challenges were to demonstrate that he could quickly change his army from a beaten, retreating horde into an effective combat force capable of stopping the enemy drive as soon as possible. At no time did he seriously entertain the thought that his army would be driven off the peninsula. He had demonstrated a cocky, aggressive attitude in tough conditions and had come through them tenaciously and successfully.

While MacArthur was superintendent at the United States Military Academy in 1919–1922, three of the principals in the American high command during the Korean War were under him: Cadet Hoyt S. Vandenberg, Captain Lawton Collins in the Chemistry Department, and Captain Matt Ridgway in the Athletic Department. But Ridgway was the only one of the three to attract MacArthur's attention at that time. "He brought me in to take charge of the Athletic Department," recalled Ridgway. "He told me right to my face to report only to him. . . . I had been very close to him there because he was so deeply interested in athletics."[1] MacArthur would remember Ridgway's aggressiveness, frankness, and decisiveness over the years, follow his career as a hard-driving airborne commander in the war against Germany, and request him to head the Eighth Army in late December 1950.

During the operations in the Mediterranean and in West Europe, 1943–1945, Ridgway stood out as an airborne division and corps leader; indeed, he and his men were often given missions as elite ground assault troops instead of as paratroops, so formidable had they proven in combat against high-caliber German outfits. Ridgway was a strikingly handsome, ramrod erect, physically robust soldier who radiated authority and drive not only by his impressive physical appearance, especially his deep penetrating eyes, but also by his dramatic communicative skills. According to one of his closest colleagues, "The force that emanated from him was awesome. . . . It was a powerful presence. He'd come into a room and you immediately felt it."[2] His superiors in the American high command rated him by early 1945 as one of the officers most likely to receive command of an army soon. The war's end that spring precluded such an appointment.

Unknown to MacArthur, by late 1950 Ridgway was not only very knowledgeable about the Korean situation but also had become critical of both MacArthur's offensive deployments in North Korea and the Joint Chiefs' reluctance to countermand him. As deputy chief of staff to Collins, Ridgway had followed the Korean operations "fourteen hours a day," and was thoroughly familiar with MacArthur's refusal to change his order of advance toward the Yalu River. "I opposed the inaction, as I saw it, of the Joint Chiefs of Staff. . . . I couldn't understand the apparent reluctance to take sharp issue with the theater commander on the dispositions there."[3]

When the Communist Chinese onslaught hit in late November 1950, General MacArthur sent to Washington widely contrasting reports that ranged from cautiously confident to wildly frantic and deeply pessimistic regarding the prospects of stopping the enemy advance. MacArthur's comments as well as the shocking news of the retreat itself had an unnerving effect on some officials in the

State and Defense departments where Dean Rusk, assistant secretary of state, and Ridgway, according to one source, played crucial roles in being "able to steady the Washington hands"[4] that
were darkly predicting evacuation from the peninsula. Ridgway
had long regarded MacArthur as one of the great captains of his
era, but he probably realized that the magnitude of the disaster, if
not stemmed soon, could lead to the Tokyo chief's replacement.
With his eye on other possible assignments next, however, he did
not foresee himself as the legendary commander's successor in the
Far East.

General Walton Walker, who was bulldoggish in both his looks
and his combat leadership, had been one of Patton's hardest driving corps commanders in the war against Germany; in fact, when
that conflict ended, Walker's troops were at Linz, Austria, the far-
thest advance eastward of any Third Army unit. Under Walker, in
the summer and fall of 1950, the Eighth Army in Korea in effect
had thwarted the North Korean offensive southward with a brilliant, stalwart defensive perimeter and then had driven deep into
North Korea. Walker, however, had picked up some critics among
Tokyo and Washington observers, who, probably too harshly, had
concluded that his defensive and offensive tactics and his officers
could have been more effective. In truth, Walker suffered from
personality feuds with key leaders of MacArthur's staff and from a
number of flawed subordinates at Eighth Army headquarters. The
shocking setback of the Eighth Army on its drive to the Yalu caused
his superiors to become even more impatient and exacting toward
Walker.

During a trip to Japan and Korea in August 1950 with Harriman,
Lowe, Secretary of the Army Frank Pace, Jr., and Lieutenant General Lauris Norstad, Ridgway expressed to Pace his "concern over
Gen. Walker's leadership, lack of force, acceptance of a mediocre
staff, and an unsound base organization." Pace "indicated clearly
his own conviction that a change ought to be made as early as possible."[5] Norstad favored Ridgway for the post. When he heard their
evaluations, Collins also concluded Walker should be replaced.
While Pace preferred Ridgway or Lieutenant General Alfred M.
Gruenther to head the Eighth Army, Collins had in mind Lieutenant General James A. Van Fleet, with Ridgway as his second
choice. Collins privately asked Ridgway if he was interested, to
which the latter replied, "If we are going to war, I would prefer to
fight in Europe."[6] Meanwhile, Harriman told Truman his choices

were Ridgway or Van Fleet, to which the President responded, "Discuss it with General Bradley." Harriman discovered that was not productive: "General Bradley and the Chiefs of Staff were afraid of General MacArthur, I think; they were very timid about it."[7]

On the other hand, MacArthur was reasonably satisfied with Walker's performance when his Naktong River defense line held and his subsequent offensive into North Korea seemed to go well. Therefore MacArthur shelved any recommendations from Washington to relieve Walker. Questions about him did not rise again until the ambush of the Eighth Army by the CCF. When MacArthur asked for Ridgway after Walker's death in a highway collision two days before Christmas 1950, Collins wrote Ridgway as he prepared to leave for Korea, "Unfortunately, one of the penalties of great ability is that it inexorably draws to itself great responsibilities. It was almost inevitable that General MacArthur should turn to you to assume command of the Eighth Army. . . . The Secretary [Pace] and I have unbounded confidence in your capacity to meet this challenge."[8]

Although at his meeting with MacArthur in Tokyo on December 26, the new Eighth Army head was assured virtual independence in his planning and operations, with the Far East chief guaranteeing the firepower and logistical support to accomplish his objectives within reason, still the vital matter of troop reinforcements was beyond MacArthur's power to provide. The Pentagon notified MacArthur that the only available division-size forces were likely to be headed to Europe. American replacement divisions for Korea would not be forthcoming until the arrival of the 45th and 40th Infantry divisions in December 1951 and January 1952, respectively.

MacArthur would make numerous trips to or near the front lines to confer with Ridgway and his Eighth Army senior officers, but the Far East chief was amazingly well behaved in refraining from interfering with Ridgway's handling of the ground forces. The good news for Ridgway was that he would not have MacArthur shadowing him, a problem Walker had faced. This, however, was offset by the doleful report from GHQ intelligence that a third Communist Chinese offensive was expected soon. As it turned out, Ridgway would have only a week with the battered, dispirited Eighth Army before the CCF assault struck.

Brigadier General Walter F. Winton, Jr., Ridgway's aide and later chief of staff of the 24th Infantry Division in Korea, said of the new Eighth Army commander: "What impresses you most about the man is the vigor and speed both of his intellect and his physical actions. He is a very decisive individual—and a very fairminded one, too. . . . But he is a little bit larger to scale than most of us in the conventional military virtues—aggressiveness, tenacity, desire to close with the enemy and put him down."[9] General Frank T. Mildren, then operations chief of X Corps and later a regimental commander, found Ridgway to be "a breath of fresh air at that time because everybody had a defeatist attitude. . . . He was confident through and through." He added, however, that sometimes he could be "like a bull in a china shop . . . a typical paratrooper."[10] Ridgway was "brusque . . . very alert, very demanding . . . competent," said Brigadier General James H. Lynch, with the 1st Cavalry Division and then with I Corps headquarters.[11] According to Major General Ned. D. Moore, who served with Eighth Army headquarters and later as a regimental commander, "Ridgway was a very ambitious man and a very knowledgeable, good soldier. He was hard on his people, but he was just as hard on himself."[12]

All of Ridgway's leadership achievements in World War II had been impressive. He had quickly adapted to the new arena of airborne warfare, turning the 82nd Airborne Division into a superlative combat force, and later in the action in Northwest Europe providing aggressive leadership for the XVIII Airborne Corps. Almost all the other American airborne officers in the European war who rose to senior positions were trained by Ridgway. Such outstanding commanders as Generals Maxwell Taylor and James M. Gavin in World War II, as well as the officers who served under Ridgway in Korea, have attested to his traits as described above. He was a dynamic pacesetter for leaders of airborne and other offensive forms of warfare. In Korea, however, this famed assault commander would meet his most difficult trials in restricted defensive combat.

Ridgway's symbols, both as army and later theater commander, were his grenade and first-aid kit worn on paratroop shoulder straps. Secretary of the Army Frank Pace, who got to know him well in Washington, found his paraphernalia rather foolhardy at the

Korean front. He regarded Ridgway as "a great chauvinist as well as a great general," but Pace asked him to remove the grenade when they went out in a Korean storm because the secretary feared it would be "hit by a hail stone."[13]

When he arrived at Eighth Army headquarters in Taegu, South Korea, late on December 26, Ridgway immediately set about the enormous task of revitalizing his staff and troops, who had become severely demoralized by the rapidity and ferocity of the Communist Chinese offensive. He visited numerous units at the front, observing "a definite air of nervousness, of gloomy foreboding, of uncertainty, a spirit of apprehension as to what the future held. There was much 'looking over the shoulder,' as the soldiers say."[14] He began developing a new spirit of confidence by exhortation and example, as well as by shipping out a number of officers who were unaggressive. He saw his mission as leading the revived, regrouped Eighth Army in a strong defensive followed by a grinding offensive that would push the enemy back with enormous casualties.

Major General James G. Christiansen, the chief engineer of the Far East Command, had noticed "a defeatist attitude especially in the headquarters [of the Eighth Army], except for Walker. . . . Ridgway took that same staff and turned it around and made it a real fighting organization." He also produced "a tremendous turnaround in the fighting morale of the army," for he himself was "first and foremost a fighter."[15] According to Chief of Staff Collins, Ridgway "was faced with a situation which suited his personality, his drive, his initiative, and everything perfectly well, and he did a magnificent job. He turned that army around; there just isn't any question about it."[16] Major General Gines Perez, one of the top regimental commanders in Korea, said, "We sensed that the running of things was headed by a very strong man when Ridgway took over. We had been withdrawing and withdrawing, and the moment Ridgway took over we stopped."[17] Lieutenant General Edward A. Craig, head of the 1st Marine Brigade, observed, "General Ridgway went to all the units personally and checked them and talked to the people. He instilled in them a will to stick there or go forward. He wasn't interested so much in real estate or getting a hill here and a hill there as he was in killing a lot of the enemy."[18]

Ridgway transformed the Eighth Army by utilizing a variety of techniques. He set a model for his staff and field leaders in determination to succeed, high professional standards, courage, and intolerance for defeatism. He spent large amounts of time and energy traveling among the troops inspiring and encouraging them by his presence and charismatic magnetism and by his informal, sincere exhortations to them. He was ruthless in relieving officers who failed to measure up to his criteria of professional competence, replacing them with men more eager to take the battle to the enemy. He established a new liaison section to oversee dealings with the ROK government and to endeavor to ensure better training and equipping of South Korean units.

The third-phase offensive of the CCF began on New Year's Eve and lasted two weeks. The heaviest attacks were initially against the American I and IX corps, which were positioned along the Imjin River and above Seoul. Unable to penetrate the American defenses, the Chinese hit the ROK divisions holding the central front where a breakthrough was achieved. The city of Chunchon fell to the CCF, and the nearby American units were in danger of being outflanked. The estimated strength of the enemy offensive was almost 500,000 troops, including a number of reestablished North Korean units. Ridgway was forced to pull his troops back to a new defensive line about seventy miles south of the 38th parallel, and the CCF seized Seoul on January 5, 1951. By then, the Eighth Army had retreated over 225 miles, suffered heavy casualties, and left behind huge quantities of heavy weapons and equipment. Chinese night infiltrations and envelopments had been frequent, paralyzing many men with fear and exaggerating the actual firepower the enemy possessed. Even as his troops were withdrawing to the new line, which ran from Pyongtaek on the west coast to Samchok on the east coast of South Korea, he was encouraging his men and constantly moving about among his outfits to boost morale and to scrutinize practices and leaders. He would comment later about this dark time: "To take over something like that was a tremendous challenge. The only way to go was up—it couldn't get worse."[19] The momentum as well as the strength in troops was to the advantage of the CCF at the time, and it was by no means certain to his superiors in Tokyo or Washington that Ridgway would be able to accomplish the feat that Walker, also a proven combat leader, had not yet begun when he was killed, namely, to regroup and seize the initiative at the front before the CCF drove to the tip of the peninsula.

In Tokyo, MacArthur was communicating daily with the JCS about the UNC options of evacuation to Japan or destruction in Korea if a last-stand defense was ordered. On January 8, perhaps the low point of the war for the Eighth Army, Ridgway sent Collins a long, emotion-laden message about the bleak situation, especially regarding American combat leadership. He reported that some of his corps and division leaders lacked aggressiveness and resource-fulness when engaging the enemy. His army had been accustomed to high standards of living in the field, necessitating the use of long and vulnerable trains of supply. The Eighth Army's movements were too largely restricted to the roads because of excessive de-pendence on mechanization and unfitness physically to move by foot across mountainous terrain. In short, he had inherited an army that was far below the level of combat readiness he had achieved in his airborne forces in World War II, and he was convinced that the latter's toughness and mobility were essential for his new com-mand to win against the hardier CCF troops, who had adapted to the rugged terrain and climate. He told Collins:

> Unless you have seen this terrain, not only from the air but from a jeep, it will be hard to visualize the difficulty of operations. Yet the other fellow manages and he seems never to lack ammunition, the heaviest load in his logistics stream, though, of course, he uses impressed human carriers and every local form of transportation— oxen, camels, ponies, and two-wheeled carts. The evil genius be-hind all this is some type of eastern mind, and whether Russian or Chinese, we shall inevitably find many of the same methods applied on major scales, if and when we confront the Slav in battle. I would say, let's go! Let's wake up the American people, lest it be too late! Let's pour on the heat in our training and, above all, let's be ruthless with our general officers if they fail to measure up.[20]

Ridgway concluded with two principal points, maintaining, first, that his forces would have to be reinforced considerably in order to defeat the CCF and North Korean units in Korea. But if assis-tance was not forthcoming to make possible an honorable outcome on the battlefield, then the U.S. government would be "forced to bail us out in shame by appeasement."[21] By the latter he meant a likely yielding of the peninsula to the enemy in return for the safe evacuation of the UN forces.

On January 15, 1951, Ridgway suddenly unleashed Operation Wolfhound, which consisted of a limited thrust by the 27th Infantry Regiment, or Lieutenant Colonel John H. (Mike) Michaelis's Wolfhounds, as his distinguished outfit was nicknamed. The unit met only moderate opposition in moving from Osan to Suwon, along the main southern route to Seoul; no large CCF forces were spotted. The main portion of the reinforced regiment returned southward into the lines of its parent 25th Infantry Division, leaving a small covering force temporarily to the north. Michaelis was strongly commended by the Eighth Army head but was quite aware of the pressure to succeed that he felt from Ridgway, who was "very forceful, very direct, very intolerant of any mistakes."[22] The operation had been brief and amounted to no more than a reconnaissance in force, but it had some significant consequences: It boosted morale in the Eighth Army, showed that the CCF was not in sizable strength in that area, and inspired Ridgway to plan a two-division attack for later that month. Operation Wolfhound, according to the Army's official history, was "a harbinger of the offensive spirit that General Ridgway was bent on developing in his new command."[23]

Wolfhound's main impact may have been on the big picture beyond the battlefield, for its launch coincided with a two-day visit by Collins and Vandenberg to the front. They found the combat effectiveness and morale of the Eighth Army to be "in good shape and improving daily under Ridgway's leadership."[24] Based on a highly favorable impression of Operation Wolfhound and of the changes in attitude and discipline inaugurated by Ridgway, Collins told some correspondents at Taegu on January 16, "As of now, we are going to stay and fight."[25] It was probably no coincidence that Ridgway had chosen the 27th Infantry: Collins had been its commander earlier in Hawaii. Buoyed by what they had observed in Korea, Collins and Vandenberg reported back to their colleagues in the Pentagon that MacArthur was wrong about the only options being evacuation or annihilation unless his proposals were adopted; Ridgway and the Wolfhounds had demonstrated that the Eighth Army could hold in Korea indefinitely.

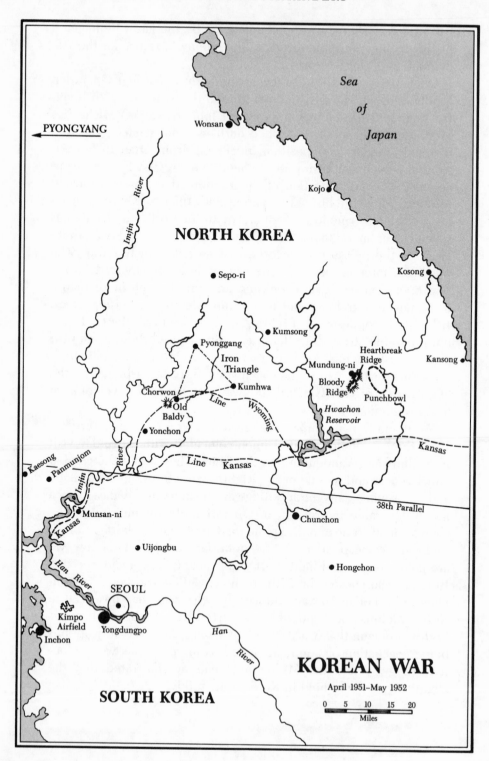

PYONGYANG ←

Sea
of
Japan

Wonsan

Kojo

NORTH KOREA

Sepo-ri

Kosong

Kumsong

Pyonggang
Iron
Triangle

Heartbreak
Ridge

Mundung-ni

Kumhwa

Bloody
Ridge

Chorwon
Old
Baldy

Line

Wyoming

Punchbowl

Yonchon

Hwachon
Reservoir

Kansas

Kaesong

Panmunjom

Line    Kansas

River

Imjin

Kansong

Munsan-ni

Kansas

38th Parallel

Chunchon

Uijongbu

Han River

Hongchon

SEOUL

Kimpo
Airfield

Yongdungpo

Han

Inchon

River

KOREAN WAR

April 1951–May 1952

0    5    10    15    20
Miles

SOUTH KOREA

The UNC strategy in early 1951, as formulated by Ridgway, called for the Eighth Army, which now included the formerly independent X Corps, to engage the enemy with annihilation of forces and equipment as the aim rather than acquisition of territory. Emphasis was to be on unleashing ground assaults only after the enemy positions had been subjected to heavy air strikes and artillery barrages. Ridgway launched Operation Thunderbolt on January 25, which was even more convincing proof of his army's new vitality. The assault began on the west side of the front, with a division each from the I and IX corps advancing northward. Two more American divisions, as well as the Turkish Brigade and two South Korean regiments, were also sent in when enemy resistance increased. The largest battle of Thunderbolt was a four-day engagement in which the 25th Infantry Division captured strategic Hill 440, near Suwon, killing more than four thousand CCF troops and losing seventy American soldiers. On February 10, elements of the I Corps reached the Han River just west of Seoul, having retaken the port of Inchon and Kimpo Airfield en route.

Meanwhile, on February 5, Ridgway had ordered the American X and ROK III corps to begin a limited drive on the central front called Operation Roundup. A strong enemy counterattack on February 11–14 stopped the ROK advance on the east side toward Hongchon, and the CCF was able to penetrate the ROK lines as far south as Chechon before Ridgway could get enough reserves into action to stop the thrust. To the west, the American X Corps, still under Almond but now part of the Eighth Army, withdrew in good order to protect its right flank. Chipyongni and Wonju were successfully retained by an American regiment and a French battalion despite repeated assaults by five CCF divisions. At Chipyongni alone the CCF lost an estimated five thousand men killed in action. Superior UN armor, artillery, infantry, and air power, highlighted by close ground support from aircraft of the Seventh Fleet's carriers and the American Fifth Air Force, exacted a costly toll on the huge CCF assault formations, compelling the enemy to retreat northward on February 18.

As it turned out, the Roundup assault had begun six days before the CCF responded, not with a limited counterattack as was first thought but with its massive fourth-phase offensive. The ability of UN forces to shift quickly from the offensive to the defensive and to thwart the big enemy drive within a week was a milestone to

Ridgway. "Despite the ferocity of the fighting and the apparent determination of the enemy," commented Ridgway, "I never had the slightest doubt over the outcome. . . . And I believe the troops shared my conviction that this time the enemy attack was going nowhere."[26]

On February 21, Ridgway's Operation Killer began with heavy artillery bombardments and devastating air strikes preparing the way. The aim was primarily destruction of enemy forces rather than capture of territory. Killer was so accurately named that Ridgway was later advised to use less apt code names. The operation employed large forces across virtually the entire front from the Yellow Sea to the Sea of Japan: the American I, IX, and X corps holding the west, west central, and central sectors, along with the ROK III and I corps manning the east central and east sectors of the front line, respectively. Altogether, Operation Killer involved ten ROK divisions, seven American divisions, three Allied brigades (Turkish, British, and Commonwealth), and two battalions (Greek and Philippine). By the end of February they had seized Kangnung on the east coast, Hoengsong in the central mountains, and control of the south bank of the Han River west, south, and east of Seoul. Almond, who was still MacArthur's chief of staff as well as X Corps commander, wrote Collins when Killer was terminated, "Matt Ridgway has infused a new spirit in the Eighth Army. This spirit was at a very low ebb when I joined it [after his independent command from Inchon to Hungnam]. I am sure that you appreciate the change, which is so evident in the results attained during the past month."[27] In contrast to Walker, Ridgway came to admire and like Almond.

Ridgway set in motion Operation Ripper on March 7, another offensive packing enormous firepower and perhaps also too appropriately named. It was designed primarily to destroy CCF forces and secondarily to drive a salient into the strategic central region. Chunchon, which was located at the northern apex, was captured by March 21. Though not a stated objective of Ripper, Seoul was reoccupied without a battle on March 15 by the I Corps when the CCF defenders pulled out to avert encirclement. On March 22, Ridgway began Operation Courageous, which in the following eight days cleared most of South Korea except for the mountains in the southwest and a small area west of the Imjin. Unlike the

controversial first crossing of the 38th parallel, this time Mac-
Arthur simply authorized Ridgway on March 23 to continue his
advance into North Korea but not to publicize it, the push carrying
forces of the ROK I and American IX corps north of the parallel on
March 27 and 31, respectively.

By that time intelligence staffs at Ridgway's and MacArthur's
headquarters were receiving strong signals that an enormous CCF
spring offensive was in the offing. The enemy's principal assembly
locale was a mountainous area just above the 38th parallel in the
central sector; it would later be nicknamed the Iron Triangle, the
locale of many fierce battles over the next two and a half years. In
an effort to keep the concentration of CCF units off balance while
his own forces prepared the strongest possible defensive entrenchments to stop the expected CCF assault, Ridgway activated Operation Rugged on April 5, which would carry his troops to a position called Line Kansas, giving them control of the high ground
just south of the Iron Triangle. On April 11, Ridgway was readying
an attack on Chorwon, the southwest point of the enemy's assembly triangle, when he received the startling news from Secretary
of the Army Pace, who happened to be visiting him near the front,
that he was to succeed MacArthur immediately as head of the
United Nations Command, the United States Far East Command,
the United States Army in the Far East, and the Allied occupation
of Japan.

The command change in Tokyo had been ordered suddenly by
the President, though the causal factors had been building toward
a collision between Truman and MacArthur for several months. It
will be recalled that, whereas the President viewed the primary
issue as one of insubordination by the Far East chief, the two held
widely differing positions on the strategy of the war and were handicapped by increasing breakdowns in communications. Truman
and the JCS believed that in choosing Ridgway as MacArthur's successor they were getting not only an extremely able, experienced,
high-level commander but also a theater chief who was in sympathy with the policies of the Truman administration in military and
foreign policy.

Because of a strong storm crossing that sector of the front line,
Ridgway was not able to fly to Tokyo until the next day, April 12.
He met with MacArthur for an hour in the library of the American

Embassy and was impressed once again by the seventy-one-year-old warrior:

> He [MacArthur] was entirely himself—composed, quiet, temperate, friendly, and helpful to the man who was to succeed him. . . . There was no trace of bitterness or anger in his tone. I thought it was a fine tribute to the resilience of this great man that he could accept so calmly, with no outward sign of shock, what must have been a devastating blow to a professional soldier standing at the peak of his career.[28]

Ridgway did not condone MacArthur's insolent challenges to Truman's authority, of course, but he was impressed by the old general's agility in shifting from rage and frustration to tranquility and gentlemanliness as he bowed out. With the four high commands he had just acquired, Ridgway also had become an officer at the zenith of his professional life so far, though his career ladder was destined to have important rungs added later.

## THIRTEEN FRUSTRATING MONTHS

Truman ordered Ridgway to succeed MacArthur on April 11. The new Far East chief would inherit a GHQ staff in Tokyo largely devoted to the ousted MacArthur and which undoubtedly would have to be replaced in many posts. It took a while for Lieutenant General James Van Fleet, who was the new commander of the Eighth Army, to journey from Florida to the Pentagon and on to Japan and Korea. He got to Taegu around noon on April 14 and assumed command from Ridgway, who returned to the Tokyo GHQ that day to take over MacArthur's positions. Major General Doyle O. Hickey, MacArthur's acting chief of staff, had functioned as acting head of the four commands in the interim.

Van Fleet boasted a long and meritorious record, including citations for bravery in the First World War and outstanding service as a commander at the regimental, then divisional, and ultimately corps levels in the offensives from Normandy to Germany in 1944–1945. He had performed ably as head of the American military advisory group in Greece in 1948–1950, helping to keep the communists from winning the civil war in that country. At the time of his appointment to the Korean command he was heading the Second Army in the United States, though on leave when Collins called him in Florida.

To Collins, Van Fleet had been "the natural selection" to succeed Walker, and the Army Chief of Staff confidentially told him at Walker's funeral that he would be his choice to succeed Ridgway, who by then had gone to Korea.[29] Meanwhile, Lieutenant General Joseph M. Swing, the hard-driving head of the 11th Airborne Division under MacArthur in the war against Japan, had been approached by his close friend Ridgway about taking the Eighth Army post in case he was transferred, possibly coming over first as deputy commander. Swing said, "There were orders coming out for me to go over there and join Ridgway," but "two days later I got countermanding orders."[30] Ridgway's version was that he had sent "a personal letter to Joe Swing, asking him would he find it agreeable. I received an enthusiastic answer back. Then I got kind of a little slap on the wrist from [General Wade H.] Haislip, the Vice Chief of Staff, that this was their prerogative in Washington." So, as for Van Fleet's selection, Ridgway admitted, "I had nothing whatsoever to do with it."[31]

The awkward beginning for Ridgway and Van Fleet would have some negative repercussions in their relationship, which would be professionally correct but personally not close. Ridgway later admitted that Van Fleet sometimes was too "political" and "aggressive," requiring him to "keep a rein" on some of his plans, but, in general, he had "the highest confidence" in Van Fleet as he proved his ability in leading the Eighth Army.[32] Ridgway admitted, "I did not agree with some of General Van Fleet's proposed tactical operations. Where I felt that way I withheld or disapproved them, but there was no difficulty there." He did feel, however, that in a Senate investigation of ammunition shortages during the Korean conflict, Van Fleet "overemphasized" the crisis, which irked Ridgway: "There was never any shortage of ammunition at the battery positions. There was never any curtailment of fire."[33]

Van Fleet would also disagree with his superior over halting UN offensive operations in June 1951, when the CCF seemed to be on the run, in order to start truce negotiations. Later, however, Ridgway said the Eighth Army commander changed his view: "There still were, of course, voices that urged that we drive on to the Yalu again . . . but Van Fleet's was not one of them. No one who was conscious of the military facts could have believed that with the limited forces at our disposal, we could have won anything resembling total victory."[34]

One of the main difficulties in the Ridgway-Van Fleet relationship was the fact that the former had revitalized the army that the latter was given, so, as Ridgway strongly implied in the following remarks, Van Fleet bore the onus to succeed: "By the time that army was turned over to Van Fleet, it was as fine as any army we ever fielded. The morale was high, the spirit fine, and their confidence in their ability to accomplish any mission assigned was all that any commander could ask."[35] Van Fleet was under more pressure than the air or naval chiefs under Ridgway. Nevertheless, he was a survivor, retaining the Eighth Army command until succeeded by Lieutenant General Maxwell Taylor in January 1953 and thus outlasting Ridgway's tenure in the Far East by seven months. In fact, Van Fleet was promoted to four-star general in August 1951, only three months after Ridgway.

The top leaders of the American Air Force in the theater did not have any difficulty adapting to Ridgway. Lieutenant General George Stratemeyer, commanding general of the Far East Air Forces, although a fervent admirer and close friend of MacArthur, adjusted well to Ridgway's aggressive, decisive leadership style. On May 11, 1951, almost a month after Ridgway assumed overall command, Stratemeyer wrote in his diary: "We have a C-in-C that isn't afraid to make a decision—and he can make it quick. My admiration continues for him—one hundred percent."[36] Stratemeyer, however, suffered a heart attack a month after Ridgway assumed command and returned to the States. Lieutenant General Earle E. Partridge, head of the Fifth Air Force, the principal unit of the FEAF, served as acting FEAF commander until the arrival in June of the new permanent air chief, Major General Otto P. Weyland, who would hold the position until the end of the war. (Weyland was promoted to lieutenant general in July 1951 and general in July 1952.)

During the Second World War, Stratemeyer had headed commendably the Army Air Forces in the China-Burma-India (CBI) theater in 1944–1945, while Weyland had distinguished himself leading the XIX Tactical Air Command, which had provided close support for Patton's Third Army. If Stratemeyer had stayed longer in command over Korean air operations, he might have become as ruffled as Weyland did over Ridgway's interference with his plans and operations. Weyland actually had "some trouble" with both Ridgway and Clark over "whether the Army ground forces would try to run the tactical air forces, or whether the Air Force would run the air forces." Ridgway, with pressure from the JCS, had "imposed restrictions" on strategic bombing, said Weyland. "Ridgway had stopped me, and I hadn't finished the job," so Weyland was delighted in the summer of 1952 when Clark gave the "Go ahead" on attacking electric power facilities near the Yalu and other strategic targets.[37] From Ridgway's viewpoint, his chief anxiety about Weyland was essentially the same as his concern about Van Fleet: a tendency to be more aggressive than Washington wanted. In view of MacArthur's disastrous encounter with his superiors, Ridgway was careful to keep Washington both well informed of his plans and assured of his intention to implement his directives strictly. Weyland, whose career, like Ridgway's, was still on the rise, became head of the Tactical Air Command after the Korean War.

Vice Admiral Turner Joy, commander of U.S. Naval Forces, Far East and head of the UN armistice delegation until May 1952, was a MacArthur admirer but confided to a friend in October 1951 that Ridgway "has ably filled his shoes."[38] He appreciated Ridgway's efforts to establish "a more truly Joint CINCFE Staff"; he also liked him because he "gets around a lot" and tries to learn "what makes the Navy tick."[39] The respect was mutual and the two men supported each other's efforts. Both men believed in a tough stance toward communists: "more steel and less silk," as Joy put it; "firmness and the will to stand on your positions," as Ridgway phrased it, each strongly endorsing the other's view on what communists "respect."[40]

Ridgway undertook some reorganization of the GHQ administrative structure of the United Nations Command and the Far East Command. Essentially, he retained MacArthur's concept of the sections whose chiefs served concurrently in both headquarters. In view of the adulation MacArthur evoked from his staff, particularly his inner circle of twelve disciples, it is surprising that his exit from Tokyo brought about the departure of only four of that dozen in the immediate aftermath of his dismissal; they were three senior aides and his pilot. Stratemeyer went back to America in late May only because of his serious heart condition. Major General Alonzo P. (Pat) Fox, the SCAP deputy chief of staff, returned to the States in June. His role had declined in significance, as did all the occupation staff positions, with the Japanese Peace Treaty scheduled to be signed in September and the occupation to be terminated the next April. Almond left as head of X Corps in July to become the commandant of the Army War College.

Hickey, who had been the acting chief of staff in Tokyo during Almond's absence in Korea, was elevated permanently to chief of staff by Ridgway, an extremely judicious move, for Hickey was widely respected by all, from MacArthur and Ridgway to field officers. Ranking with Hickey as one of MacArthur's best staff leaders was Major General Edwin K. (Pinky) Wright, his G-3, or operations chief, who also headed the important Joint Strategy and Plans Group. At first, Ridgway and Wright's relationship was marred by several minor misunderstandings, but eventually the theater commander and his operations chief worked well together. According to Wright, "We became very close" and "had the finest relationship."[41] Ridgway and later Clark wisely retained Wright in his slot; the general consensus of colleagues was that a better G-3 could not have been found.

A surprising retention by Ridgway was Major General William F. Marquat, a confidant of MacArthur who had served him loyally from the Corregidor siege onward, including the headship of the significant Economic and Scientific Section of the SCAP, or occupation, administration in Japan. Marquat blamed Ridgway for the confusion which resulted when the SCAP machinery was in process of dismantlement and the Japanese were being given authority formerly reserved to the occupation administration—a situation conducive to disorder. He felt that headquarters had become a mere "mouthpiece for Washington where all the major decisions are made."[42]

Easily the most astonishing holdover from MacArthur's inner circle was Major General Charles Willoughby, MacArthur's G-2, or intelligence chief, since 1941. Willoughby was colorful, arrogant, opinionated, hard to control, and a MacArthur adulator. He was castigated by many then and since for the intelligence failures that led to the surprises over the North Korean and Communist Chinese assaults in the summer and autumn of 1950. Ridgway, however, regarded him as "a very fine Chief of Intelligence" and maintained that the intelligence he gathered was very accurate; it was the evaluation of it which was flawed, and the work by the rest of the intelligence community.[43] Whether Ridgway and Willoughby would have continued to have a harmonious relationship is moot, for that summer the controversial G-2, exhausted after a decade of high-tension work in the Far East and savagely criticized in the press and by Washington intelligence pundits, chose to retire and return to America.

William Sebald, the State Department's senior official in Japan and chief of the SCAP Diplomatic Section, was surely the most objective of MacArthur's inner circle and was retained by Ridgway, returning to the United States in March 1952 just before the occupation ended. Ridgway regarded Sebald as a hard-working, devoted Foreign Service official, whom he could look to with confidence for advice on international aspects of the occupation. Sebald observed that "Ridgway was the perfect general to wind down the occupation. . . . There was a vibrancy about him. MacArthur was much more subtle in his leadership, but Ridgway laid down the law."[44] On another occasion, Sebald remarked:

> You couldn't tell General Ridgway how to do things, but he was very free in asking questions, asking for advice or comments, insofar as I was concerned, about anything pertaining to Japan or the Japanese in a political sense. In that respect, it was a healthy change because General MacArthur rarely asked for advice. You had to sneak in your advice to him on certain matters that didn't look right or that I felt ought to be changed or some things that ought to be done. . . . General Ridgway operated differently. He was a man who used his staff extensively and depended upon his staff to handle things.[45]

Ridgway maintained that his relations with the Joint Chiefs of Staff during his tenure in Tokyo "couldn't have been better. I knew them all personally. . . . They were all most cooperative."[46] Apparently, whatever negative feelings he and Collins held mutually were submerged for the remainder of his command in the Far East. When Ridgway succeeded MacArthur, a State Department revision of NSC 48/2, which spelled out the new aims in Korea, was in process of getting final approval by Truman and the National Security Council. According to an official source, now "the objective was an end to the fighting and a return to the status quo; the mission of the Eighth Army was to inflict enough attrition on the

foe to induce him to settle on these terms."[47] The JCS gave Ridgway nearly all the authority he asked for, including attacking Manchurian air bases if there was a major air assault on the UN Command, which MacArthur had wanted but had been denied. The
JCS official chronicle explains, "With the accession of General
Ridgway as CINCFE/CINCUNC, the Administration gained a
commander who was wholly in sympathy with the wishes of the
President, the Secretaries of State and Defense, and the Joint
Chiefs of Staff to keep the conflict within bounds."[48] Ridgway was
not as completely in harmony with his superiors as this statement
claims, but the improved communication between Tokyo and
Washington was in marked contrast to the stressful relations of the
MacArthur era.

Ridgway's Washington superiors were enthusiastic about
MacArthur's successor because of his careful delineation of objectives and parameters. He instructed his ground, naval, and air
chiefs in the limits they could attempt, exhorted them to be cautious, and told them it was their "sacred duty" to avoid extending
the conflict.[49]

Ridgway held Van Fleet's reins most tightly. He was seldom out
of touch with Van Fleet for long, and the latter felt he was "all over
the place" in Korea.[50] As MacArthur had forewarned, the Korean
front burst into flames shortly after Ridgway took over in Tokyo,
the Communist Chinese launching the first phase of their spring
offensive on April 22. Van Fleet's forces gave some ground just
below the 38th parallel, mainly because of CCF penetrations in
ROK sectors north and northeast of Seoul, but by the end of April
the CCF, suffering appalling losses especially to UN artillery, began to withdraw northward. In this first phase the enemy had lost
about seventy thousand men killed in action, the Eighth Army approximately seven thousand.

For a week, beginning May 14, the second phase of the CCF's
spring offensive, including a number of North Korean divisions,
struck the east sector of the UN front. One ROK corps collapsed,
but generally the Eighth Army held in fierce fighting, also repuls-
ing communist attacks in the central and western sectors. This time
the enemy dead totaled an estimated ninety thousand, and the
CCF was compelled again to pull back, its manpower and matériel
resources severely hurt by superior UN ground and air firepower.
Van Fleet and his men had performed well, but an anxious Ridg-

way made frequent trips to Korea all through the tense period. He would continue to keep a close watch on Van Fleet and his operations when the offensive momentum shifted to the Eighth Army, as it did in late May when the UN forces advanced north again.

Van Fleet was ordered by Ridgway to halt on May 30 at Line Kansas, extending eastward from the Imjin River above the 38th parallel to the Sea of Japan. After a number of pleas from Van Fleet, Ridgway permitted him to move on to defensive positions during the first half of June along Line Wyoming, slightly farther north in the Iron Triangle, as well as to the east near the Punchbowl, a heavily fortified hilly area. Not only Ridgway but also the JCS, NSC, State Department, White House, and America's coalition partners were nervously watching these developments, which were costing the communists frightfully in men (200,000 in the past three months) and matériel and which were provoking some threatening comments from the Kremlin. The reins on Van Fleet originated far higher in the chain of command than Ridgway, although the Eighth Army commander probably did not realize how many governments around the world were concerned by his operations, especially as the balance of military power on the peninsula seemed to be shifting strongly against the communists.

Following behind-the-scenes diplomatic maneuvering between East and West, Jacob Malik, the head of the Soviet delegation at the United Nations, responded favorably on June 23 to appeals from the UN and the United States by agreeing to a cease-fire and negotiations to settle differences. Ridgway and Van Fleet jointly decided that Line Kansas would be the most defensible line during a cease-fire but that Line Wyoming and perhaps other northward positions should be held as bargaining points during armistice talks. The JCS imposed a strict limit on advancing beyond Lines Kansas and Wyoming until the armistice negotiations began at Kaesong, northwest of Seoul, on July 10. Ridgway named Vice Admiral Turner Joy, the NAVFE commander, to head the UN truce delegation.

That day, Ridgway consulted Van Fleet about his earlier proposal to advance to a line from Pyongyang on the west to Wonsan on the east. Van Fleet hedged on whether the plan, called Operation Overwhelming, ought to be launched in view of the Eighth Army's need for more forces. The U.S. Army's official history states, "Ridgway shelved the plan, not because of Van Fleet's recommendations but out of the possibility that the two armistice delegations would reach agreement in the near future."[51] Moreover, he did not want to lose troops fighting for ground that might have to be yielded by later truce terms. He chose, instead, to forgo large-scale offensive action and to "retain the initiative through the use of strong patrols and local attacks."[52] Uncharacteristic of his bold aggressiveness in the war against Germany, this decision by Ridgway in favor of caution was in accord with his superiors' instructions but may have prolonged the war by taking the pressure of heavy combat off the enemy.

The first stage of armistice negotiations took place at Kaesong, which lay northwest of Seoul about forty miles and just within the communist lines. The Chinese and North Korean delegates were surly and uncooperative, rather obviously stalling for time while their forces regrouped and organized new positions. Most of the fighting was confined to patrol and outpost actions at small-unit levels, but occasionally the operations accelerated to large-scale dimensions. The combat was particularly heavy from August to November 1951, as both sides attempted to improve their defensive lines in the rugged region west and northeast of the Punchbowl.

In the battles of Bloody Ridge and Heartbreak Ridge, west of the Punchbowl, UN forces, spearheaded by the American 2nd Infantry Division, finally defeated hard-fighting North Korean divisions between mid-August and mid-October. The 2nd Division alone suffered 3,700 casualties, while enemy losses were 25,000. American artillery fire was crucial in driving the enemy off these ridges: One American field artillery battalion fired a record 14,425 rounds in twenty-four hours. Meanwhile, American and ROK units of the X Corps, with the 1st Marine Division in the major role, fought a three-week battle from mid-August to early September, taking the north and northeast edges of the Punchbowl. The bloody battlegrounds between Mundung-ni and the Punchbowl remained in UN control for the rest of the war, though several North Korean attacks were made later, in vain, to retake the region.

Another area of intense action that autumn was Old Baldy, a hilly area of strong CCF fortifications southwest of the Iron Triangle. Old Baldy was captured by five divisions of the I Corps, at a cost of almost four thousand casualties to about thirty thousand in the CCF divisions during the first three weeks of October. In the meantime, truce talks had collapsed in August. When they were resumed after moving the negotiating site from Kaesong to nearby Panmunjom, in the neutral zone, Ridgway subsequently ordered offensive operations to cease as of November 12. It would be the spring of 1953 before another large-scale battle developed, but losses on both sides continued to be considerable because of active defenses, an enormous growth in artillery, and a continuing buildup of manpower. When truce talks began in July 1951, Ridgway's ground troops totaled nearly 555,000, while the CCF and North Korean Army had almost 570,000; by June 1952, the UN ground strength was about 678,000, while the enemy forces had grown to over 720,000, though the former was vastly superior in firepower.[53]

The truce talks, when resumed at Panmunjom, continued to tax the patience of the UN armistice delegation and Ridgway, who stayed in almost daily contact with Joy. The communist delegates wrangled interminably over the agenda itself, questions about usage and repair of airfields, composition of the future neutral nations observer teams, use of ports to resupply forces, and a host of other topics, some of which were extraneous propaganda stratagems, such as communist charges of violations by UN planes of neutral air spaces and the Americans' resort to germ warfare. The demarcation line became the foremost heated topic in 1951, and by the spring of 1952, the principal remaining issue had become voluntary repatriation of prisoners, which the communists rejected. In April 1952, three weeks before Ridgway relinquished his command to Clark, the POW repatriation problem appeared insoluble when the UN command polled its 132,000 Chinese and Korean prisoners and announced that only 70,000 elected to return to their communist homelands. If the battlefield situation was frustrating to Ridgway as he prepared to leave for his new assignment with NATO, the Panmunjom talks seemed hopelessly stalemated. "The negotiations with the Communists," said Ridgway, "were my major concern throughout most of my remaining tenure in the Far East Command [after halting offensive operations in November 1951]. They were tedious, exasperating, dreary, repetitious, and frustrating, and I very soon lost hope of an early end to the killing."[54] As if the communists were not enough, Ridgway and his ally President Rhee had a number of tense confrontations over the stubborn ROK leader's opposition to the trend of the negotiations and his frequent threats to disrupt the truce proceedings by a belligerent or embarrassing incident that would cause the communists to terminate the talks.

On many occasions the focus of Ridgway's frustration was not the communists nor the South Koreans but his superiors in Washington, who transmitted the negotiating positions to him. He frequently protested the orders he received, regarding them as lacking in firmness and undercutting the work of the UN negotiating team. On at least one occasion, according to the official JCS history, "the Joint Chiefs of Staff felt that General Ridgway was being too intransigent."[55]

On May 7, five days before General Mark Clark was to succeed him as the theater head, Ridgway was confronted by the rioting of over sixty thousand communist POWs on Koje-do, an island off the south coast of the peninsula where compounds had been built to house the prisoners but had quickly become overcrowded. Moreover, hard-core communist leaders had been infiltrated into the compounds to take martial control. Brigadier General Francis T. Dodd, the Koje camp commander, was taken hostage. His successor, Brigadier General Charles F. Colson, gave the communists a propaganda bonus by bartering to get Dodd released, promising to rectify supposed abuses that the communists claimed but most of which were unsubstantiated. Ridgway later attributed some of the slowness in getting control of the Koje-do crisis to Van Fleet, who allegedly should have sent reinforcements faster and had not demanded the immediate release of Dodd. The affair was not settled until Clark brought in tough Brigadier General Haydon L. Boatner, who eventually restored order but not before nearly two hundred POWs and UN troops became casualties. Koje-do was a terrible send-off for Ridgway, who later referred to the incident as "a major disappointment" of his Far East command, and surely an unwelcome opening challenge for Clark.[56]

On the brighter side of Ridgway's time in Japan, he presided over the final year of that country's occupation in an efficient manner, though, like MacArthur, he was a bit disappointed at not being invited to the San Francisco Conference in September 1951 where the Japanese Peace Treaty was signed. Major General George W. Hickman, Jr., judge advocate of SCAP and the Far East Command, found Ridgway as occupation chief to be "more a doer than a contemplator" in comparison to MacArthur. "I think if Ridgway had been in charge of the earlier rehabilitation of Japan he probably wouldn't have known enough about what to do to begin to get Japan back on its feet. MacArthur seemed almost always to have the right answers on how to deal with the Japanese."[57] Edwin O. Reischauer, noted Japanese historian and later ambassador to that nation, contrasted MacArthur and Ridgway as SCAP thus: "MacArthur's role had been unique, and no one could replace him. . . . Ridgway wisely made no attempt to do so. Instead, he encouraged the Japanese to assume leadership with only a minimum of assistance and direction from the occupation authorities. The transition from occupation to independence was now fully under way" by the time Ridgway was SCAP.[58]

Ridgway was critical in implementing the President's decision regarding desegregation of the armed services. His immediate impetus came from Collins, who notified him in late May 1951: "It is my conviction that you should succeed me as Chief of Staff when I retire two years from this August. . . . It is my personal conviction, and it will be my recommendation, that we do away with segregation in the FEC. . . . The personnel of the 24th [Infantry Regiment, the principal black unit in the Eighth Army] would have to be distributed throughout your command."[59] Ridgway disbanded the 24th Infantry, as well as the 159th Field Artillery Battalion, another black outfit, in October, shifting their men into other units. Subsequently, he spurred the desegregating of other Eighth Army units. "After that," commented Ridgway with pride, "the entire United States Army adopted this long-overdue reform."[60] He later remarked of the typical African-American soldier under his command: "There was nothing wrong with him if he had the right surroundings, the right officers, the right training and the right leadership."[61] Perhaps not the most progressive view today, but in 1951, Ridgway's evaluation was unusually liberal for senior American officers.

When Eisenhower decided to leave his command of NATO forces—Supreme Headquarters, Allied Powers in Europe (SHAPE)—in the late spring of 1952 to run for President, the Pentagon rumor mill went into full swing. For a while it seemed that Ike's chief of staff and good friend, Al Gruenther, had the inside track as his successor since Eisenhower had proposed him to Bradley and Collins. Ridgway, in turn, had been told confidentially by Collins earlier that he would succeed Haislip as vice chief of staff and later get Collins's post. Once in the Far East Command slot, however, Collins and Pace informed Ridgway, ever restless and inquisitive about his next assignment, that he would have to stay in Tokyo for the duration. On April 23, 1951, only nine days after Ridgway took over in Tokyo, Pace tried to counsel patience when he brought up his future: "There are few responsibilities the equivalent of what you are undertaking at this time and still fewer officers with your ability to fulfill them."[62]

A year later, carrying a bag full of frustrations from the results on the battlefield and at the truce table, Ridgway was more than ready for a change of command. Suddenly, as he put it, "I was given the high privilege of choice: did I want to stay and retain command in the Far East or go to Europe? My decision was to go to Europe."[63] On May 12, 1952, Clark, another veteran of the war against Germany, succeeded Ridgway in Tokyo. After the two visited Koje-do, the current hot spot that Clark inherited, Ridgway, undoubtedly with great relief and high expectations, flew to Washington for high-level consultations about where he had been and where he was headed, and then he took off for Paris and his new career as NATO's second supreme commander. As his intuition probably told him, the new job would not be without its frustrations.

Thirty-three years later he would tell a senior Army historian who was interviewing him that the Korean War's main lesson for future American planning and policy was that "every war must be, if possible, a limited war—limited in objectives to the extent that political objectives must dominate the military; and that the political objectives must have a major national consensus or they will not be supported by our people under our form of government." When asked what his major achievements in the Far East had been, he replied: "Achievement of the mission assigned me. The mission assigned was very clear: expel the invader, and restore peace to the area—both of which we did."[64] Alas, it had not seemed so lucid back in 1951–1952.

CHAPTER

# 4

# *Admiral Joy: Commander and Negotiator*

## A DIFFERENT KIND OF NAVAL WAR

The West Pacific had been the scene of enormous naval surface engagements in World War II, but during the Korean conflict there were no great naval battles. Neither North Korea nor Communist China had navies of any significance, and fortunately, the Soviet Union did not loan or lease any of its considerable force of combat ships and submarines from the huge Vladivostok naval base on the Sea of Japan. American and Allied naval vessels were constantly on alert for the introduction of enemy shore batteries, mines, and occasional minor air forays. By far, Soviet-built mines accounted for the principal damage to the UNC ships. Blockading, air missions, gunfire support, and amphibious-assault functions were the activities that occupied the American and Allied fleets during the first half year of the war, while later amphibious operations were dropped, though the air sorties increased. All in all, the public focus was on the ground fighting, and the control of the seas around Korea that the American Seventh Fleet and its supporting Allied naval units achieved made possible logistical and combat support of various kinds for the UNC ground forces without which South Korea could not have been saved from communist conquest. The naval story of the Korean War lacks the spectacular

79

phenomena of large surface fleets battling each other, as at Midway or Leyte Gulf, but it is a vital facet of the struggle for the peninsula. Likewise, the man who headed the UNC naval efforts during the first and most active year of the war for the U.S. Navy was a veteran officer known for solid professional accomplishments rather than for exciting feats or flamboyant style.

Had it been known that the same officer would be required to command Allied naval forces in the Korean War and to head the UN armistice delegation, no more able man could have worn both hats than Vice Admiral Turner Joy. He possessed the personal and professional qualities that were needed during the first two years of the war to oversee the complex variety of tasks assigned to the Commander, Naval Forces Far East (COMNAVFE) and to be flexible enough to shift quickly from that command slot to the role of dealing with recalcitrant, abusive communist truce representatives at Kaesong and Panmunjom, where he lacked both power and clear instructions. Joy served as COMNAVFE from August 1949 to June 1952, while also juggling the armistice headship from July 1951 to May 1952. Few men in history have been put in such positions simultaneously as he was during the latter period. He went back and forth in these ten tension-filled months between his seven-story NAVFE headquarters in Tokyo and the often angry and humiliating truce negotiations in Korea. The admiral exercised supreme authority and was accorded utmost respect from his four-hundred-ship naval force from nine nations, while the North Korean and Communist Chinese officers could not have cared less about his distinguished naval record or the early resolution of their armistice differences. For Joy, it was like continually traveling from majestic mountain peaks to dark, boggy valleys, so different were his two domains.

Long noted for his expertise in ordnance and gunnery, Joy went into the Korean War with thirty-eight years of versatile experience in the Navy, including service in both world wars. In the Second World War he was a cruiser commander in battles in the Solomons and the Aleutians, headed the Pacific Plans Division in the Navy Department, returned to the Pacific to lead a cruiser division in the Marianas, Palaus, and Philippines operations, and commanded a task group in the naval actions off Okinawa. When the war ended, he was in charge of an amphibious group preparing for the invasion of Japan. He was a much-decorated veteran of some of the fiercest naval engagements of the war, including service as a task unit commander in the Battle of the Philippine Sea, June 1944, and the Battle for Leyte Gulf, October 1944. Among the decorations he earned was "a Gold Star in lieu of the Fourth Legion of Merit with Combat 'V'" for "exceptionally meritorious conduct" in leading his task group with great skill and valor off Okinawa in fire support, salvage, rescue, and other duties "in the face of intense enemy air and Kamikaze attacks."[1] His other 1942–1945 citations also clearly depict him as a naval professional of uncommon versatility in planning and leading diverse forces in surface bombardments, air strikes, and amphibious assaults. He was known by his peers and superiors to be one of the Navy's most widely proven admirals when he assumed the position of COMNAVFE during the tranquil summer of 1949; the crises ahead would challenge all his many talents.

When he graduated from the Naval Academy in 1916, his fellow midshipmen described Joy in the yearbook as "naturally quiet and reserved," possessing "an exterior that is not penetrated by everyone, but those who have done so have found therein a very likable fellow with all the attributes of an agreeable messmate and a capable officer." When he returned as superintendent in August 1952, he was portrayed similarly as "a modest, soft-spoken man who will avoid the limelight whenever possible."[2] Vice Admiral Felix L. Johnson, a renowned carrier leader in the Pacific War and the director of naval intelligence during the Korean conflict, was one of Joy's oldest and closest friends. Johnson said four traits of Joy's stood out: "quiet, brilliant, good sense of humor, beloved by everybody."[3] Both men were avid poker players and golfers, though Johnson admitted that Joy "taught me a lot about playing golf."[4] Major General Edwin Wright, MacArthur's operations chief, observed: "I think that at the time of the occupation and the start of the war he was the ideal man to be in naval command. I don't think he was the aggressive type in many ways, although he did very well the whole time he was there as COMNAVFE."[5] Lieutenant General Edward Craig, who headed the 1st Marine Brigade, typified the general opinion of Marines who were associated with Joy during the Korean hostilities: "He was willing to listen to you and see your views . . . a very fine type of naval officer."[6] The above traits well suited Joy to handle the challenges that his naval forces would face in supporting the UNC ground operations, the problems of cooperation and coordination with Allied naval units, and the later labyrinth of difficulties at the truce table. But the obstacles sometimes would severely tax his generous reservoir of understanding, calmness, and self-discipline.

Naval command arrangements prior to the Korean hostilities left Joy with few resources, the bulk of the American Navy's Pacific strength being stationed at bases in Hawaii and along the West Coast. The Seventh Fleet, as during the Second World War, had been the relatively much smaller and older elements under MacArthur's jurisdiction in the West Pacific. But the coming of war brought a rapid buildup of American and Allied naval units under Joy, along with several sensitive new command relationships. In peacetime, Vice Admiral Arthur D. Struble's Seventh Fleet had been under Admiral Arthur W. Radford, commander in chief of the Pacific Fleet (CINCPAC), but the fleet was transferred to Joy's control upon the outbreak of war. Joy and Struble could not have been more different. Struble was an able but strong-willed old salt who had enjoyed a mutual admiration with Fleet Admiral Ernest J. King, the domineering head of the Navy in World War II whom President Roosevelt had teased for being so tough "he shaves every morning with a blowtorch."[7] Two decades after his Korean War command, Struble still came across as a professional sailor who could be very firm and intimidating.[8] Besides having to command such a daunting character, Joy also faced the awkwardness of being below the Seventh Fleet commander in seniority. Nevertheless, the two officers managed to work together effectively through the high tensions of the Navy's largest operations of the war: the Pohang, Inchon, Wonsan, and Hungnam landings and evacuations from July through December 1950.[9]

From early 1951 onward, UNC troops were needed more along the front line, and amphibious operations became impractical without additional ground units. Naval operations, as Joy commented, became "more or less routine affairs."[10] With this decline in combat pressure, Joy turned over many of the COMNAVFE responsibilities to his top staff officers in Tokyo, especially, of course, when he became head of the UN truce team in July 1951.

In a letter to Admiral Forrest P. Sherman in February 1951, Joy admitted that he still faced problems, "the foremost of which is that of command relations."[11] By that time he was referring primarily to the quandary of what to do with Vice Admiral William G. Andrewes of the Royal Navy, who had been heading a British Commonwealth carrier-led task group in the Yellow Sea involved in blockade, escort, and other activities. The British had a different ranking system and Andrewes was very testy about ascertaining his and Joy's proper place in coalition endeavors.

When Joy arrived as a vice admiral to head NAVFE in 1949, he found a tiny force of six minesweepers, four destroyers, and a cruiser. Their peacetime tasks were mainly antismuggling patrols, showing the flag at Japanese ports, and sundry training exercises. By the start of the war he had about twenty ships, but, as he wrote a friend on September 1, 1950, NAVFE had quickly expanded to "over 150 vessels and nearly 50,000 men. It now boasts of practically every combatant vessel formerly in the Pacific Fleet as well as a number that have been sent to us from the Atlantic and Mediterranean. My staff had grown from 30 to 160 officers and will soon occupy a seven-story building where we formerly needed only two storys [sic] to satisfy our wants."[12]

By the next autumn his strength in men, ships, and aircraft would have more than doubled again, including a considerable British Commonwealth force under Andrewes, the second in command of the Royal Navy's Far Eastern Fleet. His task group, which got into action fast in the Yellow Sea blockade of North Korea, included a carrier, two cruisers, three destroyers, and four frigates as early as July 1950 and would be reinforced later.

In April 1951, shortly after Vice Admiral Harold M. Martin succeeded Struble as commander of the Seventh Fleet, Joy revamped the NAVFE command and organizational structure significantly, alleviating a number of administrative problems in the process and making the naval organization simpler and more effective. The principal results were to give more authority to the Seventh Fleet commander, to improve coordination of naval gunnery units and carrier aircraft in the campaign to interdict enemy rail and road traffic, and to work out some of the main communication difficulties with the Far East Air Forces and the Eighth Army. As the Navy's official chronicle states, "The results were not yet wholly satisfactory,"[13] but Joy's organizational reforms did make the COMNAVFE job and the naval field commanders' tasks easier for the rest of the war.

As late as March 1952, Joy was still trying to improve NAVFE's combat effectiveness: He formulated a six-point plan, with the assistance of Vice Admiral Martin and Rear Admiral George C. Dyer, the commander of the Blockade and Escort Force, because, according to a naval source, "with the number of ships available and the political and military restrictions imposed upon the conduct of the war, only an intensification of effort and improvement in technique could increase the Navy's contribution to the war." Surface ships operating with the carrier and blockade forces were to be employed more frequently for bombardment and interdiction. Closer cooperation was to be achieved between Task Forces 77 (Striking Force) and 95 (Blockade and Escort Force) in order to maximize the damage inflicted. Closer liaison was to be attained with American and ROK troops at the bomb line, so that naval gunfire support might be improved. The spotting of naval gunfire had to be improved to produce better accuracy and greater damage. More minesweeping and coastal patrolling were needed to halt enemy short-haul supply runs by sea. Better coordination of the air and ground interdiction campaign was to be attained.[14] The last, particularly regarding relations between naval aviation and the Far East Air Forces, would be the most troubling of these six continuing problem areas.

The principal duties of Joy's American, ROK, and Allied naval forces were troop-lifting, resupplying ground forces, blockading, minesweeping, bombarding with naval gunfire and carrier air strikes, defending several islands off North Korea that ROK troops held, transporting and supporting ROK commando raids, and, in the case of the Seventh Fleet's Task Force 72, patrolling the Formosa Strait to keep the Chinese Communists and Nationalists apart.

Because of a host of differences and problems in conducting air warfare, Stratemeyer, as head of the Far East Air Forces, and Partridge, the Fifth Air Force commander, were often at loggerheads with Joy and his carrier division commanders over target selection and coordination of air operations over Korea. Interservice rivalry, as well as personality differences, counted heavily in this friction that was never altogether quieted between the Air Force and Navy commanders in the Korean conflict.

On July 5, 1950, Stratemeyer described in his diary a GHQ meeting with MacArthur where the Navy representative's report was so biased that "anyone that attended that briefing might be led to believe that the Navy was winning the air war in Korea."[15]

Stratemeyer requested that all land- and carrier-based Navy aviation units except antisubmarine units be put under his control. Joy, however, vehemently opposed this move, which included giving Stratemeyer authority to choose carrier operating areas and targets. After a subsequent conference, Joy agreed to a semantic compromise whereby Stratemeyer's expanded authority was described as "coordination control."[16]

Joy and Vice Admiral Arthur Struble were not entirely satisfied with the alleged compromise, and Stratemeyer and Partridge were soon upset anew because of press reports that the admirals "are unhappy with the cooperation of FEAF." Stratemeyer wrote, "It was my impression . . . that the relationship between naval air, Admiral Joy's office, and my headquarters has been most amicable and that we tried in every instance to meet their many requests for assistance."[17] He blamed the press criticisms of the Air Force, however, on the Navy: "This was not only stimulated by Navy sources, but was even prepared by them in detail. . . . I consider it a blatant service-inspired series of misstatements."[18]

Joy seemed to do his best to better relations with the Air Force, particularly with Stratemeyer, sending him numerous messages complimenting FEAF performances. Stratemeyer, in turn, donated a generous amount of scotch whiskey for the Seventh Fleet air crews who participated in a successful joint strike with FEAF on some key enemy bridges. Joy even issued a special order to his NAVFE officers to cease all criticism of FEAF in talking to the press.[19] By November 1950, Joy was able to tell his old comrade, Admiral Johnson, naval intelligence chief in Washington: "You can assure him [Sherman, the chief of naval operations] that Rip [Struble] and I get along very well together and that other command relations are functioning equally well. We occasionally have flare-ups with FEAF, one of which is in progress at the present time, but these minor troubles are mostly due to FEAF's bad manners and poor dispatch phraseology rather than any real attempt to take charge of carrier air operations."[20]

Strangely, Stratemeyer, who appeared to most colleagues as more tactful and gentlemanly than his successor, O. P. Weyland, never did get along with Joy and his admirals as well as the latter Air Force chief. Indeed, when Joy was preparing to leave his command in May 1952, he wrote Weyland: "One of the fondest memories I will take back with me to the States will be my unbounded admiration for the way the forces under your command have co-operated with the Navy in our common cause."[21]

Navy–Air Force relations in coordination of the air war progressed but not as rosily as Joy's words suggest. Complete harmony was unlikely, according to a Navy explanation, because of fundamental differences of philosophy, techniques, and semantics between the Air Force system and the Navy-Marine system of close air support. These differences were summarized from the Navy-Marine air viewpoint by Lieutenant General Lemuel C. Shepherd, Jr., the head of Fleet Marine Force, Pacific, after a visit to Korea in 1951: "We believe in providing for a small number of on-station planes; the Air Force does not. We believe in continuous direct communication between the frontline battalion and the controlling air agency; the Air Force does not. We believe that close air support of the frontline troops should take precedence over routine interdiction missions; the Air Force does not."[22]

Joy and Struble resisted Stratemeyer's demand that the Seventh Fleet carriers put their air priority on interdiction instead of close ground support, but MacArthur "overruled" them in January 1951.[23] From then until mid-1952 the focus of Navy-Marine aviation was on interdiction, especially of enemy transportation routes in northeastern North Korea, rather than on battlefield support. Even though the Navy-Marine aviation was given its "own area of responsibility" over the large and strategically vital northeast sector of the enemy's territory,[24] Joy was never content with the arrangement, which was altered after he departed. During the remainder of the war the services did not alter their respective systems of close air support, though the dispute did lead the Air Force to reestablish its Tactical Air Command, which had been dissolved after World War II.

Target selection was an ongoing area of antagonism between the Seventh Fleet and the Fifth Air Force, which Joy tried to alleviate. In late July 1950, MacArthur approved the creation of an FEC (Far East Command) Target Selection Committee. Admiral Joy, who was to name a naval officer to the committee, would not cooperate at first. He argued that the Seventh Fleet's main job was to protect Formosa, though it would undertake some air strikes in Korea under Stratemeyer's coordination control. He believed, however, that "General MacArthur should make these decisions personally" when Seventh Fleet air power was to be used in Korea "in the light of hostile threats to Formosa."[25]

Joy made a number of trips to Formosa to confer with Nationalist Chinese leaders and the commanders of his Formosa Patrol Force (Task Force 72). Throughout his tour of duty as COMNAVFE, he, like MacArthur, demonstrated an acute awareness of the strategic value of Formosa. In early 1951, the Joint Chiefs authorized the Formosa Patrol Force to collect intelligence along the coast of the Chinese mainland, mainly by photographic reconnaissance, which Joy was happy to have his task force perform.[26] In retrospect, it is surprising that the sundry activities of Task Force 72 during the Korean War period did not precipitate more than a few small-scale hostile incidents in the Formosa Strait.

Joy was very proud of the achievements of the Navy and Marines in the largest amphibious and troop-lifting operations of the war, all of which occurred during the main maneuver phase in 1950: the movement of the 1st Cavalry Division to Pohang in July just in time to reinforce the Pusan defense perimeter; the amphibious assault at Inchon in September by the X Corps; the landing of the 1st Marine Division at Wonsan in October (as well as the subsequent lifting of the 3rd and 7th Infantry divisions there and to Iwon, farther north along the eastern coast of North Korea); and the evacuation of the X Corps from Hungnam in December. Joy maintained: "It is not an exaggeration to say that without the Navy the Pusan perimeter could never have been held. The unspectacular role of carrying personnel and supplies to Korea was perhaps the Navy's greatest contribution. Next in importance was the Navy's support of the 8th Army by bombardment, interdiction and close air support missions, as well as the timely landing of the 1st Cavalry Division at Pohang. The vital role played by our carriers in this connection cannot be overemphasized."[27]

During the several meetings in Tokyo on August 23–24, 1950, between MacArthur, his staff and field leaders, and several top brass from Washington and Pearl Harbor regarding the Inchon assault plan, Joy at first opposed the site, preferring Posung-myon to the south and warning that the proposed invasion date of September 15 would be at the zenith of the Yellow Sea's typhoon season. Nevertheless, in a session at Joy's office with Admirals Sherman and Radford and Marine Generals Shepherd and O. P. Smith, Joy and the others agreed to support Chromite, the Inchon plan, after MacArthur displayed such confidence at the earlier plenary session and refused subsequently to budge on his version of the operation. What influenced Joy most in MacArthur's presentation was his attitude toward the Navy. In May 1951, Joy wrote a friend in St. Louis:

> It would be hypocritical of me to say that I did not regret to see General MacArthur leave Japan, for I was devoted to him. He was one of the finest commanding officers I ever had, not only because he understood and admired the Navy, but also because he let me alone to run the Navy as I saw fit. It was his trust in the Navy's capabilities that prompted his decision to land at Inchon. When forewarned of the difficulties of that landing, he said: "The Navy has never failed me yet, and I know it will not fail me at Inchon."[28]

Joy was elated over the startling success of the Inchon operation, but he consistently gave the credit to Struble and especially Rear Admiral James H. Doyle. For instance, he responded to a letter of congratulations from a fellow admiral: "I can brag about the operation because all details were entrusted to Jimmy Doyle, who was the Attack Force Commander and chiefly responsible for the Navy's brilliant performance. All COMNAVFE did was to give the necessary forces and tell him the 'what, when, and where.'"[29]

Joy was alert early to the need for minesweepers and antisubmarine warfare units; he was able to garner enough vessels to form an ASW force in early 1951, and, though the threat never materialized, "his chief worry" continued to be Soviet submarines: "I hate to think what would happen if Russian submarines got into this war," he once remarked to correspondents.[30] His many requests to Washington for more minesweepers, however, were never fulfilled adequately, because, as Sherman explained more than once, there were higher priorities on other types of ships at the time. Joy's anxieties were prescient, for enemy mining of Wonsan harbor was extensive: Over three thousand Soviet-built magnetic and contact mines were laid by Soviet experts in a complex field that produced an eight-day delay in landing the 1st Marine Division and cost over two hundred casualties to clear. "The main lesson of the Wonsan operation," Joy said, "is that no so-called subsidiary branch of the naval service, such as mine warfare, should ever be neglected or relegated to a minor role in the future. Wonsan also taught us that we can be denied freedom of movement to an enemy objective through the intelligent use of mines by an alert foe."[31] Joy remembered that mines had played a significant role in operations against both Japan and Germany in the Second World

War and was concerned that, like tactical aviation, they were being neglected in the aftermath of that conflict.

Joy was personally present aboard one of the ships off Wonsan during that dangerous minesweeping operation, and though Tokyo duties caused him to miss the Inchon assault, he was present afloat and at meetings ashore at Hungnam during the frantic evacuation of the nearly 200,000 American and ROK troops and civilian refugees there as the Chinese Communist Forces approached the port. Joy was high in praise of the Hungnam evacuation as a well-executed amphibious operation in reverse that was made possible by a strong amphibious force in a state of combat readiness in the proximity. The official Navy history states that "it was in their response to the Chinese onslaught that the forces under Admirals Joy and Struble made perhaps their greatest contribution."[32] Writing to an eminent naval historian in June 1951, Joy remarked of the officer's plans for a naval account of the war: "The Hungnam evacuation is a logical place to stop unless the war ends abruptly, which seems unlikely at present. Naval operations since Hungnam, though aggressive and telling on the enemy, have not been in the dramatic category."[33]

Naval activities were important to support the UNC ground forces during the next half year, but the excitement of the amphibious stage of the war was over after Hungnam. Upon his leaving the COMNAVFE position in June 1952, Joy offered the following evaluation of the significance of the Korean War and of the Navy's role therein:

From the standpoint of battle effectiveness, the Korean War has re-emphasized lessons which were almost lost sight of in the years that closely followed World War II. We know now that there is no quick, easy, cheap way to win a war. Sole reliance on our security cannot be placed in any one weapon or in any one branch of the Services. We cannot expect the enemy to oblige by planning his wars to suit our weapons. We must plan our weapons to fight war where, when, and how the enemy chooses. The choice of time, place, and circumstances rests with him.

We need balance between the Services and balance within the Services. In the Navy, for example, we have learned that we cannot ever again neglect our minesweeping force. We cannot neglect our air arm. Inchon and Hungnam have again forcibly emphasized the vital need for our amphibious force. We cannot write off the naval gun as obsolete; the Korean War has again proved its worth. We have found a pressing need and full use for all of our naval weapons. And while the Navy's role in the war has gone unpublicized for the most part, it is sufficient to know that but for the Navy the war in Korea would come to a sudden halt. The job of getting the troops there and keeping them supplied is just as essential as it ever was, whether it makes interesting reading or not.[34]

Joy had been convinced that naval power was indispensable to victory in World War II, and obviously the Korean conflict reinforced his belief that the Navy-Marine team was not expendable in America's times of war. Unfortunately, he did not get such professional satisfaction from his other role in the Korean War; Kaesong and Panmunjom would be nightmarish experiences for a sailor who in World War II had become accustomed to associating combat with victory.

## THE FUTILITY OF IT ALL

At Kaesong in July 1951, Admiral Joy undertook a new challenge: the role of head of the United Nations Command delegation in truce negotiations with the officers representing the Communist Chinese and North Korean forces. Less than six months later he referred to his post as "without doubt the most frustrating experience of my career."[35] This opinion did not change with time. On at least two occasions he considered asking to be relieved of his duties as chief UNC negotiator.

Although he remained as COMNAVFE while in his armistice position, the naval war had become much more limited by this time and his big decisions and major operations were fewer. He moved abruptly from a situation in which he truly exercised command to one in which he was denied the power to make substantive decisions. But both roles contributed to his becoming extremely frustrated with the course of the Korean situation.

From the standpoint of the United States, the truce talks were supposed to deal with military matters. However, just as the conduct of the war was based on political as well as purely military factors, so the armistice negotiations had a dual nature, with the State Department playing an influential role. The picture of military officers working out the armistice terms was a facade, because the UNC positions were being determined largely from Washington, with Secretary of State Dean Acheson and his lieutenants in Foggy Bottom enjoying substantial input on major and minor points. Of course, the communist military negotiators were also severely limited in their freedom of decision, being under orders to check with their superiors in Peking and Pyongyang at every stage in the negotiations.

All field-grade and flag-rank U.S. officers involved on the UN side of both the truce talks and the concurrent combat operations had fought in the Second World War where they had experienced decisiveness in battle. By July 1951, many of them were exasperated with the experience of limited war in Korea. Now they faced a new frustration in having to continue the bloodshed without any immediate hope of attaining victory or even a cease-fire. Not only did many of them, including Joy, feel that their side was fighting under unreasonable handicaps imposed by Washington, but also the UN truce delegation lived with the constant and real fear of being overruled by officials of the State Department and the White House.

Just as the UN Command had to depend solely on the forces it already possessed for current and future operations, it had to draw on its own flag officers for appointments to the armistice delegation. This was due, in large measure, to the Truman administration's insistence that this be a military armistice negotiated by military officers, leaving political and diplomatic issues and officials out of the actual sessions at Kaesong and Panmunjom. Acheson and his cohorts frankly did not want the State Department entangled in a no-win situation, whether military or diplomatic. Nevertheless, just as political and diplomatic issues, along with Acheson and company, were vital elements in the direction of the war, so they were integral to the truce-making process.

Even so, it is interesting that the military officers of the truce team were chosen from the regular UN Command and not sent directly from the Pentagon. At first, the JCS and Ridgway thought the armistice would be negotiated fairly soon, so there would be no need to bring in others. There was apparently no serious consideration given to filling the slot of senior delegate, or head of the delegation, with someone from outside Ridgway's UNC-FEC senior officers. Sebald, the top State official in Japan, along with the

Joint Chiefs, advised Ridgway not to put his prestige on the line by participating personally in the negotiations. But he was empowered to name the senior delegate. On July 1, he notified the JCS that he had chosen Joy, whose official title would be "Senior Delegate, United Nations Command." The JCS and Truman quickly approved his decision.

Actually, Joy was chosen partly because he was the only senior officer in the theater high command who had been in that command before the war began. In addition to his solid performance as COMNAVFE during the first year of the conflict, he had already compiled a long and distinguished naval record that included both world wars. To his credit, too, Joy appeared to be more patient and tactful than Van Fleet or Weyland, the other two top eligible officers in the theater. Although he seemed low-key and more gentlemanly compared to the others, he would turn out, over time, to be so vehemently anticommunist that his ideological convictions would sometimes greatly incite him during the truce talks, for instance, when it was apparent that the communist delegates, for reasons dictated in Peking or Pyongyang, were stalling on points that seemed easily negotiable. It is not known if he was that opposed to communists before the negotiations began or if the communists' behavior during the talks hardened his ideological stance.

On July 10, the day the talks began at Kaesong, Ridgway wrote in a memo for the file that Van Fleet "gave me his views on the recommendations I had asked for the preceding night. He felt he should not participate in the negotiations. He stated that if he failed, he would then have to conduct operations and might be branded as a warmonger, even by his own people. I gained the impression that while he did not state so, he rather felt himself unequal to the task of senior negotiator."[36] Since Joy had already been chosen as the head of the delegation, Ridgway had apparently inquired if Van Fleet wished to join the delegation.

As it turned out, Ridgway and Joy jointly chose the original negotiating team to work with the admiral: Major General Henry I. Hodes, the deputy chief of staff of the Eighth Army; Major General Laurence C. Craigie, vice commander of FEAF; Rear Admiral Arleigh A. Burke, the NAVFE deputy chief of staff; and Major General Paik Sun Yup, commander of the ROK I Corps. Representatives from all three field commands were chosen; all the Americans had enjoyed distinguished careers in World War II. Joy was pleased with his American group and wrote an admiral-friend in August 1951: "I am fortunate in having such staunch fellows as members of the delegation. The more I see of Bill Craigie the more I admire him. Hank Hodes is likewise a tower of strength, and of course you know Arleigh's capabilities."[37] Naturally, the makeup of the delegation would change over the next two years. Joy's successor as head in May 1952 would be a member of the delegation who had been added three months earlier: Lieutenant General William K. Harrison, Jr., who, along with his superior, General Clark, would have the ignominious distinction of signing the Korean armistice agreement.

Although he enjoyed harmony with his American delegates, Joy had considerable difficulties with General Paik Sun Yup and his three successors in the ROK post on the delegation during the next ten months. The admiral wrote in his diary in late October 1951: "I had to give Maj Gen Lee [Lee Hyung Koon, Paik's successor] . . . a stern talking to . . . disapproving his request to go to Pusan to see Pres [Syngman] Rhee. . . . I told him he was subject to R's [Ridgway's] orders only and that [the] only proper channel for communicating with Rhee was through R."[38] Impatience, though often justified, frequently characterized Joy's attitude toward the ROK members of the truce team, whom Rhee tried to control tightly. In February 1952, he was upset when the ROK delegate made a public statement predicting that the communists would not comply with any armistice agreement. Although that ROK general's statement seemed to have been made primarily for the record and to protect himself, Joy was concerned that his attitude seemed indicative of that of the officials of the government of the Republic of Korea. Joy wanted to keep the ROK under firmer control. Fortunately for Joy he did not have to deal with the obstreperous ROK president when he suddenly released 25,000 communist POWs in a deliberate but vain effort to sabotage the truce talks in June 1953.

Early in their dealings Joy lost respect for the five-man North Korean and Communist Chinese delegation, which seemed always to be under the control of the Red Chinese, though the North Koreans did most of the talking and yelling and had three representatives on the team. The communist negotiators were far more experienced politically than the UN truce team, and they were not hesitant to employ blatant and crass tactics of propaganda and psychological warfare in exploiting the truce negotiations. In letters to friends and colleagues, Joy often vented his feelings about the enemy negotiators. He wrote MacArthur, for example, in January 1952: "This frustrating experience has taught me one unforgettable lesson: it is practically futile to negotiate logically and reasonably with any Communist who has not been decisively defeated on the field of battle."[39] To a naval friend he referred to them as "scum" and charged that they "have absolutely no scruples, ethics, decency, or sense of fair play. The only way to deal with them is through patience and unmistakable firmness backed by military strength, and with a pack of aces up your own sleeve."[40]

In his capacity as senior negotiator, Joy was Ridgway's executive agent. He reported directly to Ridgway and received his orders from him; he did not communicate directly with the JCS, who relayed orders and instructions from the President, the NSC, or the Department of State through Ridgway to the admiral. Ridgway and Joy had a mutual admiration relationship and continued to be supportive of each other even when they were not in agreement on an issue. Sometimes Ridgway took a harsher stand on truce proposals than did Joy; at other times Joy was tougher.

The bad situation Joy sometimes was caught in with Ridgway or Washington is illustrated in this entry from the admiral's diary in December 1951 regarding his delegation's recommendation about a neutral nations supervisory commission, which Ridgway had not passed on to Washington: "I urged [Hickey in a telephone conversation] that our views be made known even if R [Ridgway] disapproved of them. I again pointed out what a tough spot we were in. This resulted in two blasts from R to me which in effect said to carry out my orders and adopt an intransigent attitude toward [the] Commies in doing so." The perplexed admiral added, "Our contradictory directives are hard to follow! Since R told us in a despatch directing his 8-principle proposal *not* to be intransigent, I have been concerned over our present position."[41]

Neither Ridgway nor Joy was empowered to make policy concerning truce developments, though there were several instances where Ridgway exceeded his authority. The major policies seemed to be formulated in the State Department, and after consultations with the JCS, who often made alterations, they were sent to the President for final approval before transmission to Tokyo. Truman remarked: "As had been the case with reports from the field of battle, I daily received full accounts of the proceedings in the truce tent. No major steps were taken without specific approval of the President, even to the wording of announcements made by the Far East commander or the chief negotiator at crucial points."[42]

Apparently the composition of the decision-making group in Washington was initially unknown to Joy. In a letter to General Craigie in February 1952, after the FEAF officer had left the truce team, Joy indicated that he had recent new knowledge about the setup at the Washington end: "I could see from what he [Burke] wrote that we have been correct in our assumptions that the J.C.S. are not really running this Military Armistice. The more this affair progresses, the more that becomes evident."[43] Admiral Burke, another veteran of the truce negotiations, later stated that "all of our negotiating positions came through the Joint Chiefs. They originated in the State Department but went to the Joint Chiefs for transmission to us." Burke remarked further: "We were only doing the negotiating. We could recommend, but that was all."[44]

The truce talks got off to an inauspicious beginning when it took two weeks to agree on the agenda, which consisted of five items: (1) adoption of an agenda; (2) establishment of a demarcation line between the two combatant sides with a demilitarization zone as a basic condition for a cessation of hostilities in Korea; (3) concrete arrangement for the realization of a cease-fire and armistice, including the composition, authority, and functions of a supervisory body for carrying out the terms of the cease-fire and armistice; (4) arrangements relating to the disposition of prisoners of war; and (5) recommendations to the governments concerned on both sides.

When the talks began, the communists wanted the demarcation line to be the 38th parallel; the UNC wanted a more defensible line, such as the actual line of contact. And the communists insisted that this issue be settled before the other items on the agenda could be discussed. Joy and his delegation did not want a permanent demarcation line at the present line of contact. As explained in the JCS chronicle, "This would in itself amount to a *de facto* cease-fire during the time period set and time extensions would doubtless be sought by the Communists and granted by the U.N. Command for the settlement of other agenda items. A cease-fire while the negotiations were still going on would be to the great disadvantage of the U.N. Command in Ridgway's [and Joy's] opinion." They favored "the principle that the line of contact on the effective date of the armistice must be the demarcation line."[45]

Joy's delegation was ordered by Washington to agree to the communist proposal for the demarcation line (not the 38th parallel) in November 1951, with the proviso that the line would expire in thirty days if no truce had been reached. This de facto cease-fire was furiously but futilely opposed by Ridgway, Joy, Burke, Hodes, and Craigie. The demarcation line was adopted on November 27 as the communists wished it; it is no mere coincidence that Craigie left the truce delegation that day, Burke on December 11, and Hodes six days later. Joy stayed on but wrote in his diary on November 14: "Hodes and Burke feel definitely that their usefulness is ended if we are forced to accept Commie terms. The same feeling is shared by me as to my own usefulness."[46] Joy continued to believe that the demarcation line decision was an enormous blunder. He wrote to a friend in February 1952: "We are no longer negotiating from a position of strength. We took the pressure off the Communists when we agreed to a temporary demarkation [sic] line for 30 days. Except for the Navy and Air Force interdiction program we have exerted no real military pressure on the enemy since 27 Nov."[47] It is questionable whether the demarcation-line agreement and de facto cease-fire helped the communists very much militarily, though to his death Joy and many of his colleagues in the UNC high command were strongly convinced to the contrary.

It was soon evident undoubtedly to Joy and his colleagues on the truce delegation that there were disagreements and disunity in Washington about responsibility for the truce negotiations. It seemed that, as with the reversals in UNC military fortunes in Korea, no one wanted to assume full responsibility even when exercising the power. There are many exchanges in the documentary records of the State and Defense departments about what were the parameters of the Joint Chiefs' responsibility. The State officials continually tried to establish issues as pertaining to a purely military armistice and therefore of interest to the JCS. Collins tried to distance himself from some of the "Government decisions," as he called them, that the JCS had to relay to Tokyo. He admitted later that the JCS and State officials "did not see eye to eye" on truce matters "at all times."[48] Acheson and his lieutenants appeared to desire to intervene in the negotiating process to the smallest detail but without accepting responsibility for or linkage to the depressing proceedings.

In May 1952 the State Department put pressure on Joy to exploit the truce talks for propaganda blasts to counter the barrages the communists were unleashing in the world media. If the communists could accuse the UN of chemical and biological warfare and other trumped-up charges, State officials felt warranted in asking Joy to tell the press how recalcitrant the Chinese and North Korean delegates were behaving on truce negotiations. At a meeting of the Joint Chiefs with several high-ranking State officials regarding the responsibility for such propaganda, Collins argued, "This isn't really the responsibility of the Joint Chiefs, who are only supposed to give strategic guidance. . . . The JCS can transmit messages but . . . many of the things we send out are Government decisions." As to the matter of suspending the truce talks, Collins said, "This really isn't a JCS matter. . . . It is really a question for the Government." A State official countered that "it is partially a JCS responsibility."[49] Such issues of responsibility were rarely decided with any finality, much to the distress of Joy and his negotiators.

Joy and Ridgway, as well as Harrison and Clark later, were never free of the tensions resulting from misunderstandings, miscommunications, and lack of coordination and consistency in their relations with the Washington makers of their policies and guidelines for negotiating in Korea. The primary responsibility for such tensions lay with Washington, not with the truce team. Particularly frustrating were occasions when Joy would try to negotiate from a hard position, only to learn that his Washington superiors refused to establish a firm, united stance on the issue or else shifted positions and undercut him at the truce table. On two of the most critical and controversial issues, the demarcation line and voluntary POW repatriation, Joy believed the rug had been pulled from beneath him by Washington officials. He was so unhappy with his maddening tasks that he considered asking to be relieved.

One of the strongest bonds between Joy and Ridgway was their frustration with Washington. At times Joy described messages from Washington with brutal frankness (as did Ridgway). He confided in his diary in November 1951 about a JCS message received that day: "In my humble opinion this is a helluva wishy-washy despatch. If this is the sort of backing we are going to get, woe betide us in the days ahead."[50] On February 16, 1952, he penned in his diary his opinion of a new JCS radiogram: "A craven message!" Two days later his diary entry announces "Another craven message!"[51] He wrote Admiral Radford: "Trying to get something definite out of Washington is almost as exasperating as trying to get a reasonable agreement out of the Commies."[52] Besides the problem of getting the policymakers to produce, he also stayed agitated over the belatedness of responses from Washington. On December 11, 1951, he recorded in his diary: "This is the guidance we had been looking for since [the] Commies made their last proposal—8 days previously. On the 4th we had requested guidance on their proposed neutral obs. [observation] team as a matter of urgency!"[53]

Early in the negotiations Washington established the policy that the responsibility for breaking off truce talks belonged to the communists, so Joy and his team had to endure much abuse without being able to suspend the meetings. In late July 1951, Ridgway and Joy informed the JCS that they wished to give an ultimatum to the communist delegation that "the UNC would recess and await 'something new and constructive' from them." The Joint Chiefs were ready to accede to their proposed course of action, but the State Department objected, so Ridgway was told by the JCS that "it is important that, if and when breakdown of negotiations occurs, the onus for failure shall rest clearly and wholly upon the Communists."[54] The next month Ridgway again was angry and wanted to terminate the truce talks, and again the JCS refused, telling him: "It is basic to your present directives that you not break off armistice discussions without specific instructions to do so."[55] Allied and world opinion were apparently crucial factors in the State Department's consideration. Truman also thought so: "Repeatedly I made it clear that if these truce talks failed it would have to be under conditions that would make it plain to the world that the failure was caused by the enemy, not by our side."[56] This policy was continued, much to Joy's chagrin. Even in his final days as chief negotiator, in May 1952, he asked for and was denied permission to suspend the talks temporarily, although Ridgway and then Clark supported him.

The issue of prisoners of war, agenda item no. 4, was not carefully defined when the truce talks began. It became a significant moral and propaganda issue when Truman came out firmly in favor of voluntary repatriation of POWs as "the right thing to do." Besides the humanitarian factor, this position, as the Truman administration interpreted it, would be a tremendous propaganda boost for the West if the prisoners held in South Korean camps did not want to return to their homelands north of the 38th parallel. This possibility was complicated, however, by the lack of real control over some of the POW camps, especially the huge compounds on Koje-do island off the south coast of the peninsula. Some of the camps were tightly controlled by communist prisoners, a considerable number of whom, notably on Koje-do, were enemy officers infiltrated into the compounds to organize and command the POWs. Obviously, the prisoners in these compounds and camps could express no honest preference for fear of retribution. Nonetheless, the UNC screening of enemy POWs showed that only about half of the 132,000 inmates wished to be repatriated, which left the communist negotiators at Panmunjom more ill-tempered and rude than ever in dealing with Joy and his UNC delegation.

Joy, like a surprising number of the UNC senior commanders, believed the Truman administration had made a serious mistake in insisting on voluntary repatriation. He felt that the decision put the welfare of "ex-Communists" above that of UNC prisoners in enemy hands. "Since we were not allowed to achieve a victory," Joy remarked later, "I wanted the war halted. Voluntary repatriation cost us over a year of war, and cost our United Nations Command prisoners in Communist camps a year of captivity. The United Nations Command suffered at least 50,000 casualties in the continuing Korean War while we argued to protect a lesser number of ex-Communists who did not wish to return to Communism."[57] From late April 1952 on, voluntary repatriation was the only major issue not settled at Panmunjom. Interestingly, the JCS remained divided on the issue.

Once Joy felt that the UNC truce team had committed itself in negotiations to voluntary repatriation, he did not oppose it publicly for fear of causing his delegation to lose face or appear divided. In February 1952, U. Alexis Johnson and General John E. Hull, deputy assistant secretary of state for Far Eastern affairs and Army vice chief of staff, respectively, put forth a plan to solve the problem by simply releasing enemy POWs who did not want repatriation. Enemy negotiators would be presented with a fait accompli. Joy (and Ridgway) vigorously opposed the Johnson-Hull plan, arguing that it would mean abandoning voluntary repatriation, to which they were committed by this time in the negotiations, and it would endanger the lives of the UNC POWs in communist prisons. Joy remarked: "I was asked what the Commie reaction would be to a fait accompli. I condemned the idea vehemently pointing out how such an action would jeopardize the return of our own POWs held by the Commies. I claimed that it would be a breach of faith on our part which would wreck the conference."[58] He told Generals Hickey and Wright of the FEC GHQ that he was so opposed to the Johnson-Hull plan that "if I was directed to carry it out I would ask to be relieved."[59] Eventually the plan was discarded without Joy having to make more threats, real or bluffing.

With the approval of Washington, Joy in April 1952 proposed a "package deal," or complete plan covering all major items for an armistice. His plan offered one concession and asked the communists to make two concessions. He deleted any mention of airfield rehabilitation in North Korea, which was a concession to the communists. On the other hand, his plan omitted the Soviet Union as a member of the Neutral Nations Supervisory Commission, and it called for voluntary repatriation, both terms being desired by the UNC delegation. The day after he made his proposal, Joy wrote in his diary: "Now that we have made our final offer there is little left for me to do. But if there is any chance for an armistice before June 1 I should of course like to see the job through and sign the document."[60] Joy later wrote that "the final agreement [of July 27, 1953] was substantially that which I had submitted on 28 April 1952."[61]

Soon afterward riots broke out on Koje-do involving scores of thousands of enemy prisoners, much bloodshed, and the embarrassing capture and use of an American general during that island crisis. This led to the harshest communist rhetoric yet at Panmunjom and the enemy's refusal to discuss the package deal. Joy wanted to suspend the truce talks, but Washington wished him to remain and offer counterpropaganda, which he resisted. As he wrote later, "A military conference is no place to seek a propaganda victory."[62] In a message to General Clark, the new UNC-FEC chief, on May 19, 1952, Joy reported that the truce talks were paralyzed by the communists' "stream of vituperation and abuse. . . . The Koje-do situation has played directly into their hands and gives them a plausible basis on which to build propaganda which, however false, will by sheer force of repetition work to the eventual detriment of the UNC position."[63]

In his parting speech to the Communist Chinese and North Korean delegation at Panmunjom on May 22, Joy was firm, noble, and professional:

> After months of conciliation, of meeting you more than halfway on issue after issue, the UNC has told you with all firmness and finality that it will not recede from its position with respect to POWs. On the 28th of April [1952] we offered you an equitable and specific solution to the issues remaining before us. We told you then, and we tell you now, that we firmly adhere to the principles of humanity and the preservation of the rights of the individual. These are values which we will not barter, for they are one and the same with the principles which motivated the UNC to oppose you on the battlefield. No amount of argument and invective will move us. . . . The decision is in your hands.[64]

Under trying circumstances Joy had worked hard to achieve success at Panmunjom, had upheld the dignity of his position, and had shown commendable forbearance and self-discipline in dealing with the communist antagonists. Obviously Joy was burned out in his job at Panmunjom; it was time for a change. In early June, Vice Admiral Robert P. Briscoe succeeded him as COMNAVFE. In early August, after a well-deserved rest, Joy took over as superintendent at the United States Naval Academy. As a man of bedrock character and a naval leader of versatile skills he would be a sterling role model for the future officers studying at Annapolis.

Joy had made admirable, if not often successful, efforts to adapt to the exasperating conditions of the truce talks as well as to the restrictions placed upon his considerable arsenal of air, surface, and undersea weapons of naval warfare. His experience in the war against Japan, where he could achieve victories with no interference or limitation on his operations from his own superiors, had not prepared him for the Korean War, in which virtually all aspects of both naval plans and armistice negotiations had to be cleared with Washington superiors. The adjustment for Joy was made even more complicated when the State and Defense officials over him were in disagreement. Joy would have agreed with later chroniclers who called it a strange and ugly war.

# CHAPTER
# 5

# Clark: The Fading of Glory

## THE EAGLE IN TOKYO

General Mark Wayne Clark, dubbed by Churchill as "the American Eagle" (due to his sharp-nosed silhouette and piercing eyes) and remembered for his wartime command in Italy, 1943–1945, replaced Ridgway as CINCUNC and CINCFE in Tokyo on May 12, 1952. (The office of SCAP had been eliminated when the Japanese Peace Treaty became effective on April 28, 1952.) After successfully heading U.S. forces in Austria following World War II, then leading the Sixth Army, and in 1949 becoming chief of Army Field Forces, Clark was heralded by the press as "an exemplary soldier-diplomat."[1]

Clark had molded the Fifth Army into a powerful force in the Italian campaign and, along with Eisenhower, Bradley, and Patton, had become one of the most famous American commanders of the war in Europe. Although best known for his command in Italy, his greatest contribution in World War II was his 1940–1941 role in readying the U.S. Army for combat. He was an acknowledged expert in troop training, which would prove invaluable with the ROK Army. His forte in developing training programs and field exercises that realistically prepared large numbers of green recruits for battle against the Germans and Japanese was used to good advantage in South Korea where new soldiers customarily had not been provided adequate preparation before being sent into combat.

Clark was a "Marshall man." George Marshall had placed great trust in him and supported him throughout his career. They were both in France in 1918, and afterward Marshall often visited the Clarks at home in Fort Lewis, Washington, when he was serving at nearby Vancouver Barracks. Clark considered his relationship with Marshall, the Army chief of staff throughout World War II, as his greatest career break.

Eisenhower, Bradley, and Clark had been cadets together at West Point. When Clark and Eisenhower were later stationed together at Fort Lewis in 1940, they became especially good friends. They were indispensable comrades for years, but their relationship by the end of the Korean conflict was lacking in warmth due to Eisenhower's move to the White House, whereupon he collected a host of political friends and distanced himself from some of his former colleagues in the military.

The same drive and determination that enabled leaders to excel on the battlefield often turned into fierce rivalry for the coveted senior command positions in the military establishment. "Those who reach the objective . . . attract invidious remarks, pernicious slander, malevolent gossip. . . . In the case of Clark, the disapproval was excessive," observes his biographer. He continues, "Clark's rise in rank was quick, but so was Eisenhower's. Clark skipped the rank of colonel, but so did Bradley. Clark was frequently in the news, but so was Patton. . . . Ironically, Clark was a magnificent practitioner of the art of public relations, but in the end he failed to obtain a consistently good press."[2] The abnormally strong criticism of him stemmed mainly from his controversial decisions of 1942–1944 in the Mediterranean war, such as his use of pro-Vichy officials in Northwest Africa, his ordering of the 36th Infantry Division to attack across the Rapido River in Central Italy that resulted in enormous American casualties, and his opting to seize Rome and stage a victory parade rather than trap the German armies retreating from South Italy.

Collins had his eye on Clark a year before he took over the Far East Command. In a letter to Ridgway in May 1951, Collins expressed his concern, "There are rumors of offers by the University of California to Wayne Clark, which I know Wayne is seriously considering." It would be unfortunate to have him "leave the service at this time when we face a threatening international situation."[3] Actually, Clark admitted later he had expected to succeed MacArthur when he was relieved in April 1951. When he finally was appointed, he was not surprised.

Clark later explained the multiple responsibilities he assumed in moving to Tokyo:

> I wore several hats in the Far East. As Commander in Chief, United Nations Forces, I was in command of a multination army, navy, and air force fighting the Communists. I also was responsible for the conduct of armistice negotiations at Panmunjom. . . . As Commander in Chief, Far East Command, I also directed all American Army, Navy, and Air Force activities in Japan and the Ryukyu Islands. That job included preparations for the defense of all these areas. . . . A third hat made me Governor of the Ryukyus, which meant I had the responsibility of insuring a healthy civil condition among the people so that our mighty air base at Okinawa would be free from the threat of civil disturbance.[4]

Part of his time was devoted to oversight of countless logistical matters. He was ultimately responsible for overseeing maintenance of Korean highways and railroads for military use, preserving public utilities for UNC personnel, and keeping port facilities in good condition for UNC troop and cargo ships. Clark had to use limited rehabilitation funds in ingenious ways that were beneficial to the war effort. But often frustrating to him was another Korean task: "Then there was a job without a hat, and that was where I was in trouble so often with Syngman Rhee. This job was an essential corollary of my job as UN Commander."[5] Part of his duty was to maintain liaison with the ROK government in order to ascertain its interests and needs on political, economic, and military issues related to South Korea, particularly problems arising from the ROK Army's attached role with the U.S. Eighth Army.

He also had the mission of defending Japan against the Soviet Union. There were incidents of Russians seizing Japanese fishermen nearly every day. Soviet fighters sometimes flew over Hokkaido on obvious reconnaissance missions to gather intelligence on military facilities and defenses. The possibility of a Soviet invasion of Hokkaido was an ever-present threat throughout the Korean conflict.

According to one observer, "Clark brought to the job plain-spoken frankness and a deeply ingrained sense of the team player who knows that the signals are to be called in Washington."[6] His loyalty to subordinates and superiors as well as his obedience to the chain of command could be meticulously relied upon, as had been evidenced in the conflict of 1941–1945. "Whatever reservations clouded Clark's judgment of decisions reached and announced, whatever resentments, whether real or imagined, boiled beneath Clark's exterior, he was fastidiously loyal in public to the military system," states his biographer. "Clark, anguished and tormented, controlled his impulses and followed faithfully the necessities of teamwork in war."[7] Major General Frank H. Britton remembers that the Fifth Army headquarters in the Italian campaign had reflected its commander's personality: "definite . . . positive."[8] After Clark's personal intervention in the critical battles for Salerno and Anzio, wherein he had decisively changed the tactical plans and relieved two corps commanders as well as several lesser officers, he left no doubters as to his ability to act quickly and authoritatively.

Clark realized that the situation was far different in Korea than in Italy. When he visited MacArthur during the winter of 1951 to discuss the training program for South Korean soldiers, MacArthur told him about the many restrictions imposed on him, such as the noncombat duties forced on ROK troops by Rhee, the ban on using Nationalist Chinese forces, and the prohibition on air pursuit beyond the Yalu. As of May 1952, these became Clark's restrictions, with the accompanying frustrations.[9] Nevertheless, in Tokyo he would gain strong admirers among his commanders. For instance, Lieutenant General Glenn O. Barcus, commander of the Fifth Air Force from May 1952 to May 1953, concluded, "I guess if I had my favorite high-ranking Army general that I had to name, it would have to be Mark Clark."[10]

Clark inherited two problems that he had to face immediately. One was to bring order to the Koje Island prisoner-of-war camp, where control had to be restored over rebellious communist prisoners. The other was to mediate between Syngman Rhee and the Korean National Assembly in a fierce battle over South Korean political issues. Rhee was an intractable autocrat who would be one of the gravest obstacles to Clark and the United States in solving the Korean situation of 1952–1953. Yet ironically, Clark and Rhee became strong friends. This testifies to Clark's ability to compre-

hend and cope with diplomatic and domestic crises of Allied powers beyond the Anglo-American circle, as he had demonstrated in
French North Africa in World War II.

Clark and Ridgway had served together several times during
their careers in pre-1939 service schools as well as in the war
against Germany. Ridgway was anxious to leave for his NATO appointment in the spring of 1952. The outbreak of riots and violence
among the communist POWs on Koje-do presented difficult new
challenges for the incoming commander. Washington's policy of
banning a tough response to the POW ringleaders on Koje-do,
even after Ridgway's urgent pleas crossed the JCS chairman's desk,
did not escape Clark's notice as the newly appointed CINCUNC/
CINCFE. "It goes all the way into the Eighth Army and into this
headquarters, and all the way back to headquarters in Washington,
as far as responsibility is concerned,"[11] he later recalled angrily.

"Absolutely flabbergasted" by what he found at Koje-do on a
brief tour with Ridgway before the latter's exit, Clark "felt the
American Army had been disgraced." He was "horrified at the lack
of discipline and control over the rioting POWs."[12] In his memoirs
he commented: "I hadn't bothered to ask anyone in Washington
about the POWs, because my experience had been with old-fashioned wars. . . . Never had I experienced a situation in which prisoners remained combatants and carried out orders smuggled to
them from the enemy high command."[13] During the Italian campaign Clark had been relieved of POWs relatively fast; they were
shipped back to North African camps and many transshipped on to
POW camps in America.

Ridgway had reported to the JCS on April 29, 1952, that the
continuation of the POW screening program or the segregation of
the prisoners would be met with bloodshed and violence by the
well-organized and armed communist troops in the compounds on
Koje Island. "Although told of the serious situations existing in the
prison camps in Korea, neither the JCS nor any other authority in
Washington saw reason to direct specific action,"[14] states the JCS
chronicle. "Everywhere we were going, hell bent clear up to the
Yalu River, they had captured these thousands and thousands of
prisoners. . . . There wasn't any place to put them; there were just
thousands of them in one building," observed Inspector General
Edwin A. Zundel.[15]

Ridgway reprimanded Van Fleet for the POWs' riotous activities
on Koje-do, ordering him to keep them under control. On May 5,

Van Fleet told Ridgway that there was "no cause for 'undue anxiety' about Koje-do." Actually, as the official Army history attests, "For several weeks . . . the possibility of violence was no secret. Koje-do was like a chronic appendix; the Far East Command and Eighth Army . . . preferred to postpone the operation until the situation became acute." No one in the American command in Korea or Japan possessed any knowledge or prior experience to bring to bear on this complex phenomenon. Van Fleet was too busy with combat matters to give it much attention, while Dodd appeared to think that time would somehow allow the POW tensions to subside. Dodd was taken hostage on May 7 and released on May 11 through the efforts of his successor, General Colson. But "Colson traded Dodd's life for a propaganda weapon that was far more valuable to the Communists than the lives of their prisoners of war,"[16] concludes the Army chronicle.

Ridgway's last act before leaving for his new post as head of the NATO command was to call a meeting of all his staff and order that whatever force was necessary to return order must be used immediately. Even though Clark claimed that he could find nothing wrong in anything Ridgway had done as CINCUNC/CINCFE, he felt strongly that Ridgway should have protested to Washington. If he personally had seen the messages that were passing through the UN Command regarding Koje-do, Clark felt he would have refused to be a party to it. It was a bitter beginning for the energetic and eager Clark.

Clark took immediate and decisive action, instructing Van Fleet to disperse the POWs to small compounds on the islands of Koje and Cheju and on the Korean peninsula, in order to break communist control over the prisoners. Clark "felt some distaste," one source states, "at the need to deal with what amounted to a mutiny among prisoners. But he clearly recognized the necessity. He instructed Brig. Gen. Haydon L. Boatner to take action—and at once."[17] Dodd and Colson were demoted to the rank of colonel, another key officer received an administrative reprimand, and Clark moved control of the POW problem away from the Eighth Army to the Korean Communications Zone of FECOM.

General Boatner, assistant division commander of the 2nd Infantry Division, was chosen by Clark as the new commander of Koje-do. He was charged with the sensitive, dangerous job of relocating the POWs. After overseeing the rapid building of stronger prison enclosures in several locales elsewhere, he sacked and replaced every member that Dodd and Colson had appointed to the Koje-do commandant's staff. Also, he moved over six thousand Korean civilians living on the island to the peninsula mainland, and he transferred about four hundred inept UNC troops stationed on Koje-do. Although he drove his remaining soldiers hard, they caught his sense of urgency in acting fast and forcefully to avert worse rioting, and they began to improve their own morale and military discipline.

Boatner possessed two assets: Clark supported him fully in the use of force to clean up the mess and to report only to him—not to Van Fleet or anyone else in the line of command. Also, Boatner had extensive previous experience with the Chinese and knew their language. He secured control of the camp on June 12, 1952, and just in time, as it turned out—a mass breakout had been planned for June 20.

When Clark took over at Tokyo GHQ, there were mainly American Army personnel there. He formed a unified combined staff of senior officers from all three services, most of whom were men he had served with earlier and respected. Clark's entire headquarters for FECOM and UNC consisted of seven thousand personnel, much smaller than earlier staffs primarily because SCAP offices had been dissolved. By that time, the United States was an ally, not a conqueror, of Japan. He moved his GHQ to the edge of Tokyo where General Hideki Tojo's headquarters had previously been. He was glad to leave the Dai Ichi Building, which was too close to the frequent antimilitary demonstrations by Japanese radicals outside the nearby Imperial Palace.

Clark's right arm on the GHQ staff was Lieutenant General Doyle Hickey, a longtime fixture there, who had been chief of staff successively for MacArthur, Ridgway, and now Clark. Hickey was an invaluable resource for information on the situations in both Korea and Japan. Clark came to lean heavily upon him.

Robert Murphy, ambassador to Japan when Clark arrived in Tokyo and later his political aide, was a good friend and confidant. He had served with Clark in Northwest Africa in 1942–1943. Murphy remarked, "Once again Clark and I found ourselves associated in military-political-diplomatic negotiations as prickly as those with Frenchmen in Algiers. Again, I heard Clark protesting because he, 'a plain soldier,' had to spend his time on 'politics.'" He added, "But Clark understood very well why his Tokyo post was more political than military. The command he was now assuming was called the United Nations Command, and it was more complicated than SHAEF had ever been."[18] As for his longtime friend, Clark remarked, "He is an honest two-fisted, square-shooting American who has a keen grasp of military as well as political problems. He learned to appreciate the military problems during his long association with soldiers during World War II."[19]

In 1952 the limited war in Korea posed new problems. Because of military budget cuts, the Pentagon's desired levels of preparedness could not be reached until 1956, instead of 1954. The supplies and equipment going to the Far East Command were not enough. The Army faced budget reductions, and there was also a manpower shortage. The year 1952 marked the completion of the twenty-four-month tours of duty for 650,000 troops. There were only 650,000 raw recruits to replace them. Moreover, there was a shortage of ammunition because of a major steel strike back in the States.[20] Clark faced an uncertain future in fulfilling his UNC/FEC missions.

## PROBLEMS AT PANMUNJOM

Murphy and Clark, who got to the Far East after the peace talks had gone on for a year, went on an inspection tour of Korea together. Murphy recalled:

> Clark showed me the enormous difficulties of waging war in mountainous Korea, at the end of a supply and communications line 6,000 miles long, against an implacable enemy who always could take sanctuary across the Yalu River in neighboring Manchuria. Clark was convinced that the Joint Chiefs had badly misjudged this Korean situation when they started armistice parleys, and he believed we already had lost much ground by permitting the negotiations to drag on so long. What Clark personally favored was immediate resumption of a drive to unite Korea, for he was convinced that any settlement which left Korea divided would amount to a grave American defeat.[21]

Meanwhile, at Panmunjom, the main problem was to forge a plan for the release of the POWs so that cease-fire negotiations could resume. The United Nations wanted all of its own POWs to be returned quickly but was not willing to force all enemy POWs to return to Red China and North Korea. Only 70,000 of the 132,000 enemy POWs wanted to go home. The screening and re-screening of prisoners was causing an explosive situation in the POW compounds. The enemy was holding out for more returnees than could be located. Upon rescreening, the highest figure the UNC could provide of returnees was 83,000 communist POWs. This was not enough to suit the enemy negotiators.

At a meeting of the President and high-level officials of State and Defense in late September 1952, Truman listened as two differing plans were presented, each intended to end the stalemate at the peace table. Acheson's proposal provided for the immediate release of the 83,000 communist POWs in exchange for the 12,000 UN POWs, with the remaining nonrepatriates being handed over to an impartial team for interviewing. Truman, however, sided with the Defense Department's argument that any armistice must "wind up the whole thing." Defense officials recommended military pressure by "more intensive bombings, further expansion of the ROK Army, use of Chinese Nationalist forces, and amphibious landings in Korea." They "believed the time had come to inform the enemy that no further concessions would be made—to make it plain that there would be no yielding on the issue of forcible repatriation."[22]

Clark told the JCS in late September that the trouble was not the POW issue but that the UNC had not applied enough military pressure to make the enemy want an armistice. He believed that it was useless to consider a military offensive to the Yalu without a major escalation of the war. And yet he knew that the administration would never permit such an escalation. To his mind, an armistice was an objective that had to be won by military means as it had in previous wars.

The POW issue was no nearer to solution in July 1952 than it had been a year earlier despite approximately 2 million words and nearly eight hundred hours of meetings in the truce negotiations. Lieutenant General William Harrison, now served as the tough chief UN truce negotiator. "Many troublesome questions had been dealt with through compromise, but now both sides had maneuvered themselves into positions that severely limited negotiations," according to the Army history.[23]

On October 8, 1952, the talks broke down over POW exchanges and adjourned indefinitely. Clark was now ready for the use of strong military pressure, especially since Collins had reported that the United States now had tactical atomic weapons available. On October 9, the UNC chief prepared to send to Washington a team of staff officers with his plan to achieve a decisive battlefield triumph and to force a truce on UNC terms. But the timing was bad in Washington. The Democrats, with the 1952 presidential election in sight, were struggling for victories while adhering to their espousal of an honorable truce, as opposed to all-out war.

While Eisenhower was offering to stop the war if elected, Clark on October 16, 1952, put forth his Oplan 8-52 to turn the war around by resort to a military decision. He proposed to widen the war in Asia by amphibious and airborne assaults and even naval and air operations against China and Manchuria, plus a naval blockade of China. He was proposing, in essence, MacArthur's strategy of launching sufficient power against China proper to force the communists to accept the UN peace proposals.

Truman and the Pentagon began to give Clark more leeway by late 1952, less concerned now about complaints from the Allies than about the upcoming elections. Other members of the United Nations began to worry that the United States was getting too aggressive again. The Mexicans offered a proposal to end the war. But an Indian initiative in November 1952 became the dominant one considered and finally approved. It provided for a four-nation repatriation commission to be in charge of the disposition of all prisoners.

The policy of "watchful waiting" signaled by the United Nations was upheld by the new Eisenhower administration, beginning in January 1953. Seemingly, the fighting could have gone on for years under this policy. However, the unexpected death of Stalin on March 5, 1953, became a turning point which worked to the UN's advantage. Stalin's successor as Soviet head of state, Georgi M. Malenkov, was eager to end the Korean War and more profitably use the funds that had been supporting the Communist Chinese and North Korean forces with a constant flow of war matériel.

General Maxwell Taylor, Van Fleet's successor as head of the Eighth Army in February 1953, echoed the resentment of Clark and other military commanders toward the priority given to domestic considerations in wartime: "The national behavior showed a tendency to premature war-weariness and precipitate disenchantment with a policy which had led to a stalemated war. This experience, if remembered, could have given some warning of dangers ahead to the makers of the subsequent Vietnam policy." He added that "unfortunately, there was no thoroughgoing analysis ever made of the lessons to be learned from Korea, and later policymakers proceeded to repeat many of the same mistakes."[24]

In April 1953, a break occurred in the negotiations which initiated a thaw. An informal agreement was reached on Operation Little Switch, whereby both sides agreed to repatriate the sick and wounded POWs. The POW releases under Operation Little Switch began April 20 and were completed May 3 at Panmunjom. In all, the communists brought nearly 700 sick and wounded UNC prisoners; the UNC returned almost 6,700 Chinese, North Koreans, and civilian internees.

On April 26, the truce talks resumed for the first time in six months. Both Americans and Russians had new leaders in Washington and Moscow, and both appeared more flexible and eager for settlement. Clark noted the enemy negotiators were suddenly more reasonable, a marked change in attitude after Little Switch. He was confident that a truce would be forthcoming.

Clark's attitude got tougher, however, when he saw the terrible condition of the freed UN prisoners and observed the new intransigence by the communists at the truce table. He authorized Weyland to bomb irrigation dams in North Korea to further cripple the enemy's economy. He promised more air attacks if the UNC's final proposal for an armistice was not agreed upon soon at Panmunjom. On June 4, the communists accepted the UN proposals on all major remaining areas in dispute. Clark flew to Korea to tell Rhee that the United Nations would proceed with an armistice if one could be had without sacrificing the principle of "no forced repatriation."

Plan Everready, drawn up by the FEC and Eighth Army staffs, was sent to Washington by Clark to cover the worst possible contingency: if the ROK should withdraw from the UNC, as Rhee had threatened to do, and become hostile to UN forces. In order to avoid this scenario, a very liberal security pact was offered Rhee by Washington if he would accept an armistice.

The nonrepatriate issue was finally settled with the UNC's rejection of a compromise on June 4. The official Army history says of its significance:

> Regardless of how it was disguised or negatively acknowledged in the final instrument, the principle of no forcible repatriation had been recognized on the international level by the communists. . . . The establishment of the precedent had been a long and costly venture for the U.N. Command, since thousands of casualties had been suffered in the interim in the fight to protect the defectors from communism. On the other hand, the UNC had kept faith with the nonrepatriate prisoners and won a psychological victory.[25]

The UNC had won the long fight over voluntary repatriation, but Clark was soon confronted by trouble from his own camp. On June 18, in hopes of sabotaging the truce, Rhee released over 25,000 North Korean nonrepatriate POWs into the countryside of South Korea. ROK security guards did nothing to stop the escapees. American troops quickly replaced the ROK guards but were able to recapture less than a thousand prisoners.

Two decades later Clark admitted: "When old man Rhee kept threatening that he was going to release these prisoners, I secretly felt that's exactly what he should do—what I would do, if I were in his place. But being the representative of my government, I had to argue against it." The general said of the ROK president: "We saw alike on most everything. . . . Most of the things he did I liked, although I couldn't tell him so in many instances. . . . He had many fine qualities."[26]

At the peace table, however, the enemy demanded from the UNC some assurance that more trouble from Rhee and the ROK Army would not be forthcoming. The enemy was not convinced that the UNC was not a party to the release of the POWs. In letters on June 29 to the CCF and North Korean supreme commanders, Clark pointed out that the UNC commanded the ROK Army but did not have authority over the Republic of Korea, a sovereign state. Whether the truce included the ROK government, he emphasized, the armistice was a military agreement negotiated by the opposing commanders. He pledged that the United States and the UNC would endeavor to secure Rhee's cooperation and would establish military safeguards to try to guarantee observance of the truce. He proposed an immediate session to complete the final armistice arrangements.

Clark and Harrison tried to force South Korea's cooperation by threatening to pull out UN troops if the ROK forces tried to fight North Korea by themselves. Supplies and equipment were slowed to the ROK Army, so that they would see the folly of fighting without the UNC's support. According to an account of a press interview the Eighth Army commander gave, Taylor maintained that "he could extricate the U.N. forces from the battle line amicably if the ROK Government decided to continue the fighting after the armistice." The general added, though, "the Eighth Army was like a 20-cylinder automobile with a complex system of wires and cogwheels. If the U.N. forces were taken away, the ROK troops that remained would have to fashion a completely new automobile."[27]

Clark was able to use his friendship with Rhee to get an informal agreement that precluded a fight between American and ROK troops. He secured Rhee's promise that he would "support" an armistice although he could not "sign" it. Assistant Secretary of State Walter S. Robertson was dispatched to Korea to reason with Rhee. Displaying toughness and patience, Robertson met with Rhee every day for eighteen days to persuade him to cooperate.

The prisoners were always the main issue, but Rhee also wanted answers on how the future of his nation would be dealt with before it was too late. This led Clark to vow privately that it was harder to win peace than to win war, especially in the last four months of the Korean War. Rhee's opposition was more costly than it was worth to the United States. "In retrospect," states an official Army source, "it appeared that through diplomatic bargaining Rhee could have had all that he eventually won and could have avoided giving the Communists a chance to gloat over the falling out of allies."[28] Instead, Rhee pressed his two advantages in dealing with America to the hilt: He was a favorite of the Republican party right wing and his forces comprised two-thirds of the troops on the battle line.

Robertson was ultimately successful in persuading Rhee to cooperate. On July 12 the American and ROK governments announced their agreement on terms and procedures for an armistice, the disposition of POWs, and future collaboration. Robertson thanked Clark for his assistance with Rhee and the armistice progress: "To you, more than any other single individual, should go the credit for this great achievement. I think I have some idea of the difficulties you have had to surmount on all sides."[29] Harrison convinced the enemy at the peace table that South Korea would abide by the armistice provisions.

Clark insisted on having correspondents present at the Panmunjom signing. Lights from the newsreel and television cameras made the heat unbearable. At 11:00 A.M. on July 27, 1953, Generals Harrison and Nam Il entered the 159th and final session at Panmunjom to sign nine copies each of the armistice agreement. Afterward they each left without granting recognition to the other, as had been their custom in previous sessions. Several hours later General Clark signed the armistice agreement at nearby Munsan. Elsewhere, the top enemy commanders, North Korean Premier and Supreme Commander Kim Il Sung and CCF General Peng Teh-huai, also signed. The cease-fire began at 11:00 P.M. that evening. FEAF air attacks continued until the final minutes.

Murphy observed, "Mark Clark deserves great credit for restrained and intelligent handling of an assignment . . . distasteful to him . . . when he carried out, in complete silence about his personal feelings, the directive of an old friend, another Supreme Commander who was now President of the United States."[30]

Operation Big Switch, the main POW exchange, occurred from August 5 to September 6. Screening and repatriation of POWs took place at Panmunjom. The UNC delivered more than 75,000 POWs directly to the communists, and, in turn, the communists sent back over 12,000 POWs to the UNC. Two weeks later in September, the UNC transferred 22,000 nonrepatriates to the Neutral Nations Repatriation Commission, the communists turning over 350 UNC nonrepatriates to the commission.

A noted war correspondent described the final scene:

One by one, the last 160 American POWs passed through Panmunjom. These were all men who had been marked as "war criminals" by the enemy—and each of these criminals, before he went on to the tables of fruit juice, milk, and ice cream, glittering in the background, in one way or another, on his knees or otherwise, thanked God that he had returned. General Mark W. Clark was there to greet them.[31]

## COMMAND RELATIONS

During the 1952 presidential campaign, Eisenhower had promised to go to Korea if elected. The implication was that such a trip would bring about a cease-fire. The elated response from the public put pressure on Truman to sign a cease-fire before the election to get credit for the Democrats for making peace. The enemy was alert to the war's unpopularity with many Americans. Since many Americans wanted peace, the communists tried to lead from a position of strength and held out for terms acceptable only to themselves.

Having won the presidential election handily in November 1952, Eisenhower did visit Korea briefly on December 5–8. Clark asked him to be allowed "to win in our first test of arms against communism,"[32] but he never got a chance to present his broad plan for victory in Korea. Clark later wrote: "To me the most significant thing about the visit of the President-Elect was that I never had the opportunity to present this estimate for his consideration. The question of how much it would take to win the war was never raised."[33] It soon became apparent to Clark that Eisenhower was seeking an honorable truce.

On the trip home from Korea aboard the cruiser *Helena*, Eisenhower and his top advisers made plans to break the truce stalemate by compelling the enemy to need to terminate hostilities. Key advisers to the President-elect on this issue were John Foster Dulles, to be secretary of state; Charles E. Wilson, the next secretary of defense; and JCS Chairman Bradley, an old comrade of Eisenhower. Together they concluded that some way had to be devised to use or threaten to use nuclear weapons in Korea because the United States still had superiority over the Soviets in that arms category. It was thought that this would be less costly in lives and matériel and would be a persuasive influence in getting the enemy to agree to an armistice quickly.

Clark did not think that using the A-bomb in Korea would lead to Soviet intervention or to World War III. He had asked Collins in vain to allow him to include the use of tactical nuclear weapons in his planning. Clark often felt utter frustration because of the limits set in the war and the constant monitoring from Washington.

In early 1953, however, Eisenhower prepared to expand the war if necessary. Clark was advised to include the possibility of nuclear weapons in his revised Oplan 8-52. The Allies were told to be ready for a military campaign to end the war. The word was put out to the enemy that greatly expanded military operations could be the consequence of a failure at the truce table. During an NSC meeting in February 1953, the President proposed attacking the neutralized Kaesong area with tactical atomic weapons. General Clark had claimed the enemy was using Kaesong as a military base.

In May 1953, the JCS prepared extreme contingency plans in case the peace talks broke down completely. If all else failed, they recommended increased air and naval attacks against Manchuria and the use of atomic bombs. The President, however, spoke ambiguously on the issue, making it clear he was not for a wider war by then but for a peace agreement. Nonetheless, he was convinced that the U.S. government must consider "the atomic bomb as simply another weapon in our arsenal."[34]

Several eminent scholars doubt that the nuclear threat that Eisenhower and Dulles promoted would have produced the desired effect because by June 4, 1953, the communists had accepted the UN proposals on all principal issues; Peking may have not actually received these threats since they were leaked, not directly communicated; and the Korean front line was too mountainous for maximum effectiveness of nuclear weapons.

The military situation in the Far East had rapidly changed in the short time since Truman left the stage. One major development was that Soviet IL-28 jet bombers had been added to the Chinese Air Force. Their offensive capabilities were so potent that Clark felt his four-month-old Oplan 8-52 was no longer adequate. He asked for more firepower and that his ground units be brought up to authorized strength; he was down by 7 percent, or 21,000 men.[35]

The main power of the UNC in Korea was the Eighth Army under General Van Fleet. Clark described Van Fleet as "brilliant and courageous" and "a typical soldier's man who knew the problems of his men and met them." Clark "knew of the fine fighting spirit he [Van Fleet] had put into the Eighth Army."[36] Weyland remarked: "Van Fleet was a damn good ground soldier. . . . He would have liked to have attacked, and he was in a position to do it."[37] Van Fleet nourished the illusion at first that the shift in command from Ridgway to Clark might allow his army to flex its muscles in more aggressive moves. But Clark was less than eager when he proposed in late June to capture the entire Iron Triangle.

Clark was restricted by Washington, and, in turn, he had to restrain Van Fleet, who wanted to take the next hill and then the next hill. It was not worth the loss of men, according to Clark. "We just want to hold what we've got, you see, and not let them take anything away from us, nor let them get into South Korea."[38] One authority says that Van Fleet "called the static war 'a canker slowly eating at the morale of his troops' and was endlessly devising plans for offensives which were rejected on the grounds of casualties."[39] In January 1953, for instance, Van Fleet informed Clark that "he was sure that [the] Eighth Army could handle anything . . . the enemy could throw at it."[40] General Taylor commented: "A vigorous field commander with a broad experience in training foreign troops, he [Van Fleet] left his mark on the combat readiness of the Eighth Army, particularly the Korean units. In carrying out the expanded training program begun in 1951, Van Fleet had built up the ROK Army to a strength of about half a million men."[41]

Actually, to Taylor, who succeeded Van Fleet in February 1953, a defensive posture was not appealing either. But by that time there could be no changing of Eisenhower's policy. Taylor commented, "Hence, I had no hesitancy in assuring President Eisenhower, Secretary of Defense Wilson, and the other senior officials in Washington, who probed my views before my departure, that I was quite prepared to live with a defensive strategy and not kick against the pricks."[42]

Taylor was Clark's choice to head the Eighth Army and replace Van Fleet. He could count on him to carry out with frankness and confidentiality the high-level meetings of American and ROK leaders concerning the possibility of the UNC's withdrawal from Korea should Rhee insist on obstructing the armistice. Like Clark, Taylor was a specialist in preparedness: He insisted on training exercises that would make the ROK troops capable of moving out quickly from their many exposed outposts in case of strong enemy attacks.

Even though he would have liked his army to be able to prove its strength, Taylor became a strong advocate of developing limited war capability. The Eighth Army's offensive potentiality would not be tested. Its performance during the last two years of the war was better than often thought, simply because it was never allowed to undertake large-scale offensives. Close students of the military side of the war are largely persuaded that major assaults by the Eighth Army would have cost the CCF heavily.

Besides Van Fleet and Taylor, Clark enjoyed good relations and usually similar views on the war with his air and naval chiefs. He said of his FEAF commander: "Weyland was a 'can do' operator, highly efficient and willing to play on the team. . . . I had to maintain an air-ground team working as efficiently as possible." Clark praised also his NAVFE chief: "Vice Admiral Bob Briscoe [was] affable, capable, and more intent on working for the good of the three-service combined effort than in bothering about the differences of opinion that had prevailed in Washington in the past with regard to carrier-based versus land-based aviation."[43]

With the UNC offensive option ruled out in Washington, the situation in Korea for the new administration was complex: The military stalemate, the truce logjam, the interests of America's allies, and Rhee's recalcitrance all had to be weighed carefully. Also, at home Eisenhower was being held to his promise of securing a just and honorable cease-fire. He was personally convinced that the cease-fire could more readily be brought about by intimidation than by mere diplomatic means. But domestic issues, not Korea, were getting first place on the new administration's agenda. A Brookings study maintained that for the first few months of 1953 "decisions with respect to Korea were apparently made informally as the situation developed. An integrated master plan did not exist, nor was one worked out by the United States Government."[44]

Eisenhower was sympathetic with Clark's desire for victory, but he told the UNC/FEC chief, "I have a mandate . . . from the people of our country to stop the war. I want you to get an armistice." Clark asked to have the military restrictions removed so he could "pound them, . . . hit them, . . . hurt them." He argued that "when you hurt them, then the conference table is an extension of the battle." One at a time some of the limits on the air war were removed, such as the bombing of Pyongyang, electric power plants, and irrigation dams. But Clark had trouble getting official permission to break off negotiations. Finally he was allowed to present a "fair, decent American position to get an armistice."[45]

Talk of the threat or use of atomic weapons was revived in Washington as Eisenhower became more determined to bring the war to an end. Such an approach had enthusiastic support from Admiral Arthur Radford, the Pacific commander who was Eisenhower's choice to succeed Bradley as JCS chairman in August 1953, and

Secretary of State Dulles, who became known world-wide for his preference for an American global strategy based on the threat of "massive retaliation." Eisenhower's decision was, as the President put it, to "let the communist authorities understand that, in the absence of satisfactory progress, we intended to move decisively without inhibition in our use of weapons, and would no longer be responsible for confining hostilities to the Korean Peninsula. We would not be limited by any world-wide gentlemen's agreement."[46]

Besides leaks and rumors of possible American use of nuclear weapons, military pressures were undertaken in the spring of 1953 to force the communists to negotiate: B-29 missions accelerated again; Eisenhower announced that the Seventh Fleet would no longer protect Communist China from attack; Sabre jets often chased MiGs across the Yalu.

According to Clark, he did not have a problem with the JCS: "They were very good in supporting me." He added, however, "The final decision didn't rest with the JCS. You see, the State Department had an oar in there."[47] Despite Clark's positive view of the military body, a leading historian's observations typify those of a number of critics of the JCS during the war:

> The administration often failed to appreciate the military conse-
> quences of its political decisions, with the result that seemingly con-
> tradictory orders were sometimes given to MacArthur and his suc-
> cessors, Generals Ridgway and Clark. . . . For this failure . . . the
> Joint Chiefs of Staff have to assume a good part of the responsibility.
> Instead of communicating to the administration the nation's military
> capabilities and limitations in Korea, it violated another dictum of
> Clausewitz—namely that the civilian leadership had to be made
> aware of the imperatives of military operations."[48]

On the other hand, Clark was strongly critical of the State Department and the Allies. According to him, the communists after World War II were smart enough to realize that what they could not accomplish on the battlefield, they could get by going through the now powerful State Department.[49] He was also critical of the British role in Korea: "Our allies, Britain principally, were worried: Will we trigger World War III? The British, as you know, just as they were doing in Vietnam, were continuing to trade with the enemy."[50]

Under Eisenhower, Charles Wilson replaced Robert A. Lovett as secretary of defense. (Marshall had left the post in September 1951.) The Department of Defense under Lovett had held to a moderate position regarding the role of large-scale force in influencing communist judgments at Panmunjom. Admiral William M. Fechteler, who succeeded the deceased Sherman as CNO (chief of naval operations) in July 1951, had long argued for more aggressive air action to persuade the enemy to accept the UNC's version of an armistice. Even before Wilson took over the Defense Department, a number of senior officials there were convinced that "the advantages deriving from the military pressure were already apparent in the second half of 1952."[51] Clark took in stride the input of Eisenhower, Wilson, and Fechteler because he was confident by the spring of 1953 that the termination of the war was in the offing.

Most Americans seemed to be pro-war as long as the objective in Korea was victory. After the decision to end the war through an armistice, however, the stalemate on repatriation dragged on, more lives were lost, and still no truce was signed. Thus, peace became the keynote of the new administration in 1953. Requests for more money for war were denied. The Department of Defense was hamstrung financially by the concept of limited war.

While not losing faith in a successful timely ending of the war, Clark was often disappointed by the lack of clear goals displayed by the Joint Chiefs as the Korean debacle was winding down. By the time General Nathan F. Twining replaced Vandenberg as Air Force chief of staff at the end of June 1953, the Joint Chiefs of Staff lacked unity on their objectives in Korea. They were divided again, as in June 1951, on whether the main goal was to defeat the CCF below the Yalu or to create an atmosphere conducive to a cease-fire. The individual service chiefs even differed on using nuclear weapons. Twining did not join the JCS at a seemingly propitious time. All available options had flaws, or so it seemed.

## FINAL OPERATIONS

Lieutenant General William Harrison, the chief of the UN truce team since May 1952, was not bringing the communists to an agreement at Panmunjom any faster than Joy had. With the disheartening stalemate at Panmunjom, the JCS instructed Clark to "continue, within existing directives, to make maximum practicable use [of] available air strength in attacks upon all military targets in North Korea."[52]

When Clark had come on board, Truman had given consent that "opened the entire complex [of hydroelectric facilities along the Yalu] to air destruction."[53] The President had hoped vainly that these bombings would end the deadlock at Panmunjom before the November 1952 presidential election. Clark "seized on the air pressure doctrine" as offering "maximum returns for minimum losses."[54] Weyland and Clark worked together well, the former keeping the CINCFE "apprised of everything that might be considered . . . strategic" targets.[55] They had hoped thereby to bring about a compromise on the POW issue at Panmunjom, too, but the many strategic bombing missions of the summer of 1952 produced no such result. Instead, there came a six-month recess in truce talks beginning on October 8, 1952.

The strategic bombing campaign, first targeting Yalu power plants, had begun in June 1952. Vice Admiral J. J. (Jocko) Clark, the new commander of the Seventh Fleet (following Briscoe, who became COMNAVFE) coordinated his air raids with those of General Barcus, the new head of the Fifth Air Force. In the largest air strike so far in the war, on June 23, five hundred FEAF, Navy, and Marine planes hit four key dams along the Yalu, knocking out 90 percent of North Korea's power supply.

The raid was launched without prior notice to America's coalition partners, and it precipitated new anxieties among the Allies that the United States was preparing to accelerate the war again. France, India, and Great Britain especially were upset. Although it was not reassuring, Clark issued a press statement: "I note with astonishment the questions raised with regard to the bombing of the Suiho hydro-electric plant. . . . This target and any other remunerative targets in North Korea are subject to attack by United Nations forces while hostilities continue and while the enemy continues his ground attacks against our lines."[56]

On July 11, Clark and Weyland ordered a bombing campaign against the North Korean capital called Operation Pressure Pump. The FEAF and carrier planes flew over 1,200 sorties that first day against Pyongyang, dropping 23,000 gallons of napalm. The worst bombing took place on August 29, when over 1,400 sorties were flown, dropping about 700 tons of bombs. People and industry were forced underground, as Pyongyang became a city of cave-dwellers.

Clark asked for and received permission from the JCS to bomb military targets in North Korea about five miles from the Manchurian border and ten miles from the USSR. On September 1, 1952, in the biggest naval air raid of the war, planes from several American carriers attacked industrial targets at three cities in northeastern North Korea. Almost daily in September and October, land- and carrier-based American aircraft struck at industrial, communications, and transportation targets, some daringly close to the Soviet and Manchurian borders.

The communists were not cowed by this massive show of air strength; it did not force them to concede on the nonrepatriation issue. Even though the strategic bombing campaign caused disruptions and distress to the North Koreans, it was not enough to bend their will and halt the war. Because they could develop ways to counter UNC air raids, such as moving important targets underground, comments a military historian, "the air dropped conventional bomb proved as limited in the second half of the twentieth century as in the first."[57]

If the United Nations should have to recess the talks because of the stalemate in negotiations, the JCS in late September 1952 had authorized Clark to "'maintain unrelenting military pressure on [the] enemy, particularly through air action.' But . . . 'no major ground offensive action should be contemplated at this time.'"[58]

But because the enemy had been conducting vigorous ground attacks since September, Van Fleet asked Clark for permission in early October 1952 to strengthen UNC positions by taking the hills of the Iron Triangle north of Kumhwa. Thinking losses would be light (Van Fleet predicted less than two hundred), Clark approved the operation. But casualties were over nine thousand, and little ground was gained. The operation demonstrated an old principle of tactics: the futility of a ground assault without possessing superior firepower at the point of concentration. There was also severe disappointment in mid-October when a simulated landing by UNC forces at Kojo on the east coast below Wonsan turned out as futile as it was desperate.

Among the feasible political options for the Allies was the release of anticommunist POWs. Clark was able to release 27,000 civilian internees among the POWs during June-August 1952 and another 11,000 that October and November in the interest of easing tension in the compounds. Another political option was to recess the Panmunjom conference when no progress was being made and the communists were stalling. Although they were using the conference as a stage for propaganda, Clark found it difficult to convince Washington that this was an effective way to get the enemy's attention.

Clark also argued for the ability to expand and improve the ROK Army. Although he finally was allowed to enlarge ROK forces, it was not approved until October 1952, when it had become a campaign issue. After Eisenhower's victory that November, the ROK Army was expanded: The troop ceiling was lifted from 363,000 to 463,000.

Clark requested one more political option. In late May 1952 he asked that two Nationalist Chinese divisions be authorized to join the UNC in Korea. Clark said his proposal was actually "never answered by Washington. It died by pocket veto."[59]

An important decision that Clark made soon after arriving in the war theater was the setting up of the Korean Communications Zone in order to improve the administration of logistical support. He saw Van Fleet trying to run the Eighth Army and oversee the POW camps, besides endeavoring to persuade Rhee to cooperate, as well as keeping supplies coming and repairing the roads and rail lines. Clark appointed Major General Thomas W. Herren to head the new organization, which efficiently took over the care of the rear and "behind the scenes" operations, including the final disposition of the Koje-do affair.[60] Clark had established a similar organization in Italy that had proven highly successful. Kindred logistical organizations had been formed by Eisenhower's and MacArthur's supply chiefs to maintain an orderly flow of logistical matériel to the fronts in their theaters in World War II.

During the fourteen months of Clark's FEC/UNC tenure there was much ground fighting by small units up and down hills or between outposts along the front. Clark described the nature of this fighting:

> . . . The enemy was able to plan his ground operations, along the front line, with relative certainty that our forces inside Korea were inadequate to mount a decisive offensive against him. . . . No de-

fense line can be so strong that it cannot be dented by an enemy who is ready to expend the lives necessary to make the dent. When the enemy made these pushes we rolled with the punch rather than stand our ground stubbornly and be overrun. Then, if the Communists had taken terrain features important to our defense line, we had to counterattack to recapture them. That is where we suffered our heaviest casualties.[61]

A respected analyst (and veteran) of the war points out that possession of these outposts "served more political and propaganda purposes than military. In some respects it was a replay of the trench warfare of World War I, for both sides were deeply entrenched and both sides made extensive use of artillery."[62] Van Fleet wanted to be on the offensive and win objectives for the United Nations; however, Clark vowed, "The authority I had to mount limited objective attacks was a constant temptation, but I couldn't see the wisdom of paying lives for pieces of ground in Korea unless we were going all out to win the war."[63]

In late March 1953, as truce talks began to make progress, communist fighting picked up frantically. Stalin had died, and the communists agreed to an exchange of sick and wounded prisoners. Old Baldy and Pork Chop Hill, scenes of fierce earlier battles, again were hotly contested. As Taylor expressed it, "The action raged . . . on and around these relatively unimportant positions. But the battle itself soon made them important, and every soldier lost added to that importance and made their successful defense a matter of unit pride."[64] In April and early May 1953, as peace talks slowed, communist battle action subsided.

After the UNC's final proposal at Panmunjom on May 25, indicating that the truce was getting near, communist attacks started up with renewed frenzy. Clark increased artillery and air support as the enemy action mounted. There was savage fighting along the stalemated line, especially against ROK divisions. The communists were maneuvering for more defensible positions as the armistice drew nearer; loss of lives and supplies mattered little. After June 8, when the principle of voluntary repatriation was accepted at Panmunjom, the enemy initiated savage assaults until June 16, mainly in the Punchbowl area. The ROK II Corps was heavily hit and driven back. The enemy succeeded in getting better terrain positions, in giving the ROKs a black eye because they were opposing the armistice, and in exploiting the propaganda which came with the battlefield victory.

Meanwhile, on June 13–18, Clark carried out his plan to have FEAF bombers attack certain key dams to isolate important North Korean military installations. On June 24, the communists launched another offensive against ROK positions. The CCF seemed to be trying to convince the South Koreans that the war was not worth it. As the enemy assaults continued into mid-July, Clark ordered the transfer of the 24th Infantry Division and the 187th Airborne RCT (Regimental Combat Team) to Korea from Japan. Both units had seen extensive action earlier in the war.

While Clark and Robertson were still trying to bring Rhee around to accept an armistice on UNC terms, the CCF again attacked Pork Chop Hill, which the American troops had been able to hold that spring. After four days of fighting in early July, the enemy finally took control of the outpost.[65] Taylor commented: "The cost of continuing to defend Pork Chop became so prohibitive under the massed Chinese attacks that I authorized its evacuation."[66]

From July 13 to July 20, the biggest communist offensive since the spring of 1951 followed the ROK agreement on July 7 to truce terms and the resumption of peace talks on July 10. Clark later said, "There is no doubt in my mind that one of the principal reasons—if not the one reason—for the Communist offensive was to give the ROKs a 'bloody nose'; to show them and the world that 'PUK CHIN'—Go North—was easier said than done."[67] He called this communist offensive along the Kumsong River "politically inspired." Since it was directed mainly against ROK forces, he believed "the purpose was to show Rhee again how futile any South Korean fight against Red China would be. To make their point, the Communists were willing to lose 72,000 men, 25,000 of them killed. The ground gained was useless and had almost no effect on the military position when the armistice was finally signed."[68]

After the armistice was signed on July 27, 1953, Clark prepared to leave Japan and retire from the Army. Admiral Jocko Clark, head of the Seventh Fleet, told him, "I know that if your policies had been followed, we would have won more than an armistice; we would have won the kind of victory to which our country is entitled—unconditional surrender."[69] The signing of the Korean armistice was a task that no soldier of General Clark's caliber would want to be remembered for, as he later recalled the depressing occasion:

> Despite my personal disappointment that my government did not find it expedient to whip the Communists thoroughly in our first shooting war with them, I was aware of the worldwide factors which led Eisenhower to make his decision to seek an armistice.
>
> The decision having been made, I accepted it fully. There was no use continuing the frustrating stalemate where we were going no place, and suffering thirty thousand American casualties a year. . . .
>
> The Armistice was obtained and I signed it. But I would be less than truthful if I failed to record that I put my signature on that document with a heavy heart.[70]

It had been a heart-rending adjustment for a professional soldier who would have preferred an ending in World War II style, with American forces and their allies fighting with full resources and ending with decisive triumph. Even though worldwide factors made this first post–World War II conflict different, thereby requiring a new kind of resolution, this had not been Clark's kind of war, nor that of two other commanders of the last war, MacArthur and Ridgway.

# *Part II*

# THE KEY COMMAND DECISIONS

# CHAPTER
# 6

# Sending Americans to Fight in Korea

## The Uncertain Interim Between Wars

The senior American commanders in the Korean conflict all had participated in the overwhelming and triumphant demonstration of firepower in 1944–1945 that had resulted from American production and from the preference of President Franklin Roosevelt and his Joint Chiefs of Staff for a strategy of annihilation, rather than attrition, against both Japan and Germany. The victories on both sides of the world had been awesome and unconditional. It is not surprising that the postwar military leaders of the United States were prone to relive those halcyon days and to see future conflicts as similar. With the advent of the Cold War, even the younger, nonveteran career officers could envision a not-too-distant clash with communist forces that might resemble "The Good War." But the American military would have problems adjusting to the clash of arms that came to Korea, for it did not offer possibilities of supreme victory, special advantages to the larger mechanized forces, or clear-cut, morale-inspiring ideals at stake. Yet through the early stages of the Korean hostilities America would respond as if it were refighting the last war—and long afterward some of its most distinguished, if disgruntled American commanders would still wish that they could have brought their prowess of 1944–1945 to the battlefields of Korea.

The Korean War was both a civil war and a violent confrontation between the belligerents of the Cold War. The Korean roots of the conflict were exploited by major powers of the East and West to further their own strategic interests. For three years following Japan's surrender to the Allied forces, the United States and the Soviet Union sought to secure a foothold in East Asia. They not only engaged in military occupations below and above the 38th parallel in Korea but also prepared their respective zones for future peninsula-wide regimes that would be respectively capitalistic and communistic. Neither the American nor the Soviet overseers in Korea made much attempt to comprehend the seeds of civil war they were sowing among the populace by dividing them ideologically. By the time the two occupying armies pulled out of the peninsula, the tides of nationalism, communism, Western democracy, and civil unrest had become a cauldron ready to explode.

In August 1948 the Republic of Korea, headed by President Syngman Rhee, was formally established south of the 38th parallel, and a month later the Democratic People's Republic of Korea, led by Premier Kim Il Sung, was proclaimed in the north. By the end of the year Soviet troops were withdrawn from the North, leaving behind a large military advisory mission and the well-equipped and trained North Korean Army. American forces were pulled out of South Korea a half year later, in June 1949; a small U.S. military advisory group was assigned to work with the South Korean Army, which was basically a constabulary force and not prepared to meet the more powerful North Korean Army.

Influenced by the material assistance and the ideological pressures of the American and Soviet occupying forces, South and North Korea followed the political and economic systems of their former occupying powers. The American and Soviet regular troops left the peninsula quite aware that tensions between the two zones had escalated to dangerous levels during the early years of the Cold War. It was no coincidence that Rhee had been educated in America and Kim in the Soviet Union. Before and after becoming head of state, each man had often proclaimed that he intended to occupy and unite the entire peninsula by force. It is not surprising that from early 1948 onward border incidents became more frequent and bloody. When such clashes occurred, both North and South

Korea turned to their former occupation overlords to plead for more military assistance, claiming that a major invasion by the other side was imminent.

Both Rhee and Kim were preparing to reunify the peninsula by arms when the North Koreans, who had been made more combat ready by their Soviet sponsor, seized the initiative and started the war on June 25, 1950. While the Soviet Union and Communist China were major contributors to strengthening the North Korean Army and agitating domestic divisiveness between the two Koreas, the North Korean invasion was instigated unilaterally without direct orders from Moscow or Peking.

The United States was not blameless, because it had played a key role in the establishment of two separate governments in the Korean peninsula and ignored the potential for violence as well as the threat of an imminent war. Moreover, American military leaders failed to adequately anticipate the relative military strength of the two sides. But it was not just lack of foresight which prevented America from sufficiently arming South Korea. The American government was reluctant to further strengthen Rhee's military forces for fear he would strike first and invade the North. As John J. Muccio, ambassador to South Korea, recalled, "We were in a very difficult position . . . because if we gave Rhee and his cohorts what they wanted, they could have started to move north the same as the north moved south."[1]

In September 1947, with military funds scarce and American forces needed elsewhere, the Joint Chiefs of Staff had stated that the United States had "little strategic interest" in Korea, that in case of a general war "our present forces in Korea would be a military liability," and that therefore American forces should be withdrawn from South Korea.[2] For various reasons, such as the fear of Soviet forces filling the vacuum, the pullout was not undertaken, but six months later the JCS concluded that the United States should not provide any guarantee of military security to South Korea. Truman approved a policy statement that the United States "should not become so irrevocably involved in the Korean situation that an action taken by any faction in Korea or by any other power in Korea could be considered a 'casus belli' for the U.S."[3] In June 1948, only two months before the South Korean republic was established, the Joint Chiefs went on record again emphasizing "that Korea is of little strategic value to the United States and that any commitment to United States use of military force in Korea would be ill-advised and impracticable."[4]

In two press interviews in March 1949, MacArthur, whose Far East Command would no longer include Korea in its jurisdiction, observed that "our line of defense runs through the chain of islands fringing the coast of Asia."[5] The line he delineated included the Philippines, the Ryukyus, Japan, and the Aleutians. He pointedly excluded both Korea and Formosa, the latter to become the refuge for the Nationalist forces of Chiang Kai-shek when they were ousted from the Chinese mainland later that year. The President commented in a speech in early January 1950 that he was opposed to sending military assistance to Chiang's army on Formosa; he did not mention South Korea. A week later, on January 12, Dean Acheson, the secretary of state, delivered an address in which he omitted the two countries from the Pacific defense perimeter deemed vital to the strategic interests of the United States. He did say, however, that if either were attacked, American military units might be sent to their defense as part of an international force. Nevertheless, to many people and, most important, to leaders in Pyongyang, Moscow, and Peking, the various statements by the Joint Chiefs, MacArthur, Truman, and Acheson seemed to indicate minimal American interest in defending Korea. One editorialist, who probably typified the sentiments of many, claimed that Acheson's remarks constituted "an invitation to aggression against South Korea."[6] Whatever the North Korean records may someday reveal about this, MacArthur and Acheson were unwise in spelling out publicly and unnecessarily the American line of strategic commitment in the West Pacific.

The low strategic priority of Korea from the viewpoint of official Washington was due to West Europe's occupancy of center stage in the Cold War, 1947–1949, from the Greek-Turkish crises through the Berlin blockade to the formation of NATO. The foremost adversary of the free world was steadfastly seen to be the Soviet Union, and the most likely site of Armageddon was understood to be Berlin or the plains of Northwest Europe. The Soviet threat was shockingly magnified in August 1949 with the detonation by the USSR of its first nuclear bomb, at least four years ahead of the expectations of American authorities.

This news precipitated a strategic review by a State-Pentagon team, which was dominated by the civilian branch. In April 1950 the resulting document, with numerous revisions, became the National Security Council's policy paper no. 68 (NSC 68), the first significant post-1945 statement on American global strategy. It predicted that the Soviet military could be ready for conventional and nuclear warfare by 1954. NSC 68 proposed an immediate large-scale American military buildup, estimated to cost $50 billion in the first year, or nearly four times the military budget for fiscal 1950. Because of the program's costliness, final approval was still pending when the Korean War erupted.

Even within the world of East Asia, Korea's problems paled in comparison to the fast-deteriorating Nationalist position in the Chinese civil war. In the spring of 1949, Mao Tse-tung's armies launched a massive offensive so devastating that the Nationalist forces began withdrawing to Formosa by midsummer. In October, the People's Republic of China was proclaimed; in December, Chiang Kai-shek's government and troops completed their movement to Formosa; and in February 1950, Communist China and the Soviet Union entered into a thirty-year formal alliance.

Meanwhile, the United States now saw Japan as a nation with the potential to be the bulwark of communist containment in Asia that Nationalist China had failed to become. Security arrangements in Japan, Okinawa, and the Philippines got new attention, and economic as well as military aid went to these areas, especially Japan. It was feared by both American and Japanese leaders that Hokkaido, the northernmost of the Japanese home islands, was a prime target of Soviet expansionism.

In view of such portentous developments, it is no wonder that the United States did not see much positive strategic significance in Korea. Little thought was given by Washington planners to an important negative strategic value of Korea, which Moscow and Peking leaders may have envisioned: In case of hostilities there, Korea could divert American forces that might otherwise be used to counter a Soviet armed incursion in West Europe.

The Korean civil war and the Cold War were crucial factors leading to the North Korean invasion of June 1950 and the subsequent American response. But three other basic factors were involved in shaping the decision-making that led to the commitment of U.S. forces in the Korean conflict. These were the enlarged role of the State Department, the unpreparedness of the American military, and McCarthyism's impact on the Truman administration.

During the Second World War, President Roosevelt used Harry L. Hopkins as his principal adviser on grand strategy, global diplomacy, and relations with major heads of state like Churchill and Stalin. FDR treated Secretary of State Cordell Hull with cavalier disdain on such matters, relegating to him and the State Department such secondary wartime issues as Latin American affairs and United Nations organizational structuring.

On the other hand, President Truman, after less than satisfactory experiences with his first two secretaries of state, Edward R. Stettinius, Jr., and James F. Byrnes, developed great trust and respect in their successors of 1947–1953, George Marshall and Dean Acheson, as well as in several of their key lieutenants. At the same time, Truman found himself increasingly alienated from much of the military hierarchy, which was almost continually locked in interservice squabbling during the four years following World War II. Admiral Leahy, the JCS chairman from 1942 to 1949, proved indispensable as Truman's chief military confidant and as the linchpin in communications between the President and the brass. Meanwhile, Marshall, who retained Truman's esteem, tried to improve ties between the State and Defense departments. But as the Cold War expanded, the President appeared to heed more and more the counsel of Acheson and the bright leaders of State's "brains center," the Policy Planning Staff.

The Cold War demonstrated the need for greater cooperation and coordination between agencies in the diplomatic, military, economic, and intelligence fields. The National Security Act of 1947 was a significant effort to develop better teamwork in those areas; the new National Security Council and the Central Intelligence Agency were the most notable of several organizational reforms that essentially built upon the new concept of strategy as utilizing not only force and the threat of force but also political, economic, psychological, and other resources to advance national policies and interests.

All-important in policy-making for the American occupations in Germany, Japan, and Korea was an interdepartmental body called the State, War, and Navy Coordinating Committee (State, Army, Navy, and Air Force Coordinating Committee by 1947), on which State representatives often exerted paramount influence. The proclamation of the Republic of Korea in August 1948 and the ensuing withdrawal of the American XXIV Corps left American interests in South Korea under the jurisdiction of Ambassador Muccio, to whom the commander of the U.S. Military Advisory Group reported. In May 1949 the West German republic was created, and control in the American zone shifted to the State Department from the Department of the Army. John J. McCloy became the high commissioner, succeeding General Lucius D. Clay, who, as military governor, had formerly been the ranking American in West Germany. General Bradley, then Army chief of staff, notified General MacArthur in Japan of his concurrence with the expanding State role in occupation affairs: "For some time, our trend of thought here has been that we should try to get the State Department to take over the Military Government in Japan in a similar manner [to that in the American zone in Germany] as soon as the State Department is organized to handle it."[7] MacArthur, however, created such a furor in response that the matter was dropped, though in sundry subtle ways the general's authority was diminished thereafter with some shifting of responsibilities to the State Department and others directly to the Japanese government.

In virtually every area abroad where American military and diplomatic interests met, the State Department's role had gradually grown since the FDR presidency, even to the point of overseeing some key military advisory programs. In light of this trend it was not unusual for Acheson and senior State officials to have considerable input on all aspects of the decision, even military, on whether the United States should come to the defense of South Korea in the summer of 1950.

Due to pressing domestic needs, American military strength after World War II was not maintained at levels commensurate with the global commitments made by the United States in occupation, containment, and various security missions. In August 1945 the Army had 6.1 million men and 90 divisions; the Navy, 3.5 million personnel and 8,100 ships; the Army Air Forces, 2.3 million airmen with 68,400 aircraft; and the Marine Corps, 486,000 troops and 6 divisions. By June 1950 the American military establishment had shrunk markedly: the Army possessed 592,000 soldiers and 10 divisions; the Navy, 401,000 men and 238 ships; the Air Force, 411,000 personnel and 4,700 airplanes; and the Marines, 49,000 men and 2 divisions. The largest reductions had come during the first year after the fall of Japan when massive demobilization cut the total American military personnel to one-sixth of its strength in August 1945.

Because of his command's many responsibilities in Japan, South Korea, the Ryukyus, and the Philippines, MacArthur initially did not have to absorb quite as severe cuts as did American forces elsewhere: From 1.7 million Army ground and air personnel in October 1945, U.S. Army Forces, Pacific, dropped to 400,000 by June 1946. By June 1950, however, MacArthur's interservice Far East Command had suffered cuts as deep as the rest of the American military establishment. His ground forces numbered 108,000, mainly in the four divisions of Walker's Eighth Army in Japan; Stratemeyer's Far East Air Forces had 34,000 airmen and 1,172 planes, notably in the Fifth Air Force in Japan; and Joy's U.S. Naval Forces, Far East, had only about 20 major combat ships and an assortment of auxiliary vessels, most of the firepower being in Vice Admiral Arthur Struble's Seventh Fleet.

Compared to World War II figures, these were not impressive, but much of America's overseas deployment of ground, sea, and air power was concentrated in the Far East Command. Of the Army's ten divisions, for example, four were under MacArthur, five were in the States, and one was in Germany.[8] MacArthur's ground divisions, however, were understrength, inadequately trained, ill equipped, and like occupation troops elsewhere, less than sharp in physical fitness. They were hardly prepared to climb, much less fight protracted actions in the rugged mountains of Korea. Unaware of how inadequate the Far East Command was in combat readiness and striking power, Army Chief of Staff Collins, upon hearing of the North Korean invasion, "thought how fortunate it was for us that the Soviets picked for this venture the one area in the world where the United States military forces of all arms were well positioned if we should decide to intervene."[9] The Joint Chiefs of Staff, who had toured the Far East Command in January and February 1950, complimented MacArthur on "the present high standard" of his ground, sea, and air units. "The JCS and MacArthur," commented JCS Chairman Bradley, "were in nearly full agreement on most specific Far East matters. We shared the view that Korea was still of little strategic interest and that in the event of 'trouble,' the ROK Army could handle North Korea."[10] Brigadier General William L. Roberts, commander of the Korean Military Advisory Group, cockily predicted on several occasions in the spring of 1950 that the South Koreans could repel a North Korean invasion. He not only asserted that the ROK Army was better equipped but also commented on the eve of hostilities that South Korea possessed "the best doggone shooting army outside the United States."[11] Obviously American intelligence about the South and North Korean forces was woefully inadequate. Blinded by the victories of World War II, they could not realistically assess their preparedness for a new conflict.

Another factor essential to the decision to send American boys to war in Korea was the phenomenal growth of McCarthyism and its impact on the Truman administration. Senator Joseph R. McCarthy of Wisconsin began his anticommunist crusade in February 1950, charging that over two hundred communists were employed by the State Department. McCarthy commanded headlines and created a formidable political sideshow with his every act and word for the next four years. His movement's nationwide spread and its witch-hunting tactics could not be ignored by Acheson and his cohorts that spring. In early March the Senate began an investigation of McCarthy's charges against the State Department, with the aggressive Republican senator and his accusations getting front-page attention in most newspapers up to the start of the Korean War. The Senate investigating committee, headed by venerable Democratic Senator Millard F. Tydings of Maryland, terminated its hearings in July and reported no evidence to substantiate McCarthy's allegations, a fact largely ignored by the excited public.

By then, however, Acheson and his top officials had been forced repeatedly to defend their department's personnel and policies in the face of vicious smear tactics that often involved character assassination. An easy target for the McCarthyites was the Truman administration's position on China; for years pro-Chiang groups in America had pushed for greater military and economic assistance for the Nationalists in the war against the Communist Chinese. The administration had failed to render the necessary support that allegedly could have "saved" the Chinese mainland from a communist takeover, so Truman, Acheson, and numerous "China hands" of the Foreign Service were charged with softness on communism.

Truman and Acheson would probably have found it necessary for political survival at least to review their hands-off policy on China after the State Department's strong criticism of the Nationalists in its White Paper of 1949. Such a reexamination would have been likely even if the Korean War had not presented a challenge that the McCarthyites claimed was a litmus test of the administration's loyalty. Indeed, so powerful had McCarthy become in the public arena by late spring of 1950 that Truman and Acheson were being pressured to demonstrate that they, not McCarthy, actually determined American foreign policy and that they would not allow the communists to seize either Formosa or South Korea. Walter Lippmann did not overstate the issue when he said of the anti-Acheson assault by the forces of McCarthy in 1950, "No American official who has represented this government abroad in great affairs, not even Wilson in 1918, has ever been so gravely injured at home."[12] It is impossible to measure fully the torments and pressures that Truman and Acheson endured that fateful spring of 1950 and how McCarthyism impacted on their decision-making the last week of June. But it is difficult to imagine how the McCarthy-aroused public would have tolerated less than a tough stand by the administration on Korea, no matter how logical its previous position had been.

## DECIDING TO GO TO WAR

If the literal interpretation of the Constitution had been followed and a congressional declaration of war had been obtained, the time-consuming process undoubtedly would have enabled the North Korean conquest of the southern part of the peninsula to be consummated. During the first days of the North Korean invasion, ROK resistance proved spotty and mostly feeble; it quickly became obvious that only strong and quick external intervention could save South Korea. Thus Truman boldly called together a circle of fourteen civilian and military advisers in a series of meetings over the fateful six-day period of June 25–30, 1950, culminating in the full commitment of American armed forces to the Korean conflict.

North Korea badly miscalculated, acting on the presumption that the United States would not intervene, and that if it did choose to assist South Korea, its governmental machinery was so cumbersome that it would require lengthy congressional debates before voting to go to war. North Korea was not the first or last belligerent to discover that many hostilities in which the United States has engaged began with quick executive actions rather than with declarations of war by Congress. Truman's sudden reversal of strategy on Korea and his brazen bypass of the war-making power of the legislative branch would result in the hurling of American firepower into the fray just in time to prevent the overrun of all South Korea. However, it also precluded strong bipartisan support of the administration's war policies on Capitol Hill. The whirl of meetings and decisions those final days of June would cast a long shadow over the Truman administration, indeed, to its very end.

According to Ambassador Charles E. Bohlen, a top expert on the Soviets who was close to Truman and many of the advisers the President turned to that last week of June, "When all is said about Korea, however, the fact remains that the two men responsible for finally blocking the expansion of Communism were the cocky little President of the United States, and his icy-eyed Secretary of State, Dean Acheson." Regarding the thirteen other key advisers involved in the decision-making that week, Bohlen observes, "One thing is certain: they all relied heavily on Acheson, who had worked out an admirable relationship with the President. The Secretary of State came up with many of the ideas; the President, and the President alone, made the decisions."[13] Truman was frank in acknowledging Acheson's great diplomacy and his initiative in immediately calling into session the UN Security Council so that the United States would not go into Korea alone.

Acheson orchestrated the initial response of the U.S. government to the outbreak of Korean hostilities, and he continued to direct much of the process of decision-making during the period of June 25–30. Both of the Blair House conferences of Truman and his top assistants, on June 25 and 26, were characterized by Truman's presiding and Acheson's leading in introducing and pushing substantive proposals that the President eventually approved, the other advisers going along without serious objections or questions. At the meeting on Sunday evening, June 25, the main decisions were all proposed by Acheson: to empower MacArthur to provide military equipment to South Korea; to permit American air and sea forces to cover the withdrawal of American nationals from Korea, including aerial destruction of North Korean tanks and planes interfering with the evacuation; and to consider how UN members might render further help in support of the Security Council resolution that day condemning the North Korean invasion and calling for an end to the hostilities and restoration of the border.

The next evening's meeting of the President and all the advisers of the previous session except one saw Acheson offer a five-point proposal, which became the basic decisions the President then approved: to use American air and sea forces south of the 38th parallel in support of South Korea; to neutralize Formosa by interposing Seventh Fleet elements between it and the Chinese mainland; to increase military aid to the Philippines; to accelerate military assistance to French Indochina and send a military advisory group there; and to keep the UN informed of such American actions. Acheson was instrumental in formulating and getting the support for the Security Council resolutions of June 25 and 27, the latter calling for member states to give military support to South Korea. Acheson's was the strongest voice in influencing the President's decision on a number of other issues—for instance, to circumvent Congress in making war, to take a quick and firm posture of resistance to the North Korean aggression, to try to keep the conflict limited, and to avoid a direct confrontation with the Soviet Union.

The crucial Blair House meetings of June 25 and June 26 had involved the President, six officials of the State Department, and eight Pentagon leaders. Besides Acheson, the State representatives had been James E. Webb, under secretary of state (absent from the meeting on the 26th); H. Freeman Matthews, deputy under secretary of state (present only on the 26th); Dean Rusk, assistant secretary of state; John D. Hickerson, assistant secretary of state for United Nations affairs; and Philip C. Jessup, ambassador-at-large. The Defense Department was represented by Johnson, the secretary of defense who was at odds with Truman and Acheson and would be succeeded by Marshall in September; Pace, secretary of the Army; Francis P. Matthews, secretary of the Navy, who would be replaced later after calling for a "preventive war" against the USSR; Thomas K. Finletter, secretary of the Air Force; Bradley, JCS chairman who would soon get his fifth star; Collins, Army chief of staff and executive agent for the JCS in Far East affairs; Sherman, chief of naval operations; and General Hoyt Vandenberg, chief of staff of the Air Force. The State Department contingent far outshone the Pentagon delegation in sharpness, vision, and initiative at their joint meetings, the military officers being markedly inferior in communicative effectiveness. Indeed, Acheson and his subordinates did not hesitate to take the lead on matters where the Pentagon spokesmen might have been expected to dominate.

It was more than coincidental that the elder member of this Washington circle was Truman at age sixty-six, while in the Far

East Command GHQ the oldest member was seventy-year-old MacArthur. In the deliberations of the Washington and Tokyo groups that week, all deferred to the senior leader in age and rank without posing any significant challenges to his thinking. This was true even of Acheson, who spoke for his boss without saying anything at odds with what he knew Truman thought.

Amazingly, however, there was minimal friction between the State and Pentagon officials. The only known dissidence was offered by Webb, who was notably excluded from the second Blair House meeting. According to an authority, "He was said to have been 'put in the dog house' by the President because on Sunday he had attempted to precipitate discussion of American domestic political implications of the events in Korea."[14]

The National Security Council as such did not play a large part, though nearly all its individuals were deeply involved in the various sessions with the President all week. The NSC met on Wednesday, when no major decisions were made, and on Thursday, June 29, when the crucial steps were taken to authorize MacArthur to extend his air and sea attacks to military targets in North Korea and to employ limited American ground forces to secure the port and air bases in the Pusan-Chinhae area. MacArthur was also instructed to defend Formosa with naval and air operations against an invasion, and he was told that if the Soviet Union intervened in the Korean War he was to order his forces to defend themselves while he kept Washington closely posted on the situation. These proposals were presented by Johnson and were approved by the President; they had been drafted by the JCS.

Shortly after midnight of June 29–30, MacArthur's momentous report on his visit to the Korean battlefront south of Seoul was received in the Pentagon. He found the South Korean Army incapable of stopping the enemy and was convinced that American ground forces must be sent into combat quickly, first a regimental combat team and then two divisions. High-level Defense and State officials pondered the Far East commander's somber assessment for several hours. At 3:40 A.M., Friday, June 30, Collins and a Pentagon-State group began a teleconference with MacArthur and several of his senior officers in Tokyo GHQ. Collins stated that the RCT could be dispatched to the Pusan-Chinhae area under terms of the JCS directive of June 29, but the President would have to approve its use to the north as well as the two-division buildup.

MacArthur emphasized that "a clear-cut decision without delay is imperative," and Collins assured him that he should have the President's decision on the two divisions before the RCT arrived in Korea. The Army chief of staff then inquired, "Does this meet your requirement for the present?"[15] According to a reliable source, "At this point MacArthur employed a technique no other officer in the United States military service would dare to use. He simply did not respond to the last statement of the Chief of Staff. The screen remained blank."[16] Collins remarked later, "We took this to mean that General MacArthur stood by his emphatic plea for a decision 'without delay.'"[17] Collins quickly got in touch with Secretary of the Army Pace, who called the President about MacArthur's requests. It was then about 5:00 A.M., but Truman was up and quite alert. "I told Pace," stated Truman, "to inform General MacArthur immediately that the use of one regimental combat team was approved" and that he would be advised later about the two divisions.[18]

At a meeting from 9:30 to 10:00 that morning in the White House Cabinet Room, Truman met with Acheson, Johnson, the service secretaries, the JCS, Harriman, and Deputy Secretary of Defense Stephen T. Early. Truman gave MacArthur "full authority to use the ground forces under his command" in the Korean combat.[19] He also approved Admiral Sherman's proposal to establish a naval blockade of the entire Korean coast, though a warning was sent to MacArthur to make sure that his naval units stayed "well clear of the coastal waters of Manchuria and USSR."[20] Upon Acheson's urging, Truman declined an offer by Chiang Kai-shek of 33,000 Nationalist Chinese soldiers for use in South Korea because of potential international difficulties and logistical problems.

At 11:00 A.M. on June 30, Truman and an array of his executive advisers met with fifteen Senate and House leaders at which time the President explained his decisions regarding the use of military force in Korea. Senator Kenneth Wherry, Republican of Nebraska, grumbled because Congress had not been approached, even though, he predicted, "no doubt full authority and funds would have been voted by the Congress to prepare for the protection of American interests."[21] One congressman inquired whether the intervention in Korea was within the jurisdiction of the United Nations, to which Truman responded that it was and said that MacArthur would be commander of both American and UN forces.

Lt. Gen. George E. Stratemeyer, CG, FEAF *(left)*, talks with Brig. Gen. Kum Chung of the ROK Army at a South Korean air base, July 13, 1950. Stratemeyer, a distinguished air commander in the China-Burma-India Theater during World War II, enjoyed MacArthur's strong support when he headed the Far East Air Forces in the Korean operations, 1950-1951. *U.S. Army.*

Artillerymen of the 24th Infantry Division fire 155-mm. howitzers at dusk along the Naktong defense line, Aug. 9, 1950. The 24th Division, which had been on occupation duty in Japan, became the first American unit to fight in the Korean War. Major General William F. Dean, its commander, was taken prisoner in July 1950. *U.S. Army.*

Troops of the 1st Cavalry Division move up to the front in South Korea, July 13, 1950. The 1st Cavalry Division, which actually functioned in Korea as an infantry outfit, was one of the first American units to engage the North Korean Army in July 1950 and was the first American division to clash with the Chinese Communist forces that November. *U.S. Army.*

Ashore at Inchon the day after the amphibious assault, Sept. 16, 1950. *Left to right:* Brig. Gen. Courtney Whitney, Vice Adm. Arthur D. Struble, Gen. of the Army Douglas MacArthur, and Maj. Gen. Oliver P. Smith. The Inchon invasion, which was carried out by the 1st Marine Division and the 7th Infantry Division, was the turning point in the North Korean phase of the Korean conflict. *U.S. Army.*

Aboard the battleship *Missouri* off Korea, Oct. 1950. *Left to right:* Lt. Gen. Edward M. Almond and Struble. Almond commanded the X Corps, while strong naval gunfire and air support were provided to his troops by the U.S. Seventh Fleet, headed by Struble. *U.S. Army.*

Visiting the Eighth Army in North Korea on the eve of its offensive to try to drive to the Yalu River, Nov. 24, 1950. *Left to right:* Lt. Gen. Walton H. Walker, MacArthur, and Maj. Gen. Frank W. Milburn. Much to the reluctance of Eighth Army leaders, MacArthur often visited the front on the eve of major offensives, a habit that Ridgway eventually persuaded him to drop. *U.S. Army.*

Meeting with the President, Dec. 6, 1950. *Seated, left to right:* Pres. Harry S. Truman and British Prime Min. Clement R. Attlee. *Standing, left to right:* Secretary of State Dean G. Acheson and Secretary of Defense George C. Marshall. Attlee's hasty trip to confer with Truman was precipitated mainly by the President's press remark regarding consideration of the use of atomic bombs in Korea. *U.S. Army.*

JCS and FECOM leaders at Haneda Airport, Tokyo, Jan. 31, 1951. *Left to right:* Gen. of the Army Omar N. Bradley, MacArthur, Gen. Hoyt S. Vandenberg, Stratemeyer, Adm. Forrest P. Sherman, and Gen. J. Lawton Collins. By the time of this trip of the Joint Chiefs to Japan and Korea, Ridgway had impressively turned around the Eighth Army, which was now on the counteroffensive. *U.S. Army.*

Visiting the front in North Korea, early 1951. *Left to right:* MacArthur and Lt. Gen. Matthew B. Ridgway. Although MacArthur frequently visited the front, he kept his pledge to Ridgway to give him maximum freedom in his command of the Eighth Army. *U.S. Army.*

Signing proclamation making May 19 Armed Forces Day, Apr. 2, 1951. *Seated, left to right:* Truman and Marshall. *Standing, left to right:* Lt. Gen. Merwin H. Silverthorn; Sherman; Vandenberg; Sec. of the Army Frank Pace, Jr.; Sec. of the Navy Francis P. Matthews; Sec. of the Air Force Thomas K. Finletter; Bradley; and Collins. This ceremony, nine days before the relief of MacArthur, includes the principal military officials under Truman, though only five of this group—Marshall and the Joint Chiefs of Staff—were instrumental in advising the President regarding the dismissal of the Far East commander. *U.S. Army.*

UNC armistice delegation, July 10, 1951. *Left to right:* Maj. Gen. Laurence C. Craigie, Maj. Gen. Paik Sun Yup, Vice Adm. C. Turner Joy, Maj. Gen. Henry I. Hodes, and Rear Adm. Arleigh A. Burke. This was the date that the armistice talks began at Kaesong near the 38th parallel. From October 25, 1951, to the war's end, July 27, 1953, the talks were held at the nearby village of Panmunjom. *U.S. Army.*

Conference at Eighth Army Headquarters, Seoul, Dec. 1952. *Left to right:* Lt. Gen. Otto P. Weyland, Pres.-elect Dwight D. Eisenhower, Gen. Mark W. Clark, and Gen. James A. Van Fleet. Eisenhower's presidential campaign in 1952 was based, in part, on a pledge to go to Korea and bring that war to an end. He did visit Korea briefly before his inauguration, but it was largely a publicity gesture. However, he did later threaten to unleash nuclear warfare in Korea, which may have helped to bring about the armistice in mid-1953. *George C. Marshall Research Library.*

(MacArthur became head of the UN Command on July 8.) As for the President's bypassing of Congress in going to war, Truman believed that he did not need the approval of Capitol Hill, though he wanted congressional backing for his direction of the war.

Harriman later said, "I thought it was a mistake and so did many others at the time" that President Truman did not seek a resolution from Congress sanctioning the commitment of American forces to combat in Korea. According to Harriman, "Mr. Truman said he had considered such a move; if he got a Joint Resolution it would tie the hands of a successor. . . . I did not realize until later that Dean Acheson had opposed going to Congress." Ambassador Lucius D. Battle, who was special assistant to Acheson in 1950, recalled that the secretary of state "made the point that if Congress debated a Joint Resolution, it might challenge what the president had done without the Joint Resolution."[22]

A White House press release about noon referred to several decisions of the past two days and closed with a deceptively simple reference to the most important one: "General MacArthur has been authorized to use certain ground supporting units."[23] The JCS message to MacArthur that afternoon was more ominous: "Restrictions on use of Army Forces . . . are hereby removed and authority granted to utilize Army Forces available to you . . . subject only to requirements for [the] safety of Japan in the present situation, which is a matter for your judgment."[24] Even at the start MacArthur's superiors put him in a quandary, requiring him to use his forces, which were relatively lacking in combat readiness, not only to keep Japan secure from a long-feared Soviet incursion but also to save South Korea from communist conquest. MacArthur had the permission to use ground troops as he had requested, but from that message until his dismissal in April 1951 there would be miscommunication between Washington and Tokyo about what were the American strategic priorities in the Far East.

## ASSUMPTIONS AND ALTERNATIVES

American entry into the Korean conflict was influenced by the Second World War in a number of significant ways. The lack of knowledge or consideration of internal Korean political currents prevented American policymakers from seeing the military action along the 38th parallel on June 25, 1950, as anything except brazen aggression by the North Koreans. Likewise, ignorance of things Japanese had blinded the United States to all motives for the Pearl Harbor attack in 1941 except unjustified treachery. American ethnocentrism was just as influential in 1950 as in 1941 in blocking Washington leaders from comprehending all that was happening or the real issues at stake. Moreover, with the acceleration of the Cold War in the late 1940s, another adversary threatening global domination had arisen, acutely reminding Americans of the Axis totalitarians who began the previous war. Thus it was easy to move from labeling the Korean action as Moscow-directed aggression to concluding that appeasement would be no more satisfactory for South Korea and the West now than it had been in deterring Hitler, Mussolini, and Tojo in the 1930s.

Legacies of World War II for the United States included occupied Japan, along with new military bases in the Ryukyus, Bonins, Marianas, and Carolines, along with renewed military activities in the Philippines. This unprecedented American peacetime military presence in the West Pacific meant that, more than in any other region on the periphery of the Soviet Union and its contiguous satellites, the United States had ground, sea, and air forces that could be concentrated rather rapidly to meet a hostile menace. In addition, the great majority of the American military's officer corps were veterans of World War II who remained convinced by their own wartime experience and their study of American wars that they were not likely to lose any war, especially against nonwhites. Racism had been a pervading factor in the origins of the Pacific war and throughout its course, and it would likewise have an important impact on the Korean conflict, distorting each side's images of the other.

Three principal decisions propelled the United States into the Korean conflict. They were the decisions to act under the ostensible aegis of the United Nations, to commit air and naval forces, and, finally, to send ground combat units into action on the peninsula. A study of the Blair House and other meetings that last week of June suggests that the President and his fourteen key advisers on the issue of war may have had a number of alternatives that were worthy of more study than they received. In fact, the options and their what-if scenarios are more numerous than might be expected, though, of course, such speculation has the wondrous advantage of hindsight, not accorded to the original decision-makers in June and July 1950. For example, the United States could have gone to South Korea's aid without securing the UN Security Council's backing or without obtaining the support of Britain, the Commonwealth nations, and other Allies who contributed forces. Certainly UN and Allied military efforts, though of considerable value in certain supporting roles, never could carry the brunt of critical campaigns because of the small size of their contributions in men and matériel. The main UN and Allied contributions were diplomatic rather than military, putting pressure on the United States to restrain its use of force and to seek a negotiated settlement short of American aims.

Another seemingly obvious option, that of stopping with an American-led resolution or two in the Security Council denouncing the Korean invasion, was precluded by the rampaging McCarthyism of the years 1950–1953. Other apparent alternatives were a naval blockade and international sanctions against North Korea to compel her withdrawal from the South. In late 1950, MacArthur would argue vehemently for a naval blockade and international economic sanctions against Communist China, which might have been lines of action to try against North Korea first. Since North Korean imports and exports could be handled through the contiguous territories of the Soviet Union and Red China, neither a naval nor an economic blockade would have been fully effective. Besides, such efforts would have had to be quite long term in realization, and the ability of South Korea to defend itself unassisted was shattered in the first weeks of fighting. Actions against the Soviet Union in the form of attacks or threats of use of force would not likely have influenced Moscow one iota. Besides, Truman and his military chiefs knew that the American military, especially the Strategic Air Command, was then in a position to present only a hollow threat to the world's other superpower and was surely unable to take on the now-nuclear-armed USSR in a war.[25]

An intriguing alternative was proposed by one of the most esteemed historians of the Korean War. He suggests that the peninsula should have been abandoned temporarily, withdrawing the South Korean forces to Japan or perhaps the Ryukyus. There they would be provided American training and equipment, and when combat ready they would join American forces, strongly backed by American naval and air power, to launch a decisive amphibious operation at a strategic locale well up the Korean coastline.[26] He might have added that with the supremacy of the skies and seas that American air and naval forces would actually achieve, it might have been possible to employ only the revitalized ROK Army in the delayed amphibious attack, withholding American ground troops altogether.

An interesting, if also hideous, alternative might have been to give the advocates of strategic air warfare the opportunity to demonstrate whether such air power can force an enemy to do one's will. The U.S. Air Force would launch a full-scale nonnuclear strategic bombing program against North Korea from bases in Japan and the Ryukyus until Kim's regime agreed to the restoration of the Republic of Korea below the 38th parallel. It is difficult to believe, however, that the American public, much less world opinion, would have long tolerated an all-out, protracted strategic bombing of North Korea. Besides, the maximum impact of strategic bombardment is against concentrated population and industrial-military centers, of which there were only a limited number in North Korea. In addition, the Strategic Air Command's supply of long-range bombers was far smaller than imagined; the entire SAC bomber force could not have wreaked the destruction necessary to compel Kim to yield South Korea. Finally, it is hard to believe that the bulk of SAC firepower would have been diverted to Korea from the higher-priority missions around the edges of the United States and the Soviet Union.

President Truman's decision to send American forces into action in Korea resulted in a decisive defeat of the North Korean invaders; it was his later decision to conquer North Korea that expanded the conflict and led to the stalemate that satisfied none of the belligerents. It is amazing that Truman and his advisers seem to have picked the best available alternative in late June 1950 despite the fact that some of their assumptions were flawed and certain key factors were not considered adequately. The assumption that has been most criticized is that the aggression in Korea was analogous to what happened to Manchuria, North China, Ethiopia, the Rhineland, Austria, and Czechoslovakia in the thirties when the Western democracies reacted with paralysis or appeasement to totalitarian expansionism. Those aggressive moves before World War II all involved major powers' incursions into other sovereign nations. The two Koreas, however, did not view themselves as separate countries, and each looked toward reunification after the exit of the American and Soviet occupation troops. The aggressions in the thirties appeared to call for forceful intervention by the democracies on behalf of the victims, which was not forthcoming at the time. If the U.S. entry into the Korean debacle was done to contain an alleged Moscow-ordered conquest, the justification oversimplified what was occurring on the peninsula and entangled America in the affairs of South Korea for the ensuing four decades or more.

This entanglement was predicated on several assumptions held by Truman and his top counselors regarding the motivations and calculations underlying the North Korean assault. Bradley, among others, assumed that the Korean invasion was a "diversionary move" to draw American forces away from effectively responding to an impending Soviet assault in West Europe or the Middle East. Truman, as well as several State Department senior officials, assumed that the Soviets were engaged in "soft-spot probing," or "feeling out," American reactions to aggression in a strategically unimportant area. Similar was the assumption by several Blair House conferees that the North Korean invasion was a Moscow-directed test of the will of anticommunist nations, which, if not resisted, would be followed by thrusts elsewhere. Whereas the probing assumption did not imply aggressions to follow, the believers in the testing assumption compared the Korean crisis to the Rhineland reoccupation, which was seen as the first of Hitler's aggressive moves leading to World War II. Another related assumption of some of Truman's circle was that the USSR was using the North Korean assault as a "demonstration" of the strength of the communist bloc and, in turn, the weakness of the free world, thereby swaying neutral nations in the arena of world public opinion. Secretary of Defense Johnson was one of the advocates of certain aspects of both the test and demonstration assumptions. Some of the Blair House group assumed that the assault was part of a "Soviet Far East strategy" to thwart the Japanese Peace Treaty negotiations and to disrupt generally American plans to develop Cold War bulwarks against Soviet expansionism in Asia and the West Pacific.[27] All of these assumptions were based, in turn, on the same two fundamental assumptions: Moscow was orchestrating the North Korean actions, and the differences between the two Korean regimes did not precipitate the war. In recent years, however, authorities on the origins of the war have deemphasized the direct role of Moscow and heavily stressed intra-Korean tensions.

These preceding assumptions were all shaped by the last war. The German moves into the Mediterranean countries had led to Anglo-American operations to dislodge them, which had forced postponement of the Americans' top priority for decisive action against Germany—namely, the cross-Channel invasion. In the prelude to the Pacific war, Japan had engaged in clever soft-spot probing to feel out the British, Dutch, and American commands and to see if the United States especially would oppose with force a move into non-American territory in Southeast Asia. As noted, the testing assumption was seen as similar to Hitler's move into the Rhineland before World War II. The demonstration assumption was reminiscent of the pre-1939 displays of military power by Japan in handily defeating Chinese forces in Manchuria and later in North China, which intimidated several Asian nations in Japan's threatened path of conquest, including the neutrality-seeking Philippine government. Even the Soviet Far East strategy assumption had roots that could be traced back to the war against Japan, for Moscow's interest in acquiring warm-water ports on the Pacific and promoting anticolonialism in the Asian and Pacific colonies of the Western powers had long been taken for granted in Washington.

Acheson particularly nourished two assumptions that came to influence the President and his inner circle significantly: American intervention should be undertaken with a United Nations cover, and the United States could count on its allies to bear a proportionately "fair share" of the defense of South Korea. But the establishment of a military command under UN auspices and headed by General MacArthur did not appear to garner any more international backing in terms of forces and other resources for the war effort than an American-formed coalition might have produced. The UN members who contributed men and matériel to saving South Korea were the same as those who were allied with the United States previously in formal or informal collective security arrangements or in close economic ties. If it is doubtful that the UN facade was of much value, the Allies that Acheson was able to line up, notably the United Kingdom, were able to influence American policy on the Korean War far out of proportion to their input on the battlefield. British, Commonwealth, and Turkish combat units particularly made valuable contributions to the military operations, but the fact remains that the vast preponderance of the combat strength employed and the losses suffered by the anticommunist side in the war were South Korean and American.

One of the most crucial assumptions by Truman's group was that Japan would remain stable and loyal if the principal American Army, Navy, and Air Force units stationed there were sent to Korea. Japan proved to be not only dependable but vitally important. It served as a base of operations for the prosecution of the war and contributed war materials, services, and covert naval personnel, as well as base facilities and constabulary troops. MacArthur, who was instrumental in establishing the Japan Self-Defense Force, saw Japan's strong and eager support of the UN Command as a natural culmination of what he deemed to be the most successful military occupation in history. It is doubtful that many in official Washington viewed occupied Japan so optimistically, but the Blair House circle, nevertheless, assumed that Japan could be trusted and used in the war.

They assumed also that America could enter the fray without bringing about the intervention of the Soviet Union and that the war could be kept limited, averting a third world war. Astonishingly, no attention was given to the question of Communist China's reactions or capabilities. This could not have been solely because of their ignorance of Peking's motives and plans, because, while discussing the Soviet threat cautiously, they actually knew no more about goings on in Moscow than in Peking.

As it turned out, both sides were deeply concerned about restricting the war. Perhaps because of the clash between MacArthur and Washington over the latter's prohibitions on "hot pursuit" of enemy aircraft across the Yalu, bombing targets along the North Korean border, and entering Soviet or Chinese land, air, and sea spaces, the myth has been perpetuated that the war was limited primarily because of American policy. Actually, the communist restraints were just as important in preventing the war's escalation, such as refraining from use of bombers against key bases, ports, and transportation centers in South Korea, especially Pusan, and from deployment of submarines against Allied naval elements in the Yellow Sea and the Sea of Japan. It would have been relatively easy for the Soviet Union to have transferred large quantities of such weapons to Chinese or North Korean control for a very destructive scale of air and undersea warfare.

It is clear that the failure of the two superpowers to resort to atomic weapons was the most important and obvious restriction on the Korean War. Although Moscow and Washington limited the conflict for different reasons, their decisions were based less on battlefield considerations than on internal politics and international repercussions the war might produce. In view of each side's distorted perceptions of the other, the assumption that the war could be kept limited was risky and maybe reckless, even if it luckily turned out to be correct.

The number of factors that Truman and his advisers did not consider adequately (or at all) during their sessions at the start of the Korean hostilities were many, which is not surprising in view of the short span of time that elapsed between the outbreak of fighting and the decision to commit American forces. They failed to assess accurately the myth of global monolithic communism and the reality of a high degree of independence of Peking and Pyongyang from Moscow. They misread the nature of the war's origins as more international than Korean, more rooted in global East-West tensions than in differing interest groups on the peninsula. They underestimated the dangerous extremes to which MacArthur would go to secure his way on the war's direction. They did not foresee the reticence of the Joint Chiefs of Staff in dealing with MacArthur and Acheson on policy and strategy. Leaders in Tokyo and Washington discounted, in part, the alarming state of America's military unpreparedness because of deep-seated ethnocentric convictions that the North Korean forces could be repelled by an inconsiderable American military commitment. They were also unable to take into account the extent of Truman's political vulnerability during the bizarre but powerful McCarthyism excitement, which left him unable to find a way to victory in the war or even a formula for ending it honorably.

Possibly the most important presumption influencing the decision to go to war was the strong ethnocentric, if not racial, bias that underestimated Asian capabilities and that persisted despite the lessons learned in 1941–1945 from the Japanese. If the communist side badly misjudged the American government's readiness to change direction on Asian policy and come to South Korea's defense, MacArthur and his superiors in Washington underestimated the forces required and the duration of fighting that would be needed just to gain a stalemate. Uncomfortably similar to the attitude of American military leaders in the autumn of 1941 that the Japanese were not capable of a raid on Pearl Harbor and simultaneous wide-ranging combat operations in the West Pacific and Southeast Asia, so in June 1950 the Washington and Tokyo leaders made a commitment to the ground war which they believed could defeat the enemy by employing only two divisions and a regimental combat team. That number of troops would turn out to be about half the number of Americans who would die and less than a tenth the total of Americans who would serve in the Korean War. Unhappily, a third war pitting Americans against Asians lay a decade ahead when, again, the former would tragically underestimate the fighting capabilities of the latter and probably, again, because of the blinders of ethnocentrism and racism.[28]

Another factor that was not weighed adequately was that the Achilles' heel of a republic is the divisiveness that grows during a war that becomes protracted and indecisive. In the case of the Korean situation, the loss of bipartisan support would be augmented by the frustrations of its limited nature, the popular notion of the American tradition of warfare being hostilities that are quick, all-out, and decisive, even annihilative. Of course, in June 1950 there was no way to know that the Korean fighting would last three years and end without a clear-cut triumph. Truman could have protected himself, however, if from the beginning he had involved Senate and House leaders more in the decision-making process, instead of merely informing them after the fact. Indeed, at the start of the war, majority opinion of both Congress and the people appeared to be in favor of the United States making some positive effort to save South Korea. As public support for Truman, Acheson, and the war effort seriously eroded, beginning with the Chinese intervention that fall, the President may well have wished by campaign time in 1952 that for his own sake, as well as the Democratic party's, he had undertaken a limited-liability approach to the direction of the war.

Not only should Congress have actively participated with the executive branch in the overall administration of the war, but also the Truman administration desperately needed to set up an agency that would incorporate ways of explaining to the people the aims of the war and the changes in strategy and policy. Admittedly, neither the Office of War Information in World War II nor the Committee on Public Information in World War I performed those functions well; in fact, in its own way each became the target of severe criticism, which may have deterred Truman from setting up another such agency. The savagery of McCarthy's attacks on the Truman administration also may have made the President reluctant to open his policy-making more to the scrutiny of Capitol Hill or the public. Nevertheless, it seems imperative when a republic becomes entangled in a limited, drawn-out war that Congress be involved as much as feasible in policy-making and that the people be educated. To do otherwise is to invite the bipartisan bitterness on Capitol Hill and the public antiwar movement that were born after November 1950, though only mild harbingers of the dissent of the ensuing American war in Asia. In the later stages of both wars Congress and public opinion became sensitive barometers of the reluctance of Americans to expend lives in poorly justified wars, however just they might be.

Less directly relevant to the decisions made in late June 1950 were several factors which should nevertheless not be forgotten. Among them is the fact that the Joint Chiefs did not demure that week when Truman and Acheson abruptly set aside the JCS position that Korea was strategically of little worth. Of perhaps more importance, Acheson's lieutenants did not object to the drastic change in policy toward Nationalist China. In late 1949 the State Department's position had been one of virtually abandoning the Nationalists, who were expected to be overrun on Formosa by Mao Tse-tung's forces in the summer of 1950. Now Truman had charged the Seventh Fleet with patrolling the Formosa Strait to keep the two Chinese armies apart, thereby committing the United States to a dual-China policy that would be like an albatross for years to come in America's international relations. Moreover, the presence of Seventh Fleet ships in the Formosa Strait would lead to engagements with the Communist Chinese, which may have been a causal factor in Peking's rising anxiety about America's military presence in Korea.[29]

A final factor that was not considered sufficiently at the time was Truman's adaptation of Roosevelt's plan for a postwar world order to be patrolled and kept peaceful by what he perceived to be the great powers—the United States, the Soviet Union, the United Kingdom, and Nationalist China—who would become "the four great policemen" of the post-1945 era.[30] Of course, only two great powers emerged after the Second World War, and their systems were so antipodal as to preclude any cooperative global policing. In taking the United States into the Korean conflict, however, Truman, upon Acheson's urging, attempted to salvage the American role as a world policeman by having its intervention by force sanctioned by the United Nations. The military element, though predominantly American, was to appear to be a truly international force and to represent a large segment of global opinion regarding the particular crisis. Actually, the UN guise at the high-command level was so thin in 1950 that MacArthur used the same officers to head the principal sections—for example, intelligence, operations, and personnel—in the headquarters of both the United Nations Command and the United States Far East Command. He was under strict orders to issue his periodic reports to the UN Security Council through the JCS, which freely edited and censored them; and he was to have no direct communication with the Security Council whatsoever.

Four decades later the United States would turn to a variant of this scheme again, acting as policeman in the Iraq-Kuwait affair and providing a large majority of the combat forces of the coalition whose mission was to enforce a dozen UN Security Council resolutions regarding Iraq's aggression. In 1950 and again in 1991 the United States would undertake a military task enjoying UN sanction and claiming to have world opinion largely behind its use of force. During and after the Korean War some thoughtful observers questioned whether the compromises, complications, and resources drain involved in trying to maintain the roles of the global policeman and the international command were realistic and successful in furthering American strategic interests.

If the President and his advisers in June 1950 could have been blessed with the foresight to see what lay ahead by July 1953, they probably would have still committed American forces, but the rationale would have been difficult to explain to the nation or the world. Whether the ground war in particular was worth the price is still hotly debated. The human and material losses were high for America, Communist China, and especially the two Koreas. Ironically, the highest price in deaths and property destruction was paid by the Korean civilians, most of whom were indifferent to the issues of either the civil war or the Cold War. The global communist front suffered a serious crack when Red China and North Korea became alienated from the Soviet Union, partly because of the disappointing wartime support from Moscow. After mid-1953, South Korea developed an increasingly strong economy but continued to spawn repressive political regimes whose practices were often far from democratic. Meanwhile, the United States shouldered the burdens of large troop commitments in South Korea and massive military and economic aid to that nation for the indefinite future. Frankly, no one had much to show for the three years of killing and destruction. It was a war that was not won nor was its ending a time for celebration.

# CHAPTER
# 7

# *MacArthur's Grand Obsession: Inchon*

## THE MOMENTUM SHIFTS

When the Allied offensive was in full swing in the Southwest Pacific theater in 1943–1945, MacArthur's VII Amphibious Force carried out numerous operations against the Japanese. Then he had to rely on Army troops in such assaults, but in the summer of 1950 he was blessed with a brigade of the 1st Marine Division and the promise of the rest of the division. With his well-deserved reputation for launching brilliant amphibious envelopments and with the elite amphibious outfit soon to be on hand, MacArthur, not surprisingly, turned early to the possibility of striking behind the North Korean lines with a decisive seaborne attack. Fortunately, his senior naval officers had participated in numerous Pacific amphibious operations of the Second World War. MacArthur's supreme act of refighting the last war would be the most spectacular of all his amphibious envelopments—at Inchon, the port for the South Korean capital of Seoul.

In its brazen invasion of South Korea, beginning June 25, 1950, North Korea gambled on its ability to conquer the southern portion of the peninsula before an effective defensive line could be established below the 38th parallel. Fortunately for President Syngman Rhee's republic, four American divisions (40 percent of the U.S. Army's strength), along with the relatively strong U.S. Fifth Air Force and Seventh Fleet, were stationed close by, mostly in Japan with other American units available in the Ryukyus and Philippines. Luckily also for South Korea, President Truman decided quickly to commit American forces to the peninsula war, General MacArthur acted swiftly to implement the administration's decision, and Secretary of State Acheson quickly rallied support among America's allies to send troops and war matériel to supplement the rapidly mounted American military buildup in defense of South Korea. The result was that, despite desperate fighting along the Naktong River line in the southeast corner of the peninsula through most of the summer, the North Korean offensive was halted.

By September 1, the United Nations Command in the Naktong perimeter numbered 180,000 troops, almost double that of the North Korean Army facing them across the Naktong, while the ratio of armored and artillery strength had grown to five to one in favor of MacArthur's forces. A historian of the war observes that the North Korean forces' "logistics and communications were a shambles. The wonder of the period is not that they collapsed so quickly [after the Inchon envelopment], but that they did as well as they did before the collapse came."[1] Having lost its first-stage gamble, the North Korean command had no alternative plan, and the momentum, though then barely perceptible, swung to the United Nations Command.

As South Korean and American soldiers retreated before the North Korean invaders in the early summer of 1950, many Pentagon leaders who looked ahead to a counteroffensive recalled the Italian campaign of 1943–1945, particularly the torturous route up the mountainous peninsula and the near-disastrous efforts at Salerno and Anzio to speed up the advance by amphibious envelopments. On the other hand, MacArthur remembered his own experiences with fighting on a peninsula and launching fifty-six amphibious assaults in the Southwest Pacific war. His singular peninsula campaign had been Bataan, where the enemy had the advantages of ground, air, and naval supremacy as well as proximity to reinforcements. In Korea, these advantages would be with MacArthur, not with his adversary. If a firm perimeter could be held in South Korea, he could attack the enemy far in the rear where, unlike the Anzio crisis, his presumed buildup of forces would give him such dominance on the ground, in the air, and at sea that it would not be crucial to achieve an early junction of the perimeter and amphibious forces. Moreover, as in mid-1943 when MacArthur inaugurated his amphibious leapfrogging with Operation Cartwheel, so by late summer of 1950 the enemy had greatly overextended himself, left his lines of supply long and exposed to air attack, and faced shortages of manpower and matériel resources at the front.

The plight of the South Korean, American, and Allied forces that were backed up in the southeast corner of the peninsula was destined to provide key roles for a man and a service that some considered outmoded by mid-century: MacArthur and the U.S. Marine Corps. The general had enjoyed considerable success in administering the occupation program in Japan during the first two years, but by 1948–1950 the State Department and Pentagon had drastically altered the occupation's objectives, making it difficult for MacArthur to adjust, culminating in a gradual but steady diminution of his influence in controlling policy implementation in occupied Japan. In addition, in 1949, MacArthur's XXIV Corps had been withdrawn from South Korea, and the State Department henceforth had held the principal American hand in dealing with President Rhee's new republic, its armed forces, and the small American military advisory group. MacArthur had also seen his presidential ambitions virtually obliterated after his disappointing showing in early Republican primaries in 1948 where he could gain the backing only of part of the party's right wing.

The Marine Corps, in turn, had seemed to find its raison d'être in its well-conducted, hard-fought amphibious operations in the South and Central Pacific, 1942–1945. But the heated struggle between the services over the provisions that ultimately went into the National Security Act of 1947 and its amendment in 1949 saw much questioning of the Marines' role in aviation and its place in the Naval Establishment. The Army's leaders took a dim view of the necessity of the Corps even for amphibious functions. Before the House Armed Services Committee in the autumn of 1949, JCS Chairman Bradley had ventured the prediction that "large-scale amphibious operations . . . will never occur again."[2] An angry Marine Corps and a seventy-year-old Army general in Tokyo would find their needs for renewed appreciation fulfilled in an unlikely partnership in what may have been the most brilliant amphibious operation in the history of each. This was certainly MacArthur's sense of Inchon's significance among his military operations, and, as for the Marines, General Lemuel Shepherd observed: "It was the best thing that ever happened to the Marine Corps. We were at a very low ebb at the time, but the Inchon landing and our courageous fight on the Chosin Reservoir saved the Corps from becoming only a ship landing force under Navy control."[3]

## BIRTH OF CHROMITE

On June 27, two days after the war began, MacArthur sent a fifteen-man mission headed by Brigadier General John H. Church to Suwon, thirty miles south of Seoul, to observe and report on the combat situation and the logistical needs of the ROK Army. The next day Church relayed to Tokyo GHQ the dismaying news that Seoul had fallen and North Korean divisions had achieved major breakthroughs on the central front. Church advised that the South Korean defenses were collapsing fast and that American forces would be needed to stop the North Korean offensive.

On June 29, MacArthur flew from Tokyo to Suwon to investigate the situation himself. He was accompanied by six of his main general and flag officers. In a small schoolhouse they met with Rhee, Church, Ambassador Muccio, top ROK officers, and American military advisers. After listening to the disheartening reports of a number of the conferees, MacArthur remarked, "Well, I have heard a good deal theoretically, and now I want to go and see these troops that are straggling down the road."

According to Lieutenant General Edward Almond, MacArthur's group went in "three old broken-down cars" to a point on the south bank of the Han River at Yongdungpo, where they could see "the enemy firing from Seoul." Almond said, "We were within probably a hundred yards of where some of these mortar shells were falling." He remembered MacArthur's commenting about the ROK soldiers they observed for an hour or so, "It is a strange thing to me that all these men have their rifles and ammunition, they all know how to salute, they all seem to be more or less happy, but I haven't seen a wounded man yet."[4] While watching "the pitiful evidence of the disaster I had inherited," MacArthur said, he came to several important conclusions before leaving the scene of chaos and devastation at the Han: His divisions in Japan would have to be dispatched to Korea after getting the President's authorization, and he would begin planning an amphibious assault to "envelop and destroy" the main North Korean invading forces—"a counter-stroke that could in itself wrest victory from defeat," though his forces "would be outnumbered almost three to one."[5]

The next day, June 30, he reported to the Joint Chiefs of Staff:

> . . . The Korean army and coastal forces are in confusion, have not seriously fought, and lack leadership through their own means. . . .
>
> The Korean army is entirely incapable of counter action and there is grave danger of a further breakthrough. If the enemy advance continues much farther it will seriously threaten the fall of the Republic.
>
> . . . To continue to utilize the forces of our Air and Navy without an effective ground element cannot be decisive.
>
> If authorized, it is my intention to immediately move a US regimental combat team to the reinforcement of the vital area discussed [near Suwon] and to provide for a possible buildup to a two-division strength from the troops in Japan for an early counter-offensive.[6]

Truman quickly gave MacArthur "full authority to use the ground forces under his command"; a proviso was added in the Joint Chiefs' subsequent message to the Far East chief that "such use was qualified by the need to protect Japan."[7] Acheson somberly observed, "We were then fully committed in Korea."[8] He and the President saw the sending of American ground troops into action as potentially the first stage of a global conflict. MacArthur, on the other hand, was already thinking in the narrower dimension of a theater strategy that could trap the enemy army by a surprise amphibious envelopment.

Three days after returning to Tokyo from Korea, MacArthur set to work with Almond, his chief of staff, and Wright, his operations head, on planning the broad outlines of an assault from the Yellow Sea on Inchon, the port for Seoul. Wright's Joint Strategic Plans and Operations Group (JSPOG) bore the brunt of the planning details of Operation Bluehearts, as it was named. MacArthur intended to use the 1st Cavalry Division and a Marine regimental combat team he had just requested. On July 10, Bluehearts was dropped because the two units would not be available for the projected assault on July 22: The 1st Cavalry Division had to be thrown in to slow down the North Korean drive, and the Marine RCT would not arrive in Korea until early August. MacArthur instructed Wright and his planners to keep working on contingency plans for an amphibious envelopment, still targeted for Inchon, with the units to be designated later.

MacArthur raised his demand for reinforcements to four divisions on July 9, which would give him a total of eight American divisions. With only four divisions left in the United States, Truman and the Joint Chiefs decided that the Far East Command's needs should be investigated further before dispatching any of these units to Korea. Generals Lawton Collins and Hoyt Vandenberg, the Army and Air Force chiefs of staff, accompanied by four other Pentagon officers, were appointed to go to Tokyo and South Korea for conferences with MacArthur and Lieutenant General Walton Walker, the Eighth Army commander.

When they met at Tokyo GHQ on July 13–14, the conferees also included Almond; Lieutenant General George Stratemeyer, commander of FEAF; and Admiral Arthur Radford, head of the Pacific Command and the Pacific Fleet. MacArthur brought up his Inchon scheme, which got a lukewarm response from Collins, who thought the very high tides at Inchon precluded it as an assault site, though he did think the 1st Marine Division could probably be employed if an amphibious operation were undertaken. MacArthur was advised to tailor his plans to his available forces plus the Marines in view of the critical depletion of the remaining ground forces in the States. Collins described MacArthur as "cool and poised as always. He spoke with confidence and elan as he paced back and forth in his customary fashion. He always gave me the impression of addressing not just his immediate listeners but a larger audience unseen."[9]

In spite of his reservations about Inchon, Collins did a good job of selling MacArthur's need for more troops when he returned to Washington. The Pentagon's response was not inconsiderable: the Far East Command received the 2nd and 3rd Infantry divisions in July and November, respectively; the rest of the 1st Marine Division in August; and the 187th Airborne Regimental Combat Team in September. The personnel strength of U.S. ground, air, and sea forces in Korea grew from 45,000 at the end of July to 148,000 a month later to 233,000 by late September, and to nearly 360,000 by April 1951 when MacArthur left the theater. In addition, nineteen nations allied with South Korea and the United States contributed combat and support forces to the United Nations Command, the principal early ones being a British and a Turkish infantry brigade.

On July 23, the day after he originally intended to launch Bluehearts, MacArthur informed the Joint Chiefs of his latest plan to assault Inchon; it was code-named Chromite and, if approved, would be set for September 15, with the 2nd Infantry Division and 5th Marine RCT as the main strike forces. He told the JCS: "I am firmly convinced that an early and strong effort behind his [the enemy's] front will sever his main lines of communications and enable us to deliver a decisive and crushing blow. . . . The alternative is a frontal attack [from the Naktong line] which can only result in a protracted and expensive campaign to slowly drive the enemy north of the 38th parallel."[10]

Unhappily, he had to send the JSPOG planners back to the drawing boards again when these two outfits reached Korea near the end of July and had to be sent to the front forthwith, so threatening was the Naktong situation. The 5th Marine RCT was reinforced and redesignated the 1st Provisional Marine Brigade, becoming the indispensable mobile defense force for Walker's Eighth Army in plugging gaps and thwarting breakthroughs along the Naktong perimeter. With General Shepherd, head of Fleet Marine Force, Pacific, working zealously to round up more Marines for Korea, MacArthur learned in early August that he would receive the 1st and 7th Marine regiments. Thus he would be able to spearhead the Inchon assault, if the landing were authorized, with the entire 1st Marine Division, its third regiment, the 5th, to be withdrawn from the Naktong perimeter as late as possible.

After MacArthur's controversial visit to Formosa, July 31–August 1, Truman dispatched Ambassador Harriman to "discuss the Far Eastern political situation" with the theater commander in Tokyo. The mission also included Generals Ridgway, Lowe, and Norstad, together with several aides, and visited South Korea as well as Tokyo on its brief Far East itinerary, August 6–8. When queried about the possibilities of the Soviet Union or Communist China entering the conflict, MacArthur speculated that the Soviets probably would not become engaged, but they were "likely to try to get the Chinese involved."[11] He believed that with the Inchon envelopment, America could win quickly and Communist China would not risk involvement.

Ridgway was quite impressed by the Far East commander: "In

a brilliant 2½ hour presentation, made with utmost earnestness, supported by every logical military argument of his rich experience, and delivered with all of his dramatic eloquence, General MacArthur stated his compelling need for additional combat ground forces," particularly for Chromite.[12] "MacArthur made it very plain," according to Harriman, "that time was of the essence, that we had to take a bold step, and that, although the Navy was very much opposed to the operation because of the high tides, the risk was worth taking." Later, Ridgway confided to Harriman, "I had great doubts about it, but his dramatic and convincing manner persuaded me fully that it was an operation that should be undertaken." While Lowe remained in Tokyo as presidential liaison with GHQ, Harriman recalled that he, Ridgway, and Norstad "came back determined to recommend" Chromite to the President. Truman, in turn, instructed Secretary of Defense Johnson and JCS Chairman Bradley to "act on it rapidly."[13]

MacArthur sent the Pentagon a new edition of Chromite on August 12, which called for the 1st Marine Division and a still-to-be-named Army division to conduct the Inchon landing, followed by the capture of Kimpo Airfield and Seoul, while the Eighth Army broke out of the Naktong perimeter and linked up with the Inchon invaders south of Seoul. Major General David G. Barr's 7th Infantry Division was soon designated for Chromite. It was the fourth and last of the American divisions in Japan to go to Korea. Since the other three divisions had been about one-third below strength when ordered to the peninsula, elements of Barr's division had been added to them, leaving the 7th Division short almost nine thousand men.

MacArthur instructed Walker to inaugurate the KATUSA (Koreans Attached to the U.S. Army) plan, whereby South Korean civilian volunteers were sent to Japan for a quick program of training and integration on a "buddy" system with the Americans of the 7th Division. Barr did a remarkable job of trying to prepare the KATUSA element in the short month that remained before the Inchon attack, but the 7th Division's level of combat readiness did not reach that of the Marines, as would be demonstrated in the Inchon-Seoul fighting. Nevertheless, MacArthur was sufficiently satisfied that he continued to incorporate KATUSA in other American units later.

Despite MacArthur's enthusiasm for Chromite and his seeming suasion of some of his high-level visitors, the Joint Chiefs and their planners, while trying to provide him with the means for a future amphibious envelopment, remained skeptical about the wisdom of landing at Inchon. They were concerned primarily with persisting questions about navigating the narrow port channel that might be mined, coping with the huge tidal problem, draining men and matériel from the Eighth Army, and linking up with Walker's army from the Naktong area. The ghosts of Salerno and Anzio seemed to bother Bradley, Collins, and other senior officers in the Pentagon. Many of them also remembered MacArthur's unjustified optimism about defending the Philippines in 1941 and other cocky predictions of his during the Southwest Pacific war that proved in reality less rosy, notably the reconquest of Luzon. MacArthur was widely regarded as the Army's main proponent of the power of positive thinking. Moreover, the Joint Chiefs were troubled that few specific details of the new modifications of Chromite were relayed to them by MacArthur.

They decided the time had come for a final showdown with the Tokyo chief about what he was planning. Collins, as the JCS executive agent for Far East affairs, and Sherman, CNO and the JCS member most knowledgeable about amphibious operations, were designated to meet with MacArthur and other key leaders involved in Chromite.

## TIME FOR DECISIONS

Collins and Sherman arrived in Tokyo on August 21, by which time MacArthur had appointed Almond, his chief of staff, to head the newly formed X Corps, which would carry out the assault, and Rear Admiral James Doyle to lead Task Force 90, the Chromite attack force, with Struble, the Seventh Fleet commander, in overall charge of the Inchon armada. MacArthur went over the latest version of Chromite with Collins and Sherman, emphasizing, "I expect to close this operation up much more rapidly than most people estimate." Some discussion ensued about the risk of intervention by the Soviets, though, interestingly, not by the Communist Chinese. A confident MacArthur assured them that he did not believe Russia would risk war. Collins, perhaps facetiously, said, "I am glad to hear your concept for a settlement of the Korean War."[14]

When Major General Oliver P. Smith, commander of the 1st Marine Division, reached Tokyo GHQ on August 22, he found that planning and preparations were well under way on Chromite despite the lack of authorization to launch the operation. Smith's first meeting was with Admiral Doyle, at the end of which the two agreed that there were many logistical problems and other difficulties associated with a landing at Inchon, that the preferred landing site was Posung-myon, twenty miles south of Inchon, and that the target date for the amphibious operation at whatever location should be postponed a week at least, to September 22. A staff officer under Doyle summed up the sentiments of many Navy and Marine officers acquainted with Chromite: "We drew up a list of every conceivable and natural handicap, and Inchon had 'em all."

Later that day Smith met with MacArthur; the Marine was primed and eager to criticize Chromite. He was ushered into MacArthur's office in the Dai Ichi Building, according to an official source, where he was told "that the Inch'on landing would be decisive and that the war would be over in one month after the assault." Smith was not given much chance to make his case, and, in any event, it was apparent MacArthur would not have yielded. Smith later observed of MacArthur, "It was more than confidence which upheld him; it was supreme and almost mystical faith that he could not fail."[15]

By August 23, the date set for the crucial conference on Chromite at Tokyo GHQ, the gathering of general and flag officers from Washington and Pearl Harbor consisted of Collins, Sherman, and Lieutenant General Idwal H. Edwards (representing Vandenberg), along with several Pentagon staff planners, and a Pearl Harbor delegation led by Radford and Shepherd. The Far East Command was represented by Generals MacArthur, Almond, Wright, Hickey (deputy chief of staff), and Major General Clark A. Ruffner (to become X Corps chief of staff), as well as Admirals Joy, Struble, and Doyle; there were also three JSPOG planners and nine briefing officers from Doyle's staff.

Marine Generals Shepherd and Smith were oddly excluded even though the spearhead of the Chromite ground assault would be the 1st Marine Division. Both of the generals were strong admirers of MacArthur, so the reason for their omission is especially puzzling. MacArthur had thought in advance of the meeting that Admiral Sherman might be the principal leader of the opposition because of his experience in the war against Japan with amphibious warfare. Unknown to the general, however, Sherman had visited Struble aboard his Seventh Fleet flagship anchored at Sasebo Naval Base two days earlier and had confided, "I'm going to back the Inchon operation completely. I think it's sound."

The meeting at MacArthur's Dai Ichi headquarters on August 23 was actually a briefing on Chromite, but the ultimate decision by Truman and the JCS would be heavily influenced by the reports brought back by the representatives from the Pentagon together with the impressions obtained from the Pearl Harbor officers present at this and other Chromite meetings in Tokyo that week. The Dai Ichi assembly began with a presentation by Pinky Wright, MacArthur's able operations chief and head of JSPOG, who outlined the fundamental Chromite plan, particularly the ground forces' roles. He was followed by Doyle's briefing officers, who covered the naval, air, and amphibious phases of the operation, including naval gunfire support, aerial targets, intelligence about enemy dispositions, navigation and communications aspects, transit of the channel to Inchon, landing formations, and a number of technical subjects. Their tone was decidedly pessimistic.

Admiral Doyle then stood and, looking at MacArthur, declared somberly, "General, I have not been asked nor have I volunteered my opinion about this landing. If I were asked, however, the best I can say is that Inchon is not impossible." He went on to explain the dangers for the armada in Flying Fish Channel, the narrow sea approach to the port, stressing that it might be lined with enemy shore batteries and also heavily mined. Surprising many of those present, Sherman interrupted Doyle to declare, "I wouldn't hesitate to take a ship up there." A delighted MacArthur exclaimed, "Spoken like a Farragut!"

Collins, who had earlier expressed reservations to MacArthur about the Inchon site, stated later in the session that he preferred Kunsan, a hundred miles south of Inchon, because it was nearer the Eighth Army's defense perimeter along the Naktong. He warned that unless the X Corps and Eighth Army linked up quickly, the amphibious operation might become a "disaster." Collins probably was remembering Anzio.

Except for several one-sentence comments during the first hour or so of presentations and discussion, MacArthur had remained silent, puffing on his pipe. After everyone had apparently had his say, the officers all looked at the Far East chief, but for another minute or two MacArthur remained seated and continued to smoke without saying a word. Then he slowly rose and began speaking in a low voice, gradually escalating in force. Soon he was pacing back and forth, gesturing dramatically with his pipe, and displaying to the assembly the fabled MacArthur rhetorical approach. For forty-five minutes he orated without notes while speaking eloquently and commanding every officer's attention.[16] A powerful speaker with memorable orations during his long career, MacArthur may have given his best on that critical occasion:

> . . . The very arguments you have made as to the impracticabilities involved will tend to ensure for me the element of surprise. For the enemy commander will reason that no one would be so brash as to make such an attempt. Surprise is the most vital element for success in war. . . .
>
> The Navy's objections as to tides, hydrography, terrain, and physical handicaps are indeed substantial and pertinent. But they are not insuperable. My confidence in the Navy is complete. . . . The Navy's rich experience in staging the numerous amphibious landings under my command in the Pacific during the late war, frequently under somewhat similar difficulties, leaves me with little doubt on that score.
>
> . . . By seizing Seoul I would completely paralyze the enemy's supply system—coming and going. This in turn will paralyze the fighting power of the troops that now face Walker. . . .
>
> The only alternative to a stroke such as I propose will be the continuation of the savage sacrifice we are making at Pusan, with no hope of relief in sight. Are you content to let our troops stay in that bloody perimeter like beef cattle in the slaughterhouse?
>
> . . . It is plainly apparent that here in Asia is where the Communist conspirators have elected to make their play for global conquest. The test is not in Berlin or Vienna, in London, Paris or Washington. It is here and now—it is along the Naktong River in South Korea. . . . Actually, we here fight Europe's war with arms, while there it is still confined to words. . . . Make the wrong decision here—the fatal decision of inertia—and we will be done. I can almost hear the ticking of the second hand of destiny. We must act now or we will die.[17]

The general concluded, "I realize that Inchon is a 5,000 to 1 gamble, but I am used to taking such odds. . . . We shall land at Inchon and I shall crush them!"[18] A period of silence followed MacArthur's speech, until Sherman spoke for most when he arose and said, "Thank you. A great voice in a great cause."[19]

On August 24, Admirals Sherman, Radford, Joy, and Doyle conferred with Marine Generals Shepherd and Smith in Joy's office. All thought that MacArthur's presentation the previous day had been impressive; however, they preferred to change the landing site to Posung-myon. Shepherd visited with MacArthur later that day but argued in vain the Navy and Marine leaders' case for the alternative assault site. Reporting his lack of success to his colleagues of the earlier session, Shepherd concurred when the group decided to capitulate on the Posung-myon issue and pledged to do their best to make the assault at Inchon a success.

When they got back to Washington, Collins and Sherman discussed the Chromite plan and the Tokyo sessions with President Truman, Secretary Johnson, and the other JCS members, Bradley and Vandenberg. On August 29, the Joint Chiefs sent MacArthur a tentative, lukewarm approval of Chromite:

> . . . We concur in making preparations and executing a turning movement by amphibious forces . . . either at Inchon . . . or at a favorable beach south of Inchon if one can be located. We further concur in preparation, if desired by CINCFE [MacArthur], for an envelopment by amphibious forces in the vicinity of Kunsan. . . .
>
> We desire such information as becomes available with respect to conditions in the possible objective areas and timely information as to your intentions and plans for offensive operations.[20]

The final sentence of this limp endorsement was a chastisement for MacArthur's previous refusals to update the Joint Chiefs quickly on the many changes in his plans. The Far East commander wondered why they could not have been more decisive on the more important issue at stake, a major assault being readied for launching in two weeks.

The next day MacArthur issued his Chromite operational orders, delineating the units to be used and their objectives. Almond would head the Chromite ground force, X Corps, which would consist of the 1st Marine Division and the 7th Infantry Division, along with artillery, armor, and support forces totaling 71,300 troops. At least until the two forces linked up, the X Corps and Eighth Army were to be separate commands. Almond was allowed to retain his powerful position in Tokyo GHQ as chief of staff of the Far East Command, United Nations Command, U.S. Army Forces in the Far East, and the Allied occupation of Japan. Hickey, his deputy, would handle most of the responsibilities of chief of staff in Tokyo while Almond was in Korea, but the dual hats worn by the latter gave X Corps significant advantages in future allocations of men and matériel vis-à-vis the Eighth Army. It is no wonder that Walker and many of his men considered MacArthur's decisions injudicious in giving Almond concurrent field and staff positions and in freeing him from Walker's control.

Struble's invasion armada was to consist of 260 ships, divided into task forces and task groups; the various naval units, in aggregate designated Joint Task Force 7, would assemble at three Japanese ports and at Pusan, rendezvousing off the southwest tip of Korea. Thirty-seven of the forty-seven LSTs (landing ship, tanks) were operated by Japanese crews, a fact said to be unknown in Washington until after the assault. Air support for Chromite would be provided by four American carriers and one from the Royal Navy. The Far East Air Forces would be available for emergency missions but during the Chromite operation would be flown primarily in support of Walker's Eighth Army, which was due to launch an all-out offensive along the Naktong peninsula on September 16, the day after the Inchon landings. Elements of the Seventh Fleet, including the battleship *Missouri*, were to conduct diversionary coastal shellings of targets along the east coast, and landing feints were to be staged at several points on both coasts to draw the enemy's attention away from Inchon.

In the first two weeks of September, MacArthur and the Chromite leaders had to cope with innumerable difficulties, such as late arrivals of various items of equipment and weaponry, which were endemic in such a large amphibious operation prepared in so short a time. In addition, the Far East Command chief had to deal with disputes among some of his field commanders and continued waiting for final approval of Chromite from his Washington superiors. Walker and Almond had clashed in Japan before the Korean War over professional and personal differences; not only did these collisions increase once the war began but also Smith and his Marine officers quickly found that they could not often reconcile their differences with their sometimes unreasonable and arrogant corps commander, Almond.

Smith requested Almond on August 30 to obtain the release of the 5th Marines, now at the Naktong front, but Walker responded that the unit was the key to his mobile defense of the perimeter and the North Koreans were now mounting their strongest attacks along the Naktong line. Almond then offered Smith a regiment of the 7th Division to be attached to the 1st Marine Division, but, not surprisingly, the Marine general rejected it. Finally, Admiral Struble found a compromise that suited the now angry disputants: The 5th Marines would join the rest of the 1st Marine Division for Chromite, while a regiment of the 7th Division would be retained as a floating reserve in Pusan harbor to be sent to the Naktong front in case of a North Korean breakthrough.

In spite of their chiding of MacArthur in their message on August 28, the Joint Chiefs heard nothing in the next few days, and so they again reminded him on September 5 that he must keep them informed of his Chromite modifications. MacArthur responded that "the general outline of the plan remains as described to you" and that by September 11 they would receive from him a courier-delivered copy of his detailed Chromite operational plan.[21]

The Joint Chiefs were deeply concerned about the North Korean attacks along the Naktong that Walker reported were still increasing in fury and the adverse impact on his defense when the 5th Marines were pulled out for the Chromite operation. On September 7 the JCS asked MacArthur to submit an estimate of the chance of success of his operation. "We are sure that you understand," they wrote, "that all available trained Army units in the United States have been allocated to you" except for the 82nd Airborne Division. They warned him that it would be at least four months before any partially trained National Guard divisions could arrive in Korea in case his plan did not work and the Eighth Army and X Corps did not join.[22] MacArthur later commented that the JCS message "chilled me to the marrow of my bones" because it "expressed doubt of success and implied the whole movement should be abandoned."[23]

On September 8 he replied to the Joint Chiefs, emphasizing once again the strategic assets of Chromite and demonstrating more patience with his superiors' caution than he actually felt:

There is no question in my mind as to the feasibility of the operation and I regard its chance of success as excellent. . . . It rep-
resents the only hope of wresting the initiative from the enemy and
thereby presenting an opportunity for a decisive blow. . . . There
is no slightest possibility, however, of our forces being ejected from
the Pusan beachhead. . . .

The embarkation of the troops and the preliminary air and naval
preparations are proceeding according to schedule. I repeat that I
and all of my commanders and staff officers, without exception, are
enthusiastic for and confident of the success of the enveloping
operation.[24]

The Joint Chiefs of Staff, according to Collins, were "impressed
by this firm reiteration of confidence from the responsible field
commander." On September 8 (Washington time, which was fourteen hours behind the time in Tokyo, where it was already September 9), the JCS finally sent MacArthur the message that "with
growing concern" he was awaiting: "We approve your plan and
[the] President has been so informed."[25] MacArthur concluded,
perhaps erroneously, that the Joint Chiefs' "last-minute hesitancy"
originated with the President. The Far East commander speculated at another time that Admiral Sherman was instrumental in
obtaining for him the Joint Chiefs' support.[26]

## CHROMITE AND ITS CONSEQUENCES

Although the Chromite authorization was not granted until September 8, the planned air attacks against the Inchon area had begun four days earlier and the slowest ships of the invasion force
had left Yokohama on September 5. On September 10, Lieutenant
Colonel Lynn D. Smith, the courier bearing the final Chromite
operational plan that MacArthur had promised to send the JCS,
departed from Tokyo, the Far East chief cautioning him not to arrive in Washington "too soon." It is not known whether Smith delivered to the Joint Chiefs MacArthur's oral message: "If they say
it is too big a gamble, tell them I said this is throwing a nickel in
the pot after it has been opened for a dollar. The big gamble was
Washington's decision to put American troops on the Asian mainland." Smith met with the JCS on September 14; if the Joint Chiefs

had decided against the assault, it was too late that day to stop it because the many questions they put to Smith about the plan made the session last until late afternoon. The first wave of Marines hit the shore of Wolmi-do in Inchon harbor at 6:30 A.M., September 15, Seoul time, which was 5:30 P.M. on the 14th in Washington.[27]

MacArthur, whose good luck in most of his military ventures in both world wars had become legendary, found that Chromite further buttressed his affinity with favorable fortune. A typhoon with winds of 110 miles per hour hit Honshu during the final preparations and loading; it did widespread damage to ships and dock facilities but not severely enough to delay or halt the operation. An even larger typhoon was on a collision course with the Chromite armada after it had entered the Yellow Sea en route to Inchon, but at the last minute it veered away from the ships. MacArthur's luck held, too, as he had gambled that the North Koreans would be taken by surprise: They had neither placed in Flying Fish Channel the large shipment of Soviet mines they had stored nearby nor reinforced the garrison of two thousand in Inchon and the vicinity.

MacArthur and his senior officers watched with binoculars from Doyle's flagship, *Mount McKinley,* as the Marines easily took Wolmi-do, the small island offshore from Inchon, on the morning of September 15. Late that afternoon the 1st Marine Division braved the thirty-one-foot tide, among the highest in the world, secured beachheads directly on the waterfront of Inchon, and seized a third of the city by nightfall, suffering relatively light losses. Three days later the Marines captured Kimpo Airfield, and the next day they took Yongdungpo, the grimy city situated across the Han River from Seoul. In the meantime, the Army's 7th Division had come ashore at Inchon and was advancing eastward on the right flank of the Marines. The conquest of Seoul was slow and bloody, the North Koreans having reacted by then and deploying in the city 20,000 soldiers and considerable artillery. Seoul was finally secured on September 28, the X Corps having suffered 3,500 casualties during the previous two weeks of the Chromite operation, most of them being Marines and the majority of them suffered in the battle for Seoul. About 14,000 North Korean troops had been killed and 7,000 captured in the Inchon-Seoul area from September 15 to 28. Meanwhile, Walker's Eighth Army had encountered strong resistance in its effort to break out of the Naktong perimeter; it was not until September 27 that elements of the 1st

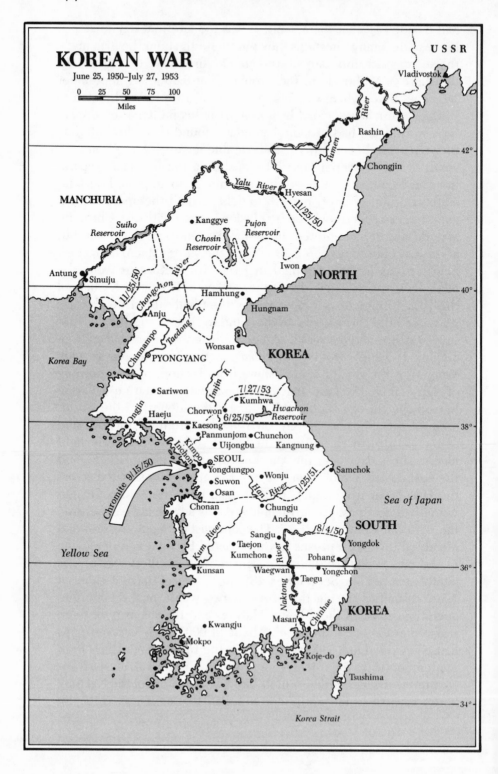

KOREAN WAR

June 25, 1950–July 27, 1953

0    25    50    75    100
Miles

USSR

Vladivostok

Rashin

Tumen River

42°

Chongjin

MANCHURIA

Yalu River    Hyesan

11/25/50

Suiho
Reservoir

Kanggye

Pujon
Reservoir

Chosin
Reservoir

Iwon

NORTH

Antung
Sinuiju

11/25/50

Chongchon River

Hamhung

40°

Anju

Taedong R.

Hungnam

Chinnampo

Wonsan

KOREA

Korea Bay

PYONGYANG

Sariwon

Imjin R.

7/27/53

Kumhwa

Chorwon    Hwachon
Reservoir

Haeju

6/25/50

38°

Ongjin

Kaesong

Panmunjom    Chunchon

Kimpo

Uijongbu    Kangnung

Inchon

SEOUL

Yongdungpo

Chromite 9/15/50

Suwon    Wonju

Han River

1/25/51

Samchok

Osan

Chonan    Chungju

Andong

Sea of Japan

Kum River

8/4/50

SOUTH

Sangju    Yongdok

Taejon    Naktong River    Pohang

Yellow Sea

Kumchon

36°

Kunsan    Waegwan    Yongchon

Taegu

KOREA

Kwangju    Masan    Chinhae

Pusan

Mokpo

Koje-do

Tsushima

34°

Korea Strait

Cavalry Division, from the Naktong line, linked up with Barr's 7th Division between Seoul and Osan.

MacArthur received congratulatory messages from a host of high-level civilian and military leaders, including such international figures as Churchill and Prime Minister Shigeru Yoshida of Japan. Instantaneously, it seemed, Truman and the Joint Chiefs abandoned the camp of the doubters and joined the ranks of his adulators: "No operation in military history," exuded the President, "can match either the delaying action where you traded space for time in which to build up your forces, or the brilliant maneuver which has now resulted in the liberation of Seoul."[28] The Joint Chiefs, in turn, were equally rhapsodizing: "Your transition from defensive to offensive operations was magnificently planned, timed, and executed. . . . We remain completely confident that the great tasks entrusted to you by the United Nations will be carried to a successful conclusion."[29]

In the immediate glorious afterglow of Chromite, MacArthur and many other military leaders in South Korea, Japan, and the United Nations members involved in the war were convinced that the Inchon envelopment and subsequent breakout of the Eighth Army had virtually destroyed the North Korean Army. Indeed, when Communist China later entered the fray, MacArthur would proclaim that it was the beginning of a new war, the one against North Korea having been won. It was true that temporarily the North Korean Army had been reduced to scattered regimental-size and smaller units that were functioning somewhat autonomously in the mountains of southwest South Korea or above the 38th parallel, having fled the intended trap between Inchon and the Naktong River before it could be closed by Almond's and Walker's forces. It was later determined, however, that not only most of the senior North Korean officers but also about a third of their troops had managed to get back to North Korea. There they would be reorganized and strengthened with the addition of 125,000 reserves to constitute a formidable enemy in partnership with the Communist Chinese later in the Korean War.

Now that the Rhee government had been restored in Seoul and South Korea, except for the enemy guerrillas in the southwest region, had been freed of the invaders, the morale of the South Korean people and their troops, as well as the ésprit de corps of the UN forces, was bolstered immensely. Perhaps the most crucial changes in outlook were those of MacArthur, whose self-confidence soared, and the Joint Chiefs, who indulged in optimism about the Korean outcome in the wake of MacArthur's seeming invincibility. Collins admitted, "The success of Inchon was so great and the subsequent prestige of General MacArthur so overpowering, that the Chiefs hesitated thereafter to question later plans and decisions of the general, which should have been challenged."[30] During the subsequent advance of the United Nations Command into North Korea, Ridgway, then on duty in the Pentagon and worried about Chinese and Soviet reactions to MacArthur's spurning of JCS warnings against using non-Korean troops in his offensive spearhead, asked Vandenberg after a meeting why the Joint Chiefs did not just "send orders to MacArthur and tell him what to do." According to Ridgway, Vandenberg responded, "What good would that do? He wouldn't obey the orders. What can we do?"[31]

The consequences of Inchon were momentous in the expansion of the war in the autumn of 1950. They included not only the costly house-to-house battle for Seoul, the smashing defeat of the North Korean Army, the seeming unassailability of MacArthur, the restoration of the South Korean government, and the morale boost to South Korea and its defenders but also the unsound Wonsan amphibious operation, the subsequent logistical handicap to the Eighth Army's offensive, and the divided command in the advance toward the Yalu River.

After the success at Inchon, MacArthur ordered the X Corps to take Wonsan, an excellent natural harbor on the southeast coast of North Korea with good road connections to Seoul as well as to Hungnam, farther up the coast of the Sea of Japan. Almond would continue to report directly to MacArthur instead of coming under Walker, as the latter thought the case would be. The dual command structure of the UN forces in moving northward through North Korea was justified by MacArthur as necessary because of the virtually impassable Taebaek Mountains that formed the spine of North Korea and prohibited a connected advance by the Eighth Army on the west coast and the X Corps on the east.

Logistical nightmares for the Eighth Army accompanied the outloading of the 1st Marine Division, which was to go by sea to Wonsan, thwarting for a crucial period the unloading at Inchon of supplies for the Eighth Army. Walker's forces also encountered snarls and paralysis of the road network from Pusan to Seoul while the 7th Division was transported to Pusan by truck and then by ship to Wonsan. Temporary, if sometimes alarming, shortages of ammunition, equipment, and various supplies plagued the Eighth Army during its push toward Pyongyang, the North Korean capital, though, fortunately, North Korean resistance was not heavy. A number of MacArthur's senior officers, including all his top naval officers, objected in vain to the Wonsan plan, especially the assault by sea. One naval source comments, "When the Navy argues for an overland assault on an enemy coast and the Army, with compelling finality, insists on going by sea, a certain Alice-through-the-Looking-Glass element enters into military planning."[32]

Bradley also was critical of the Wonsan scheme: "MacArthur threw away an opportunity for decisive hot pursuit, bringing operations to a standstill for almost three weeks; sent X Corps off on a secondary mission of doubtful value, assigning the primary mission to the least prepared of his two forces; divided his force and command; and created an unnecessary logistical logjam of monumental proportions at a time when logistics were crucial to operations." Bradley admitted, however: "The JCS shared my reservations; nevertheless we did not raise any formal objections. . . . What a terrible mistake this would prove to be."[33]

Actually, MacArthur did not seriously consider the option to send the relatively fresh X Corps toward Pyongyang instead of Walker's tired Eighth Army. He also did not consider placing the X Corps under Walker in the advance up the west coast, leaving Wonsan to be seized by the ROK Army, nor did he think to send the X Corps overland to Wonsan. Fast-moving ROK forces, in fact, took Wonsan on October 11, exactly two weeks before the Marines entered the port, the latter having been prohibited from entering the harbor for six days due to extensive mine-clearing operations. The 7th Division also made an administrative rather than assault landing four days later at Iwon, a port 120 miles to the north and already secured by South Korean troops.

The Wonsan operation, although getting the approval of the Joint Chiefs, the President, and the new secretary of defense, General Marshall, was as unwise as Chromite was brilliant. Bradley believed that "MacArthur's vanity got in the way of good sense. . . . Had a major at the Command and General Staff School turned in this solution to the problem, he would have been laughed out of the classroom."[34] MacArthur's Inchon performance, as it turned out, would have no encore.

Another alternative to Inchon that might have been wiser was also ignored. MacArthur was right in arguing against the other landing sites proposed by various planners and leaders of the Navy, Marines, and Army, mainly because they would have sacrificed much of the element of surprise and would have been less strategically valuable envelopments. But no major consideration seems to have been given to using the Chromite divisions in a concentrated assault on a weak point of the Naktong line. Penetration and breakthrough might well have been achieved with great success and with the Eighth Army's logistical situation in better shape than after the Inchon operation. Records now available indicate that the North Korean Army along the Naktong was in much worse condition than was known at the time; indeed, shortly after the Inchon landing, the North Korean line on the Naktong cracked like a hollow shell. Some of Walker's officers at the time believed the enemy defenses were on the verge of cracking, but MacArthur gave no consideration to such an "unimaginative," less dramatic way of seizing the momentum in the war. In view of all that happened adversely in the wake of Inchon, especially the invasion of North Korea that led directly to the war's escalation, it might have been discreet to have considered striking northward solely through a Naktong breakout.

The Inchon operation had proven decisive to defeating the North Korean Army and driving most of its remnants in disarray back across the 38th parallel. In a way, MacArthur was right in saying that the CCF's later intervention marked the beginning of a new war, for Inchon had dramatically ensured the military outcome of the war with North Korea below the 38th parallel. MacArthur had been deferred to by his superiors in the Inchon planning, but his days as a vital force in the decision-making on the strategic direction of the war were numbered thereafter, so vain and flawed were some of his subsequent decisions.

CHAPTER

# 8

# *The Liberation of North Korea*

## LOOKING BEYOND THE DESPERATE DAYS

The idea of freeing North Korea from communist rule must rank in quixotism with the Bay of Pigs invasion of 1961 among joint State-Defense brainstorms. Popular beliefs to the contrary, MacArthur's contribution to the North Korean crusade's origin was limited to the flurry of excitement he caused in Washington upon achieving his smashing success at Inchon. Both he and his superiors now believed that he was invincible, and his egotism and their giddiness came together in the Washington plan to have the UNC forces conquer North Korea. After all, the virtual annihilation of the North Korean Army seemed near. Intelligence reports did not indicate a likely Soviet intervention if North Korea were invaded, and the impressions of senior military leaders in Tokyo and Washington were amazingly confident regarding the capability of MacArthur's command to cope with any Communist Chinese attempt to defend North Korea. Reminiscent of the superior, unrealistic attitude of the American high command regarding Japan's military capabilities on the eve of the Pearl Harbor attack, the American senior commanders from Washington to Tokyo (but excluding those on the battlefield) were convinced that American firepower, especially in artillery and planes, would be awesome against the Communist Chinese.

179

The United Nations had been deeply involved in efforts to make Korea one nation again for quite a while. The General Assembly had passed resolutions by large margins in November 1947, December 1948, and October 1949 calling for the freedom and unity of Korea. The State Department, under the aegis of Marshall and then Acheson, had backed such action as a UN political objective as long as it had strong UN support and did not risk war with the USSR or Communist China. The JCS, as well as MacArthur, however, had been in favor of withdrawing American forces from South Korea and not making a commitment to employ force in an area so strategically valueless. The right and left arms in official Washington were not working in coordination because, in contrast to World War II, State, not Defense, had been the dominant department in formulating long-range national security and strategic policies since 1947. Marshall, who had served as head of State and then Defense, embodied a balance of military and diplomatic concerns in decision-making on security and strategy, but Acheson made little pretense of considering military leaders' views on the military wherewithal needed to fulfill political or diplomatic aims. Both Truman and Acheson were influenced instead by McCarthy's charges of softness on communism, when they pondered the obviously aggressive and risky invasion of a communist state that might be able to draw either or both of the world's foremost communist powers into the fighting.

Although Walker and his troops considered their defense of the Naktong perimeter a desperate, precarious, and costly struggle in the summer of 1950 and MacArthur viewed his Inchon plan as a high-risk gamble, back in Washington there was a surprising amount of euphoria among senior State officials, who were quite confident of ultimate victory over the North Koreans even while the enemy army was still advancing. As early as July 1, John M. Allison, director of the Office of Northeast Asian Affairs, expressed his opinion to Dean Rusk, assistant secretary of state for Far Eastern affairs, that "we should continue right on up to the Manchurian and Siberian border, and, having done so, call for a UN-supervised election for all of Korea."[1] By August many in the State Department displayed no doubt that the North Koreans would be driven out of South Korea and that the decision to cross the 38th parallel would have to be faced soon. After the news of the Inchon success and the breakout along the Naktong, the Pentagon became optimistic as well.

By mid-September, when those two operations were launched, the first objective of the United Nations, as expressed in the Security Council resolution of June 25, was within sight, namely, the repulse of the invaders from South Korea. Much earlier in the summer, however, State and NSC staff members had seen in the Security Council's resolution of June 27, which called for UN members to help defend South Korea and to "restore international peace and security in the area," the legal basis for taking the military action above the 38th parallel.[2] The justification from the viewpoints of MacArthur and the JCS was that, notwithstanding the recapture of Seoul on September 28 and the fact that the North Korean Army was no longer effective at the corps level and above, numerous small units were still functional, the enemy high command remained intact, and the enemy forces could regroup and emerge again as an army-level organization. MacArthur emphasized not only his Inchon plan but also the necessity of destroying the North Korean military remnants above the 38th parallel when Collins and Vandenberg conferred with him in Tokyo in mid-July. The three of them were in accord on allowing the UN troops to enter North Korea to wipe out its military units and to occupy the land briefly. Collins and Sherman agreed similarly with MacArthur on an August visit.

Even while Walker's hard-pressed soldiers were fighting off repeated enemy attempts to penetrate the Naktong perimeter, in the UN Security Council, Warren R. Austin, the U.S. ambassador to the United Nations, delivered speeches on August 10 and 17 reemphasizing "the determination of the United Nations to insure that Korea shall be free, unified and independent."[3] Truman also called for a "free, independent, and united" Korea in a nationwide radio broadcast on September 1, as did Acheson in a number of public statements that month.[4] Several influential members of the British Parliament also delivered speeches calling for the liberation of North Korea from communist control and for subsequent reunification of the two Koreas. It is not altogether understandable how the excitement to reunite Korea forcibly became so widespread before the balance had shifted in favor of the UN forces on the battlefield.

Guidance for operations in North Korea came in NSC 81, which was circulated on September 1, and after JCS modifications to provide more operational flexibility, was approved by Truman on September 11 as NSC 81/1. This was a crucial policy statement that

contained seven principal provisions. UN forces would be authorized to advance north of the 38th parallel "for the purpose of destroying the North Korea forces." If Soviet or Communist Chinese
military units moved into North Korea first, the UN troops were
not to cross the 38th parallel. If Soviet intervention took place
north or south of the 38th parallel, MacArthur was to order his
men to go on the defensive and to consult the JCS immediately. If
Communist Chinese troops advanced south of the 38th parallel
(oddly, no mention of their movement south of the Yalu), Mac-
Arthur was to continue action "as long as he believes his forces
capable of successful resistance." The policy forbade UN naval and
air, as well as ground, operations in Manchurian or Soviet territory.
Further, it stated that only ROK troops should be used in the drive
into the northern border provinces of North Korea and that
MacArthur should develop contingency plans for the occupation of
North Korea, relying mainly on ROK units. In conclusion, the document said that "final decisions cannot be made at this time concerning the future course of action in Korea," because they would
depend on "the action of the Soviet Union and the Chinese Communists, consultation and agreement with friendly members of the
United Nations, and appraisal of the risk of general war."[5]

On the day the 1st Marine Division went ashore at Inchon, September 15, the Joint Chiefs sent MacArthur the basic provisions of
NSC 81/1 and alerted him that a directive would soon be forthcoming based on this document. On September 27, MacArthur received the JCS directive authorizing the invasion of North Korea.
Much of the phraseology was the same as in NSC 81/1, a notable
exception being that, "as a matter of policy," non-ROK ground
forces would not be in the forefront of the drive to the Yalu. The
directive had the firm backing of not only the NSC and JCS but
especially Truman, Acheson, and Marshall, the last having succeeded Johnson as secretary of defense on September 21. Several
Allies, including the British, French, and participating British
Commonwealth governments, had been consulted about the directive before it went to MacArthur. "Your military objective," the
directive stated in unmistakable terms, "is the destruction of the
North Korean Armed Forces. In attaining this objective you are
authorized to conduct military operations, including amphibious
and airborne landings or ground operations north of the 38° parallel in Korea."[6] It went on to restate from NSC 81/1 what his re-

sponses were to be in case the equation of belligerent powers changed. He was told to submit his plans for operations above the 38th parallel and for the occupation of North Korea. This directive was not born of Washington's euphoric reaction to Inchon, because although the UN commander received it twelve days after the Inchon assault, it was heavily based on NSC 81/1, which was approved by the President four days before the Inchon operation.

Laying to rest the myths about MacArthur is like scraping barnacles off a hull: They are numerous and often difficult to dislodge. Even in the UNC's attempt to reunify Korea, a decision made above his level in all its aspects, MacArthur is popularly linked to its beginning and end. The canards that continue to appear in print include two that were spread by the press in the autumn of 1950: MacArthur sold his superiors on the idea of crossing the 38th parallel, and he sent his troops in a reckless invasion of North Korea with no authorization from above. However, the effort to unify Korea was far more complex than can be explained by one man's doings.

MacArthur promptly sent his operational plan to the JCS; his Joint Strategic Plans and Operations Group had been instructed by him some time previously to prepare a plan for this eventuality. The next day after receiving it, September 29, the JCS approved the plan, though in the months ahead they would sharply assail it. But it should not have been difficult at the time to predict that MacArthur's intention for the Eighth Army to strike up the west coast toward Pyongyang and ultimately Sinuiju on the Yalu, while Almond's independent X Corps fanned out across northeast North Korea from the Chosin Reservoir to the Yalu and the Soviet border, was overly ambitious. Plainly, his men would be spread too thin in a vast mountainous region to coordinate effective offensive or defensive operations. Moreover, his plan for the X Corps to take Wonsan, on the east coast, by amphibious assault could have been foreseen to cripple the Eighth Army's advance logistically by tying up the port at Inchon and railroads from Inchon to Pusan with the X Corps' movements. Continuing to have Almond report directly to MacArthur, moreover, spelled further trouble in producing cooperation between the Eighth Army and X Corps since Walker and Almond often were vying for the same matériel, which, not surprisingly, usually went to the X Corps. All in all, the plan for the conquest of North Korea had a number of flaws that the JCS should have insisted the FEC chief correct before granting approval. The Joint Chiefs' after-the-fact criticisms rang hollow to MacArthur when the ensuing Chinese storm broke.

September 29 was also the day Marshall sent a strangely worded message to MacArthur, telling him to "feel unhampered tactically and strategically" in his invasion of North Korea.[7] Marshall was referring to Walker's proposal to issue a public proclamation that he was stopping the Eighth Army at the 38th parallel to reorganize and await orders to cross into North Korea. Marshall meant to assure MacArthur that the Eighth Army was not required to halt its advance while waiting for subsequent directives. Washington did not want MacArthur or Walker to make a public pronouncement about crossing the parallel for fear it would trigger a UN debate over the issue. But, as well he might from his perspective, MacArthur interpreted the secretary of defense's words as assurance that Washington would not interfere with his operations. Thus his reply to Marshall: "The logistical supply of our units is the main problem which limits our advance [caused by his Wonsan venture he might have added]. . . . I regard all of Korea open for our military operations unless and until the enemy capitulates."[8]

For some time, however, foreboding clouds had been gathering over the Yalu Valley. Willoughby's Far East Command intelligence, the Central Intelligence Agency, State Department intelligence, the American armed services' intelligence organizations, and the Nationalist Chinese intelligence system all had been reporting since April 1950 that large troop movements were under way from South China northward. In fact, as early as March 10, Willoughby warned that "the North Korean P.A. [People's Army] will invade South Korea in June,"[9] but he reported two weeks later there would be no war that spring or summer. Sightings of Red Chinese seagoing craft of all types were reported that spring in ports and inlets of Fukien Province on the mainland opposite Formosa, which appeared to be preparations for an invasion of the island. With the coming of war in Korea and the interdiction of the Seventh Fleet in the Formosa Strait, Peking apparently postponed its amphibious assault on Formosa. It began a cumulative shift of armies toward Manchuria in July when it became clear that the North Korean offensive had been critically blunted.

Nationalist and American intelligence estimates rose fast in the next months; even his intelligence adversaries would have considered Willoughby's figures conservative when on August 31 he reported "total Chinese strength in Manchuria estimated to be 246,000 Regular and 374,000 Militia Security forces."[10] By mid-October, various intelligence sources put the strength of Chinese regulars in Manchuria as high as 450,000; they included the Fourth Field Army and elements of the Third Field Army, reputed to include the best of Red China's combat units. MacArthur's estimate of 300,000 at the Wake conference was on the lower end of the intelligence community's analyses, but rather close to the figures recently reported by the CIA and known to Truman.

Beginning in early July, Peking launched the "Hate America" campaign of gradual mobilization of its populace against the United States and its coalition pitted against North Korea. The Red Chinese Foreign Office orchestrated the propaganda drive, and all public media avenues were exploited to reach the masses. The preliminary decision to commit Communist Chinese troops in Korea was made in late August, with the initial war alert coming in early September, and the acceleration in redeployment of armies to south Manchuria in mid-September. A subtle but important shift in the bellicosity of the propaganda campaign took place toward the end of August when the Hate America publicists shifted from the verb *fan tuei*, meaning "to resist" in a nonviolent manner, to *k'ang fei*, which also means "to resist," but with violence.[11]

On September 30, Premier Chou En-lai proclaimed in a Peking speech the strongest official word yet of possible Red Chinese entry into the war, maintaining that his people "will not tolerate foreign aggression, nor will they supinely tolerate seeing their neighbors being savagely invaded by imperialists."[12] He told K. M. Panikkar, the Indian ambassador in Peking, on October 3 that the presence of ROK troops above the 38th parallel was not threatening but that an intrusion by Americans into North Korea would be met by Chinese armed resistance. Panikkar passed the ominous news on to his superiors, who notified Washington. Unfortunately, Panikkar had relayed garbled reports previously, and it took quite a while to get a consistent and reasonably accurate record of what the premier had actually said.[13] Most high-level State and Defense officials, who had a low opinion of Panikkar's credibility, did not put much stock in his latest report. Some figured that Chou was either bluffing or trying to sway opinion in the UN against support of South Korea. Chou's warning was sent along to MacArthur, who, like leaders in Washington, discounted it along with the many other rumors of possible use of force by Communist Chinese that he heard.

The decisions by Washington to cross the 38th parallel and by Peking to cross the Yalu were inextricably linked by each side's ethnocentrism and miscommunication that made the Communist Chinese leaders exaggerate the threat that American troops in North Korea would pose to China's security and that led American officials, enjoying the recent smashing of the North Korean Army, to ridicule the supposed inferior fighting capacity of the CCF. MacArthur's comment to Truman at Wake Island typified much of the attitude of the American military leadership: "Now that we have bases for our Air Force in Korea, if the Chinese tried to get down to Pyongyang, there would be the greatest slaughter."[14] Those who did not underestimate Chinese strength mistakenly believed the intervention unlikely. The absence of direct and candid communications between Peking and Washington was about to cost both sides dearly in men, matériel, and long-lasting hatred.

## NORTH TOWARD A NEW WAR

With MacArthur's and Walker's approval, ROK forces crossed the 38th parallel on October 1 and began advancing up the east coast of North Korea against sporadic resistance. Within two days South Korean spearheads were more than fifty miles deep in North Korea. Meanwhile, on October 1 and again on October 9, MacArthur, as authorized by the JCS, broadcast surrender ultimatums to Premier Kim Il Sung's regime but got no reply either time. American and British units delayed their entry into North Korea until the completion of a UN maneuver that the Truman administration, particularly Acheson, deemed important to the form, if not the substance, of the highly sensitive invasion of the communist state.

In June and July, thanks to a Soviet boycott of the UN Security Council over its failure to seat Communist China, the United States and its alliance had enjoyed smooth sailing in getting their way in that body. On August 1, however, Jacob Malik, the Soviet delegate, returned to take his rotation as president of the Security Council. Malik quickly threw the body into a state of chaos and paralysis in promoting moves to censure South Korea and Formosa, as well as American bombing of North Korea. The Soviet Union, India, and other communist or neutralist nations also sponsored a flurry of plans to settle the Korean conflict by diplomacy, but none of them was approved. While personally endorsing the liberation of North Korea, Acheson took the high ground with his "Uniting for Peace" address to the Security Council on September 20 that denounced aggression in vague, global terms but really was a plan to strengthen the General Assembly in collective security efforts in Korea if the Security Council was paralyzed by a Soviet veto. The plan eventually was approved in November, but weeks earlier the American government had gotten what it wished from the General Assembly regarding Korea for the present.

Acheson, Austin, and their subordinates worked successfully behind the scenes in getting eight friendly nations, led by the United Kingdom, to sponsor a resolution on September 30 changing the UN's objective in the war. Whereas since late June the aim had been to restore the status quo antebellum on the peninsula, now the United States got the multilateral backing it wanted when the General Assembly, by a wide margin of forty-seven to five, with seven abstentions, passed the resolution on October 7 that plunged the international body into the Cold War cauldron of liberating North Korea. The resolution called for appropriate action "to ensure conditions of stability throughout Korea" and to bring about "the holding of elections, under the auspices of the United Nations, for the establishment of a unified, independent and democratic government in the sovereign state of Korea."[15] It was true that three UN resolutions had been passed in 1947–1949 calling for unity, freedom, and democracy in Korea, but this one would commit the UN to achieving unification by force—or so it seemed.

The Joint Chiefs transmitted the text to MacArthur and stated that "it was considered that the resolution provided support for operations north of the 38th parallel." They instructed him "to transmit the text of the resolution to the North Korean authorities and to call upon them to lay down their arms."[16] MacArthur did so in his second surrender ultimatum on October 9, which got no response from Pyongyang.

The American intrusion into North Korea was more critical than the UN resolution of October 7 in influencing Peking to order its troops to cross the Yalu. The secret CCF move into North Korea, however, began the day after the resolution was adopted and, oddly, the day before the Eighth Army crossed the 38th parallel. Between October 8 and the end of the month, 180,000 to 228,000 soldiers of the Fourth Field Army moved south of the Yalu. By mid-November the CCF had from 270,000 to 340,000 troops in North Korea, but the UN forces totaled 440,000 and had superior firepower, even if their ROK units were not as combat effective as the Chinese.

Peking was getting serious and blatantly so, making no attempts to hide its Hate America campaign, the redeployment of its armies from South China northward (if not revealing their movement below the Yalu), and the numerous public threats by Chou and other high-ranking officials. Nevertheless, a CIA report on October 12 concluded that Communist Chinese entry into the war, while it was "a continuing possibility," was "not probable in 1950." It added that Red Chinese support of North Korea "will probably be confined to continued covert assistance."[17] Willoughby's intelligence report two days hence did not contradict the CIA evaluation; the Far East intelligence chief concluded the recent threats by Peking belonged "probably in a category of diplomatic blackmail." But he also acknowledged, "The decision is beyond the purview of combat intelligence; it is a decision for war on the highest level, i.e., by the Kremlin and Peiping."[18] MacArthur also stressed this on several occasions, but official Washington preferred to blame Tokyo intelligence for the June and October-November failures than to admit the primary responsibility lay with the CIA and State Department for knowledge of a nonbelligerent power's activities.

After a five-day battle for Kumchon, not far above the 38th parallel on the west side, the Eighth Army encountered only scattered North Korean resistance. Pyongyang fell to American and ROK units on October 19, while Kim Il Sung and his officials moved the seat of government to Sinuiju, on the Yalu River opposite the Manchurian city of Antung, and still later went on to Kanggye, deep in rugged mountains to the east. The ROK 6th Division, facing light opposition, reached the Yalu not far from Kanggye on October 26. The optimistic UNC and ROK commanders thought this would be only the first of many of their divisions to draw up to the banks of the Yalu, but it would prove to be the only unit of Walker's Eighth Army to reach the river.

It was fortunate, indeed, that the Eighth Army did not meet heavy resistance en route to Pyongyang, because it faced serious supply shortages, particularly ammunition, which was often thousands of tons short in forward supply depots. Walker's men had advanced so fast they had outrun their logistical support, which was sorely handicapped to the south by the outloading of the X Corps for the Wonsan amphibious operation on the east coast. On October 9, the day the first Eighth Army unit, the 1st Cavalry Division, crossed the 38th parallel, the 1st Marine Division embarked at the port of Inchon for the long voyage around the peninsula, while the 7th Infantry Division, the other division of Almond's X Corps in the Inchon-Seoul campaign, went by truck and rail to Pusan and there boarded transports to go far northward. A ROK unit took Wonsan on October 11; the Marines did not get to disembark there until October 26 due to minesweeping that was needed in the harbor; the 7th Division, meanwhile, was shipped on to Iwon for an unopposed landing, 120 miles farther up the North Korean eastern coast. The X Corps also included two ROK divisions and shortly would get the 3rd Infantry Division from Japan, but it still would not have enough men to maintain more than a thin and often broken line of advance through the ever-widening expanses of the rugged northeast area of North Korea.

Although covering a smaller front line with more troops than the X Corps, Walker's Eighth Army was vulnerable to infiltration and outflanking because of the scattered deployment of its units. Walker used the American I Corps and the ROK II Corps in his drive toward the Yalu; he assigned the U.S. IX Corps to battle the large number of North Korean troops and guerrillas still at large in the mountains of southwest South Korea. At the front for the Eighth Army's advance were the American 1st Cavalry and 24th Infantry divisions, along with two ROK divisions on their right, while, in turn, the ROKs had an exposed right flank that extended seventy miles to Almond's nearest units moving northward. Attempts were made to link the lines of the Eighth Army and X Corps, but it was so futile in the extremely rough and almost trackless terrain that later the Communist Chinese soldiers also avoided the backbone of the Taebaek Range in central North Korea.

As the UN Command moved through North Korea with mostly mop-up operations, talk turned to issues of peace. Beginning October 10, there was a busy traffic in messages between the JCS and MacArthur concerning forthcoming problems associated with the reconstruction and rehabilitation of all Korea, the occupation of

North Korea, and the expected roles to be played by Rhee's troops and officials in the occupied north pending Korea-wide elections and establishment of a unified, democratic government. There was also much discussion about possible war crimes trials in the aftermath of the fighting. In contrast to later Chinese behavior, the North Korean forces had committed numerous grisly atrocities against American soldiers as well as South Korean military and civilian personnel.

The anticipated end of hostilities brought wildly premature decision-making on pulling UN forces out of Korea. On October 20, the JCS informed MacArthur that he had to yield the 2nd and 3rd divisions "as soon as military operations permitted" because of "requirements elsewhere in the world." As MacArthur probably expected, he was told that "it was particularly desired that the 2nd Division be redeployed to the European Command by the end of the present calendar year." MacArthur responded agreeably, for him: He wished to keep the 2nd Division until the cessation of hostilities and the 3rd Division for occupation duty until May 1951. He said that it was the only American division he planned to assign to occupation chores, the ROK Army being counted upon for most of those duties. Also on October 20, Major General Oliver P. Smith, head of the 1st Marine Division, learned that two of his regiments were to go to the States and the third to Japan when combat ceased. MacArthur told the Joint Chiefs that "upon the close of hostilities, the Eighth Army should be withdrawn to Japan" and that, hopefully, this redeployment "would start before Thanksgiving and be completed before Christmas."[19] Shortly he instructed Stratemeyer to release two of his B-29 "Stratofortress" groups to return to the States.

Allied forces were also to be cut, though most of them had arrived recently or were expected soon. By October 20 there were about 9,000 men in ground, sea, and air units from Great Britain, Australia, Turkey, Thailand, and the Philippines serving in Korea, the principal units being the 27th Commonwealth Brigade and the Turkish Brigade (both attached to Walker's Eighth Army). On October 24, Pentagon leaders decided that only 15,000 non-ROK non-American troops were required for the UN Command, so the donor nations were informed that 21,000 of the 27,000 personnel about to depart or en route to Korea would not be needed. Upon hearing this news, some UN nations that had pledged future men and matériel to the war effort canceled their commitments. The feeling of euphoria over the impending triumph was widespread, and one of the developments that nourished such elation was the Wake Island conference of Truman and MacArthur on October 15.

The Wake meeting came at an opportune time for the President, MacArthur, and a number of key participants in the decision-making process to reconsider realistically what the United States and the United Nations were attempting to accomplish in the Korean War. If the American-led side pursued to the end its conquest, occupation, and unification objectives, bringing about the first forcible separation of a state from the communist orbit, would the major communist powers tolerate the new situation or would one or both of them respond by entering the conflict? Would the Allies stand firm in supporting America and South Korea in a combat escalation that would become far costlier than the war against North Korea? These and other questions that were profoundly disturbing could have been examined soberly and in depth. Unfortunately, Truman came to Wake on the suggestion of some of his aides that "it was good election-year stuff," admitted Charles S. Murphy, Truman's special counsel.[20] According to Robert Sherrod of *Time*, many of the attending journalists felt they had witnessed "a political grandstand play."[21] Acheson, Marshall, Collins, Sherman, and Vandenberg were invited by Truman but declined to make the trip. Later, Acheson commented of the Wake meeting: "The whole idea was distasteful to me. I wanted no part of it, and saw no good coming from it."[22]

Undoubtedly if the meeting is remembered for one thing, it is MacArthur's ill-advised and overly confident assurance that the Communist Chinese were not likely to intervene and if they did, they would be prevented by American air power from becoming a menace to the ground forces. Actually, half of the time in the preliminary forty-minute session between Truman and MacArthur, as well as the Truman-chaired general meeting later, was devoted to the political and economic reconstruction of Korea after the expected imminent termination of fighting. The better-authenticated general session had no agenda, and Truman moderated it in such an informal manner that the conferees hopped quickly and usually illogically from one subject to another, covering a bewildering variety of topics but with such brevity and shallowness that the scenario should have been embarrassing to all. MacArthur fielded

nearly all the questions, in fact—thirty questions in ninety minutes. Even when MacArthur made his erroneous prediction about
Red China, it provoked no follow-up questions or challenges. The
group moved on to possible war crimes prosecution, introduced by
Harriman; after a brief response by MacArthur, Truman brought
up the Japanese peace-treaty negotiations, and so on it went in this
sham of a high-level conference. They even ranged over problems
in French Indochina and the Philippines in pellmell fashion. In
fact, MacArthur was right when he looked back on the discussions
as dealing with "nothing on which my views were not known. No
new policies, no new strategy of war or international politics were
proposed or discussed."[23]

General Lowe, the President's liaison with UNC, who was sincerely dedicated to building good communications between Truman and MacArthur, suggested ahead that he brief Truman in Hawaii en route about the latest developments in Tokyo GHQ. The
President rejected Lowe's idea for a get-together. The two principals displayed a facade of harmony in public comments after
leaving Wake, but, revealingly, in letters to family members on
October 13 and November 17, Truman referred to MacArthur dis-
paragingly, while MacArthur told his staff at Haneda Airport in
Tokyo upon his return that he had not changed his mind about
anything as a result of the Wake conference.[24] This most costly of
summit meetings might have been a chance to seriously reappraise
policy, but instead it was only political theater.

No sooner did MacArthur get settled back in his Dai Ichi office
than he was in trouble with Acheson again. Three days after Wake,
American planes spotted nearly one hundred MiG-15s at an air
base near Antung, Manchuria. Also, the CIA reported that it was
believed that the Communist Chinese were prepared to fight to
defend the Suiho Reservoir hydroelectric facilities near Sinuiju, on
the Yalu in North Korea, opposite Antung. That same day, October
21, the JCS relayed to MacArthur a message from Acheson: "It is
suggested that Gen. MacArthur make a special report to the SC
[Security Council] to the effect that it is the intent of the Unified
Command not to interfere in any way with the present operations
of the plant and the existing arrangements for the distribution of
electric power." In his report, said Acheson, the general should
state that "he presumes" that the UN Commission for the Unifi-

cation and Rehabilitation of Korea, established after the resolution of October 7, "will consult with all interested parties [including Communist China] on this and the many other problems" the commission would face.[25] MacArthur responded that he could not disavow the possibility that the Suiho hydroelectric plant might have to be destroyed in the future if it was used for "hostile military purposes." As for the announcement about the commission, he said that he could not speak for that body and found it "inadvisable to issue any statement" on its affairs "at this time."[26] The JCS did not bother him further about this.

In the JCS directive authorizing MacArthur's invasion of North Korea he had not been given a specific restraining line above which non-ROK forces were to be excluded. On his own he had established that line across the waist from Chongju on the west to Hungnam on the east, which many planners considered to be the most defensible line above the 38th parallel as for satisfactory terrain conditions and frontline length. Two days after his return from Wake, with his commanders reporting rapid advances almost everywhere, MacArthur changed the position above which non-ROK forces were not to go to the Sonchon-Songjin line, which was about forty miles north of the Chongju-Hungnam line. Far more important, the new line meant that the UN divisions would have twice as long a front line to cover, even considering the seventy-mile gap in the middle. The lengthening exterior lines of supply on which the UN units were operating yielded the advantage of interior lines to the Communist Chinese armies that were now taking positions furtively in the mountains of the northern provinces of North Korea. Another liability in the northward drive was the widening contours of North Korea as its terrain blends into the Asian mainland, not unlike the broadening of the peninsula of Italy as it joins the European continent south of the Alps.

The Joint Chiefs were not at all pleased with MacArthur's report on October 24 that he had ordered non-ROK, mainly American, forces to move through the ROK troops in the final advance to the Yalu. If they were to encounter Chinese forces, as he reasoned, it would be far better to have the less dependable ROK divisions in reserve than in the forefront. Generally, previous ROK combat performances warranted such a conclusion, but MacArthur had been instructed to lead with ROKs. He gave the JCS a rather labored rationalization, which, surprisingly, they accepted for the moment, though later they would mark this as his first clear violation of a JCS directive during the war. The episode did not turn into a serious confrontation between the general and his superiors at the time because of the "First-Phase Offensive," as the CCF designated it, that struck the Eighth Army and X Corps on October 25.

On the west side of the peninsula on October 25, the northernmost ROK division, the 6th, was ambushed and virtually annihilated in the next two days. The other two divisions of the ROK II Corps were attacked fiercely also, resulting in a complete collapse and disintegration of the ROK right flank of the Eighth Army. In Walker's first report to MacArthur about the disaster, the Eighth Army commander stated clearly that the attacks were made mainly by "fresh, well-organized and well-trained units, some of which were Chinese Communist Forces." He noted that the ROKs had built up an "intense psychological fear of Chinese intervention."[27] There was considerable doubt at Almond's headquarters on the east side of the peninsula, when his units were also ambushed that day, whether the CCF was participating, though in the 1st Marine Division there was no question, having a number of CCF prisoners soon as clear evidence. Willoughby seems to have been reluctant to admit the intrusion of the CCF at first, and he may have influenced his chief, for MacArthur, though wavering in his initial reactions to the turn of events, was slow in coming to the realization that the CCF was the principal adversary now. The attackers disappeared into the northern mountains on November 7 as quickly as they had emerged, having decimated a regiment of the 1st Cavalry Division and several ROK outfits in the two weeks of vicious fighting.

When the Communist Chinese preliminary offensive struck on October 25, the grandiose campaign to liberate North Korea from communist control had ended. The UN Command would send probing patrols northward in the next few weeks, but the main forces would remain in holding positions well below the Yalu. Refusing to admit defeat, MacArthur was still determined to complete his conquest of North Korea and was looking toward launching an end-the-war offensive on November 25. It is incredible that the White House, the National Security Council, and the Joint

Chiefs of Staff did not order him to pull back his forces to defensible positions across the waist of the peninsula and give up his planning for what would prove to be the north-toward-hell offensive.

The decision to liberate North Korea is so irrational from both military and diplomatic perspectives that the roots of it must lie in a phenomenon of groupthink among Truman and his inner circle of advisers. The causal links between the decision and the accelerating impact of McCarthyism's charges of the administration's softness on communism may go far to explain the desperation, even panic, that seem to pervade this case. Politics, indeed, was never far from the minds of most of those who advised the President on the strategic direction of the war.

# CHAPTER
# 9

# *MacArthur's Dare*
# *Is Called*

## DIFFERENCES IN STRATEGY

The dismissal of General MacArthur in April 1951 is a watershed in the history of American strategic direction in the Korean conflict. For the ensuing two years and three months of hostilities and truce negotiations no major challenge would be offered to the Truman administration's manner of limiting the war except by a few Allied leaders who urged more compromises with the communists at Panmunjom than the Americans wished to make for the sake of a quicker end to the fighting. With the removal of MacArthur, moreover, the post-1945 trend of increasing input by the State Department in military policy was accelerated. By the bellicose nature of his criticism of the Truman administration's direction of the war, MacArthur had placed himself in the position of championing a military solution in Korea in the American tradition of preferring strategies of annihilation, instead of attrition. He left the scene as an uncompromising warrior, though, in actuality, his differences with Truman were not as simplistic as they appeared. During World War II, as in the Korean conflict, for instance, he had argued for a balanced global strategy that accorded high priorities to not only Europe but also Asia and the Pacific. In view of the sites where American boys have died in combat since 1945, perhaps that and other arguments of the fiery old general need not have been dismissed so lightly.

Contrary to popular accounts, the strategic aspect of the Truman-MacArthur controversy was not based on the President's advocacy of limited war and the general's alleged crusading for a global war against communism. MacArthur wanted to carry the war to Communist China in air and sea operations of restricted kinds, but he never proposed expanding the ground combat into Manchuria or North China. Both Washington and Tokyo authorities were acutely aware that the Korean struggle could have escalated into World War III if the Soviet Union had gone to war, but at no time did MacArthur wish to provoke the USSR into entering the Korean War. He predicted repeatedly that none of his actions would lead to Soviet belligerency, which, he maintained steadfastly, would be determined by Moscow's own strategic interests and its own timetable.

Yet there were significant strategic differences between Truman and MacArthur. The "first war," against North Korea, did not produce any major collisions between the general and Washington except on Formosa policy, which did not reach its zenith until the Communist Chinese were engaged in Korea. The strategic plans of MacArthur for a defensive line at the Naktong, for an amphibious stroke through Inchon and Seoul, and for a drive north of the 38th parallel all had the blessings of the President and the Joint Chiefs before they reached their operational stages. Even the Far East commander's plans for separate advances by the Eighth Army and the X Corps into North Korea and for an amphibious landing at Wonsan, though they raised eyebrows in Washington, did not draw remonstrances from his superiors, who viewed such decisions as within the purview of the theater chief. Sharp differences between MacArthur and Washington leaders only emerged after the euphoric days of October 1950 when it seemed the North Korean Army was beaten and the conflict was entering its mopping-up phase. Perhaps because of the widespread optimism that prevailed most of that month, neither Tokyo nor Washington officials were aware of a strategic chasm developing between them.

On September 27 the Joint Chiefs, with unmistakably clear wording, directed MacArthur, whose troops were to enter North Korea within four days, to employ only ROK forces in the provinces bordering Siberia and Manchuria. Two days after returning from the Wake Island conference with Truman, the general proclaimed on October 17 a line from Sonchon to Songjin north of which non-ROK units would not be used; the new line was well above a more defensible belt across the narrow waist of North Korea, which was still deep in North Korea. The latter line was preferred by the JCS, but the theater commander was not challenged, though Collins later called it "the first, but not the last, stretching of MacArthur's orders beyond JCS instructions."[1] Then came a bombshell for the Joint Chiefs one week hence when MacArthur abolished the Sonchon-Songjin restraining line and ordered his ground commanders "to drive forward with all speed and full utilization of their forces" in order "to secure all of North Korea."[2] The JCS promptly informed him that he had violated the directive excluding non-ROK units from the border provinces; he was told to explain his action, which was "a matter of some concern" to them.[3] He brazenly responded, "There is no conflict that I can see with the directive . . . [which] stated: 'These instructions . . . may require modification in accordance with developments.'" He argued that ROK units involved in the drive were not of adequate strength or stability to secure the region, and he reminded them that Secretary of Defense Marshall had told him on September 30 "to feel unhampered tactically and strategically" in advancing through North Korea.[4]

"The Joint Chiefs of Staff," attests the JCS chronicle, "apparently accepted his defense of his latest action; at any rate, they did not countermand his order."[5] Since Red China's impending intervention was precipitated in part by the American spearheads approaching its border, the JCS might well have considered more carefully the ramifications of MacArthur's bold advance toward the Yalu River. At the Senate hearings on the Far East chief's dismissal later, Collins testified that this was the first of a number of violations of directives by him during the Korean conflict and that it showed that MacArthur was "not in consonance with the basic policies" of the administration.[6] "In any event," Collins remarked subsequently, "it was too late for the JCS to stop the movement of American forces north of the restraining line."[7]

Perhaps it might not have been too late to avert war with Communist China if the Joint Chiefs had focused less on MacArthur's impudence toward them and more on the strategic consequence at stake in the Far East commander's move, namely, the escalation of the war by Communist China rather than by the USSR. While

MacArthur had largely discounted the possibility of the Soviet Union's entry into the war, he had not seemed greatly concerned about Communist China's possible belligerency. As he had cockily assured the President at Wake, his air power would decimate the Chinese Communist Forces if they tried to advance south of the Yalu. The aggressive move up to the border with American troops in the lead was imprudent adventurism on MacArthur's part, but, on the other hand, the Joint Chiefs' timidity toward him and their priority on his effrontery to them at such a critical strategic juncture left them fully as liable as he was for the decisive provocation of Peking.

Communist Chinese units in unknown strength struck the Eighth Army and X Corps in savage but brief attacks, October 25–November 7, and then disappeared into the mountains of North Korea. When the JCS told MacArthur that the CCF intervention, though limited, might lead to a new directive altering his current mission to liberate all of North Korea, he replied heatedly, "It would be fatal to weaken the fundamental and basic policy of the United Nations to destroy all resisting armed forces in Korea and bring that country into a united and free nation." He said that his final push to the Yalu would begin soon and that its curtailment "would completely destroy the morale of my forces"; indeed, South Korean resentment would be so strong that the ROK Army "would collapse or might even turn against us."[8] The JCS and the National Security Council decided not to change his directive. MacArthur's tactics of intimidation and hyperbole could be quite effective at times, particularly when his superiors were unsure of their position. Acheson observed in hindsight, "Here, I believe, the Government missed its last chance to halt the march to disaster in Korea. All the President's advisers in this matter, civilian and military, knew that something was badly wrong, though what it was, how to find out, and what to do about it they muffed."[9]

On November 18, MacArthur notified the JCS that six days hence the United Nations Command would begin an offensive toward the Yalu, which he hoped would bring the war to a swift end. On November 21, high-ranking officials of the Defense and State departments met at the Pentagon to consider changing MacArthur's directive and halting the offensive, especially in view of mounting concern among UN members over Peking's repeated threats of intervention and growing interest in a British plan for a demilitarized zone along the Yalu in North Korea. But the meeting produced no new orders to MacArthur. "Once more we adhered to the custom," said Bradley, "of yielding to the recommendations of the man on the scene."[10] At the time even Truman commented, "You pick your man, you've got to back him up. That's the only way a military organization can work."[11]

As the Eighth Army and X Corps began their widely separated pushes northward on November 24, the Joint Chiefs sent the UNC commander a list of suggestions, "on the assumption that your coming attack will be successful," regarding the problems of how to unify Korea without further involvement. They timorously informed him that they would appreciate his observations on the postoffensive course of action.[12] MacArthur replied that he understood and shared their concern over finding the means to limit the war. But he then went on to dismiss most of the JCS suggestions for lowering the risk of escalation, for example, pulling his force back from the banks of the Yalu after the offensive. He reiterated his opinion that neither the Soviets nor the Red Chinese would oppose with force his march to the Yalu. In fact, he confidently assured the JCS that "resolutely . . . accomplishing our military mission" was the "best—indeed only—hope that Soviet and Chinese aggressive designs may be checked."[13]

MacArthur visited the front on November 24 and buoyantly told several officers that he hoped to "get the boys home by Christmas," whereupon some correspondents who were present dubbed the operation the "Home by Christmas Drive." Meanwhile in Tokyo, that day his public information officer released a communiqué written by MacArthur before his flight to Korea that announced the opening of "the United Nations massive compression envelopment in North Korea," which was expected to be "decisive" and "should for all practical purposes end the war."[14]

On the night of November 25, the United Nations offensive came to an abrupt end when 180,000 CCF troops attacked the Eighth Army on the west side of the peninsula and 120,000 others hit the X Corps on the east side. MacArthur frantically notified the JCS: "We face an entirely new war. . . . Our present strength is not sufficient to meet this undeclared war. . . . The resulting situation presents an entirely new picture which broadens the potentialities to world-embracing considerations beyond the sphere of decisions by the Theater Commander." He declared that he was ordering his forces to "pass from the offensive to the defensive," and he urgently requested new policy guidance from Washington.[15] The JCS approved his shift to the defensive but recommended that the UN forces set up a continuous line of defense across the waist of North Korea, the narrowest width of the entire peninsula. He countered, however, that such a cordon defense could be penetrated easily and got approval instead for the Eighth Army and X Corps to withdraw to beachheads around Pusan and Hungnam, respectively. There, he stated ominously, his troops could try to make defensive stands and, if unable, could be evacuated by sea to Japan.

So far in this fast-developing drama MacArthur and his superiors agreed that their intelligence systems had not provided sufficient warning of the impending CCF assaults, while they differed on whether the Yalu offensive should have been led by ROK, instead of American, troops and whether, once the UNC drive had been thwarted, their forces should stand and fight along the waist of North Korea or should retreat to the port beachheads. The latter alternatives were soon beyond choosing by Tokyo or Washington authorities. With the notable exception of the 1st Marine Division's masterful fighting withdrawal from the Chosin Reservoir, most elements of the Eighth Army and X Corps began rapid movements southward that some correspondents labeled "bugouts," with many units breaking contact with the enemy and abandoning large quantities of weapons and supplies. This disastrous setback was caused primarily by swift Chinese infiltration and envelopment more than by panic and confusion among the UNC soldiers. Once the necessity to pull out of North Korea became quickly evident, neither MacArthur nor his Washington superiors could consider long-range strategic plans until the issue of stopping the Chinese or evacuating the peninsula was settled.

With the British and other Allied governments urging restraint in responding to the Chinese intervention, the Truman administration began to back away rapidly from its aim of liberating North Korea. In the absence of a new directive from Washington, however, MacArthur continued to believe that his ultimate strategic objective was to conquer North Korea for the purpose of reunifying the peninsula under a free and democratic government, presumably the not-quite-liberal regime of President Syngman Rhee of South Korea. Seoul would be recaptured by communist troops on

January 4, 1951; another ten days would pass before the Eighth Army, now under the command of Lieutenant General Matthew Ridgway, would stop the Chinese advance considerably south of the 38th parallel. MacArthur, not realizing the wondrous turn-around Ridgway was about to accomplish, was in desperate search for ways to regain the initiative in the ground war. He hit upon five, each of which accelerated his collision course with Washington over strategy: expanding air operations, employing naval surface forces directly against Red China, taking advantage of the Nationalist Chinese divisions on Formosa, getting four divisions in the United States that were earmarked for NATO shipped to the Far East Command instead, and raising the specter of abandoning the Korean peninsula if he did not get approval of some or all the above ways to bring relief to the battered UN ground forces in Korea.

Ever since the air war over Korea had picked up dramatically in early November with the appearance of Soviet-built MiG-15 fighters of the Communist Chinese Air Force, as well as bombing of targets along the Yalu, especially bridges, by MacArthur's ground- and carrier-based aircraft, the UNC chief had been putting increased pressure on the JCS to remove prohibitions against his planes engaging in "hot pursuit" of enemy planes across the Yalu and hitting their bases in Manchuria. MacArthur argued that enemy planes were afforded "a complete sanctuary" and "the effect of this abnormal condition upon the morale and combat efficiency of both air and ground troops is major."[16] Lieutenant General George Stratemeyer, head of Far East Air Forces and a key member of MacArthur's inner circle of confidants, joined him in complaining about the restrictions. The Joint Chiefs were in favor of permitting FEAF planes to pursue Chinese aircraft up to eight miles into Manchuria, but permission was never granted because of the opposition of the State Department, which did not like the international implications even of short-distance pursuit above the Yalu. According to State officials, Allied opinion was strongly against it, and, besides, it would be seen in Peking as the first step in expanding the combat into Communist China itself. Needless to say, MacArthur's proposal in late December to launch a strategic bombing campaign to wipe out "China's industrial capacity to wage war"[17] was voided by the Truman administration for similar reasons as well as Vandenberg's admission that he lacked the strategic bombers for such a grandiose project.

Another possible avenue of relief for his beleaguered ground troops, according to MacArthur, was to bring in additional units of the United States and Allied navies to set up a blockade of Communist China and to bombard military and industrial targets along the coast of the mainland. The Navy Department maintained, however, that such warships as could be spared from other stations would be inadequate to institute an effective blockade or to wreak much damage in shore bombardments. The British vehemently objected to a blockade because it would interfere with their lucrative trade ties with Hong Kong and Red China. Moreover, a naval blockade would have little impact because much of Communist China's export-import traffic went overland across the long Sino-Soviet border.

While the administration dismissed MacArthur's ideas about further use of naval power, Truman during the first week of the war had approved the precarious insertion of a task force of the Seventh Fleet in the Formosa Strait where it would serve as a buffer between the Communist and Nationalist forces. Its presence precipitated a number of tense skirmishes between American and Red Chinese naval and air units, including the shooting down of an American patrol bomber. Undoubtedly it would have become embroiled in combat if either Chinese side had attempted an amphibious assault across the Formosa Strait. The U.S. Navy's presence in those waters influenced the belief of Communist China's leaders that America and its coalition were staging a major offensive threat against the Peking regime by its actions in Korea.

For some time before the Korean fighting erupted, MacArthur had been interested in preserving and possibly utilizing Chiang's troops that had fled to Formosa. On June 14, 1950, he completed a lengthy position paper on the strategic importance of Formosa, including both the island and its newly arrived Nationalist forces. A few days later he gave copies of the paper, accompanied by eager oral suasion, to Johnson and Bradley for the Pentagon and to John Foster Dulles for the State Department when those officials visited Tokyo on the eve of the North Korean invasion. "Formosa in the hands of the Communists," he argued, "can be compared to an unsinkable aircraft carrier and submarine tender located to accomplish Soviet offensive strategy and at the same time checkmate counteroffensive operations by United States forces based on Okinawa and the Philippines." He warned that "the domination of Formosa by an unfriendly power would be a disaster of utmost importance to the United States, and I am convinced that time is of the essence."[18]

At the end of July, MacArthur, with JCS approval, visited Chiang on Formosa to discuss his security needs. In the ensuing weeks back in Tokyo, he vigorously promoted the case for strong defense links between the United States and Chiang's regime. A message from MacArthur to the annual VFW convention containing more pro-Formosa remarks was withdrawn upon orders from Truman but not before the main news magazines had advance copies to publish. Briefly Truman gave "serious thought" to "replacing him with General Bradley" as UNC commander while leaving MacArthur over the occupation in Japan; the President said he demurred because it might present "the appearance of a demotion, and I had no desire to hurt General MacArthur personally."[19] That autumn, however, MacArthur began the drum beat again for American defense aid to Formosa and for use of Nationalist troops in Korea and on the Chinese mainland. His outcry became shrill after the massive Red Chinese offensive struck in late November. When his pleas through official channels were rejected or unheeded, he began sporadic attacks on Truman's Asia policy in general through interviews, releases, and letters.

On December 6, an irate President issued two directives: the first decreed that all American officials abroad must hence clear public statements on foreign or military policy through the State or Defense departments, respectively; the second ordered such persons "to exercise extreme caution in public statements, to clear all but routine statements with their departments, and to refrain from direct communication on military or foreign policy with newspapers, magazines, or other publicity media in the United States."[20] MacArthur's continued violations of these directives, especially in March and April 1951, exhausted Truman's tolerance of the defiant old warrior. To his last days MacArthur would argue that Chiang's forces ought to have been used, mainly to preserve the lives of American boys. Truman and his senior advisers, in turn, continued to insist that involvement of the Nationalist Chinese would have resulted in diplomatic and logistical nightmares. The successes of the rejuvenated Eighth Army under Ridgway and then Van Fleet from January to June 1951 did not decide the rightness of either side on this issue, but they surely made MacArthur's argument academic.

The final manpower source MacArthur hoped to tap was the contingent of four American divisions said to be going soon to Europe. In correspondence and public statements during the Great Debate in Congress, MacArthur gave his support to the Wherry-Taft faction that opposed the administration's plan to send the units to NATO. While MacArthur found it impossible to comprehend the Pentagon's word to him that he could expect no sizable reinforcements in Korea, Secretary of Defense Marshall announced in mid-February that Eisenhower would establish NATO's supreme headquarters near Paris in April and that four U.S. Army divisions would be transferred to West Europe during the coming months. It seems more than coincidental that the Senate's approval of these moves took place on April 4, exactly one week prior to MacArthur's dismissal. With its firm positions on the Great Debate and on MacArthur, the Truman administration made unmistakably clear its limited commitment to the war in Korea.

While the Great Debate was heating up on Capitol Hill, the beginning of MacArthur's end occurred when Collins, his Army superior and the executive agent for the JCS in Far East matters, visited Tokyo and the Korean front on January 15–17, accompanied by Vandenberg, the Air Force chief. Their trip had been precipitated by a false dilemma MacArthur had posed to his superiors the previous week: As Truman saw it, the Tokyo commander declared the only alternatives were to "be driven off the peninsula, or at the very least suffer terrible losses."[21] Collins reported that during their meeting at MacArthur's GHQ in Tokyo, MacArthur again appealed for the four divisions. Upon visiting Ridgway and his troops in Korea, however, Collins found a renovated force preparing to go on the offensive. He was able to return to Washington with the good news, backed by Vandenberg's findings also, that MacArthur was not only uninformed about the situation at the front but also deceitful in posing the false dilemma of evacuation or annihilation if they did not approve his proposals and troop requests. Ridgway's counsel, rather than MacArthur's, was thereafter increasingly sought by the Joint Chiefs and the President.

MacArthur had been found wanting in both strategy and stratagem. Far more crucial, the U.S. government had reaffirmed its foremost global priority to be the security of its Atlantic coalition. Similar to his plight during the Second World War, MacArthur again was arguing in futility for greater American strategic concern about Asia and the Pacific against a predominantly Europe-first leadership in Washington. Having spent over twenty-five years of his career in the Far East, MacArthur may have been biased in speaking out for a higher priority on American interests in that region. There is little question, however, that communist expansionism was mounting in East and Southeast Asia and that American leaders knew little about the susceptibilities of the peoples of those areas. To MacArthur, his struggle to get Washington's attention focused on the Pacific and Asia must have seemed as frustrating as the efforts by him and Fleet Admiral Ernest King to get more resources allocated to the war against Japan.

Despite the warmongering allegations leveled against him, MacArthur never proposed resorting to nuclear weapons while he was Far East chief. In December 1952, he did suggest in a private talk with Eisenhower and Dulles, the President-elect and the next secretary of state, that a line of radioactive waste materials be air-dropped along the northern border of North Korea, to be followed by conventional amphibious assaults on both coasts as well as atomic bombing of military targets in North Korea to destroy the sealed-off enemy forces. He saw this as "the great bargaining lever to induce the Soviet [Union] to agree upon honorable conditions toward international accord."[22] It must be remembered, however, that he had been out of command for twenty months, and, besides, Eisenhower and Dulles scorned his counsel and never sought it again.

In truth, Presidents Truman and Eisenhower, not MacArthur, both considered the use or threat of nuclear force in the Korean War. On November 30, 1950, Truman remarked at a press conference that use of the atomic bomb was being given "active consideration,"[23] but Allied leaders, with British Prime Minister Clement R. Attlee in the forefront, exhibited such high states of anxiety over his comment that the President never openly discussed that option again. In January 1952, however, he confided in his diary that he was considering an ultimatum to Moscow to launch atomic raids against Soviet cities if the USSR did not compel the North Koreans and Red Chinese to permit progress in the Korean truce negotiations. "This means all out war," he wrote angrily but wisely reconsidered the next day.[24] In the spring of 1953, President Eisenhower tried to intimidate the Chinese and North Koreans into signing an armistice on UN terms by threatening to use nuclear weapons, which by then included hydrogen bombs. MacArthur had nothing to do with these nuclear threats. Nevertheless, the canard of MacArthur as a warmonger who was eager to employ nuclear weapons in the Korean conflict has persisted in popular and scholarly writings over the years.

## A THREAT TO CIVIL-MILITARY RELATIONS?

MacArthur's record of arrogant and near-insubordinate conduct during the previous decade on the world stage was well known to the leaders in Washington in 1950–1951. During World War II, President Roosevelt and General Marshall, the Army chief of staff, had been greatly annoyed when he attempted to get Prime Ministers Churchill and Curtin to press for more American resources to be allocated to the Southwest Pacific theater in 1942. MacArthur appeared to encourage anti-Roosevelt groups in American politics who tried in vain to stir up a draft of him for the Republican presidential nomination in 1944. As for defiance of his military superiors, MacArthur launched a number of amphibious operations prior to obtaining authorization from the Joint Chiefs. Admiral Morison observes that "the J.C.S. simply permitted MacArthur to do as he pleased, up to a point" in the war against Japan.[25]

On several occasions during the early phase of the occupation of Japan, MacArthur defied Truman's instructions for him to come to Washington for consultations, the general pleading his inability to leave "the extraordinarily dangerous and inherently inflammable situation" in Japan.[26] Truman was so irked that he quoted two of the general's declinations in his memoirs written nearly a decade afterward. In 1948, MacArthur again appeared willing to run against his commander in chief, but his right-wing supporters were unable to secure the Republican nomination for him. His dissatisfaction with Washington directives during the later phases of the occupation almost led to his replacement by a civilian high commissioner. His growing alienation from administration policies during the first eight months of the Korean fighting gave rise to speculation that he might head an anti-Truman ticket in the 1952 presidential race.

The administration officials who testified at the Senate hearings on MacArthur's relief clearly indicated that they viewed his attitude and conduct as insubordinate and a threat to the principle of civilian supremacy over the military. Secretary of Defense Marshall, probably the most admired of the witnesses representing the administration, was adamant about MacArthur's unparalleled effrontery toward his superiors:

> It is completely understandable and, in fact, at times commendable that a theater commander should become so wholly wrapped up in his own aims and responsibilities that some of the directives received by him from higher authorities are not those that he would have written for himself. There is nothing new about this sort of thing in our military history. What is new, and what had brought about the necessity for General MacArthur's removal, is the wholly unprecedented situation of a local theater commander publicly expressing his displeasure at and his disagreement with the foreign and military policies of the United States.
>
> It became apparent that General MacArthur had grown so far out of sympathy with the established policies of the United States that there was grave doubt as to whether he could any longer be permitted to exercise the authority in making decisions that normal command functions would assign to a theater commander. In this situation, there was no other recourse but to relieve him.[27]

The evidence accumulated in the Senate investigation of May and June 1951 demonstrates that virtually all of his transgressions fell under the category of disobedience of the President's "muzzling directives" of December 6, 1950. The general's responses, in turn, had revealed his deep opposition to administration policies. The press had widely publicized his blasts; indeed, many of his missives had gone to national news magazines and major newspapers by way of interviews with and correspondence to their publishers and senior editors or bureau chiefs. His false dilemma about evacuation or annihilation, which was rankling enough to his superiors since he seemed to pass responsibility to them, was a frequent theme in his flagrantly defiant public statements. McCarthyism had already left the national press in a feeding frenzy, so it was natural for reporters eager to exploit the popular hostility against Truman and Acheson to give lavish attention to the antiadministration barbs of one of the nation's greatest heroic figures of World War II.

Most heinous to Commander in Chief Truman were the general's ultimatum to the head of the Chinese Communist Forces on March 24 and his denunciation of administration policy read in the U.S. House of Representatives on April 5. The general had been told that Truman would soon announce a new diplomatic initiative to get a Korean truce before Ridgway's army advanced across the 38th parallel again. MacArthur arrogantly and deliberately wrecked this diplomatic overture by issuing his own public statement directed to the CCF leader, which scathingly criticized Red China's "complete inability to accomplish by force of arms the conquest of Korea," threatened "an expansion of our military operations to its coastal areas and interior bases [that] would doom Red China to the risk of imminent military collapse," and offered "at any time to confer in the field with the commander-in-chief of the enemy forces in the earnest effort to find any military means whereby realization of the political objectives of the United Nations in Korea . . . might be accomplished without further bloodshed."[28]

In sixteen or more instances in the previous four months the volatile Far East chief had made statements sharply chastising the administration for its errors or absence of policy in the Far East. MacArthur was bent now upon some dramatic gesture to salvage his waning stature. By late March, the UN commander became so paranoid that he believed that he had ruined a plot created by some in the United Nations, the State Department, and high places in Washington to change the status of Formosa and the Nationalists' seat in the UN.

Upon reading MacArthur's shocking statement of the 24th, the President firmly but secretly decided that day to dismiss him; only the procedure and the date had to be settled. Truman heatedly remarked to an assistant that the general's act was "not just a public disagreement over policy, but deliberate, premeditated sabotage of US and UN policy."[29] Acheson described it as "defiance of the Chiefs of Staff, sabotage of an operation of which he had been informed, and insubordination of the grossest sort to his Commander in Chief."[30] Astoundingly, however, the President, through the JCS, sent him a brief and mildly worded message on March 25 reminding him of the directives of December 6 and telling him to contact the Joint Chiefs for instructions if the Chinese commander asked for a truce.

The message from Washington on March 20 alerting him to the impending peace move also set off MacArthur's second climactic act of self-destruction in his endeavor to redirect American foreign and military policies to a greater focus on Asia's significance to the self-interests of the United States. That same day the general wrote Representative Joseph W. Martin, Jr., the House minority leader and a strong Asia-first and Nationalist China crusader. Martin had asked for comments on a speech by the congressman hitting Truman's weak support of Formosa, his limited-war strategy in Korea, and his plans to strengthen NATO. In his letter, MacArthur endorsed his friend Martin's views with enthusiasm but offered nothing new, even admitting that his positions "have been submitted to Washington in most complete detail" and generally "are well known." What made the general's comments different this time were their coincidence with the sensitive diplomatic maneuvering, Martin's dramatic reading of the letter on the floor of the House, and the front-page headlines MacArthur's words got. Widely quoted in particular was the following passage, which the Truman administration had already heard in varied forms from the Far East commander:

> It seems strangely difficult for some to realize that here in Asia is where the Communist conspirators have elected to make their play for global conquest, and that we have joined the issue thus raised on the battlefield, that here we fight Europe's war with arms while the diplomats there still fight it with words; that if we lose this war to Communism in Asia the fall of Europe is inevitable; win it and Europe most probably would avoid war and yet preserve freedom. As you [Martin] pointed out, we must win. There is no substitute for victory.[31]

At the Senate hearings, MacArthur claimed the letter to Martin was "merely a routine communication."[32] On the other hand, Truman penned in his diary on April 6: "MacArthur shoots another political bomb through Joe Martin. . . . This looks like the last straw. Rank insubordination. . . . I call in Gen. Marshall, Dean Acheson, Mr. Harriman and Gen. Bradley before Cabinet [meeting] to discuss situation."[33] Acheson exclaimed that the Martin letter was "an open declaration of war on the Administration's policy."[34] When Truman conferred with the above "Big Four," as he called them, he did not reveal that his mind had been made up for some time; instead, he encouraged a candid discussion of options and expressed his desire for a unanimous recommendation from them as well as the three service chiefs, Collins, Sherman, and Vandenberg.

Over the weekend Truman talked to key members of the Cabinet to solicit their opinions, while top State and Defense officials met in various groupings to discuss the issue. At the meeting of the President and the Big Four on Monday, April 9, the relief of General MacArthur was found to be the unanimous verdict of the President, the Big Four, and the service chiefs. At the session Bradley read the following statement he had composed with input from and concurrence of the rest of the JCS as spelling out "the principal reasons why they thought from a military point of view he should be relieved":

a. . . . General MacArthur had shown plainly that he was not in sympathy with the decision to limit the conflict to Korea and might not be sufficiently responsive to the directives given him for this purpose.

b. He had failed to comply with the instructions of the President to clear statements of policy with the Government before making public such statements and had taken independent action in proposing to negotiate directly with field commanders to that effect, knowing that the President still had such a proposal under consideration.

c. . . . It was difficult to have General MacArthur do certain planning for eventualities. . . . [The reluctance of the JCS to inform him that across-the-border air attacks had secretly been authorized but none undertaken was given as an example.]

d. All members of the Joint Chiefs of Staff have expressed from time to time their firm belief that the military must always be controlled by civil authorities. They were all concerned in this case that if General MacArthur were not relieved, this civil control would be jeopardized.[35]

In early May, after Truman abruptly replaced him with Ridgway on April 11, MacArthur testified before the Senate's Armed Services and Foreign Relations committees, professing on each of his three days that he was mystified as to why his superiors had become so excited over his remarks and actions. At one point he told the senators, "Any idea that a military commander in any position would possess authority over the civil functions of the Government is a treasonable concept in my mind." When one senator inquired if he doubted whether the President had the right to relieve him, the general replied, "Not in the slightest. The authority of the President to assign officers or to reassign them is complete and absolute. He does not have to give any reasons therefor or anything else." On another occasion he informed the senators, "I do not know why I was recalled. . . . So far as I know, I have completely implemented, to the best of my ability, every directive, every policy that was given to me." In his most startling profession of innocence he proclaimed, "I have . . . to the best of my ability, carried out every order that was ever given me. No more subordinate soldier has ever worn the American uniform."[36] To Truman and his senior advisers the last sentence must have been unmitigated gall, but MacArthur's rationale, amazingly, was comprehensible to himself and his fiercely loyal GHQ leaders.

MacArthur was the first to testify at the Senate hearings, and when he expounded on the harmonious relationship and identity of strategic views between him and his military superiors, he seems to have believed this sincerely, if naively. One by one, Marshall, Bradley, Collins, Sherman, and Vandenberg would later tell the senators that they were not in accord with MacArthur on matters of the direction of the war, relations with civilian officials, the value of the European allies, and the priority of the war in the global picture, among other differences. Not aware of how united and devastating against him his uniformed superiors would be, MacArthur set about describing a dichotomy in the leadership of the war from Washington, with Truman, Acheson, Harriman, and other ranking civilians of the administration, especially the State Department, which tended to have unprecedented input in military affairs by 1950–1951, being responsible for the policy vacuum, indecisiveness, and protracted, costly stalemate. On the other hand, he and the Pentagon leaders, along with most of the other senior American officers of the various services, wanted to fight in less limited fashion and gain a decisive triumph in order to deter future communist aggression.

MacArthur, thinking he spoke for his military colleagues, told the senators that Truman and his "politicians" favored "the concept of a continued and indefinite campaign in Korea . . . that introduces into the military sphere a political control such as I have never known in my life or have ever studied." He argued that "when politics fails, and the military takes over, you must trust the military." Later he added: "There should be no non-professional interference in the handling of troops in a campaign. You have professionals to do that job and they should be permitted to do it."[37] As for his recommendations for coping with the entry of the Red Chinese onto the battlefield, he maintained that "most" of them, "in fact, practically all, as far as I know—were in complete accord with the military recommendations of the Joint Chiefs of Staff, and all other commanders." Referring to a JCS list of sixteen courses of action that were under consideration on January 12, which included three of the four he had recommended on December 30, he claimed with some hyperbole, "The position of the Joint Chiefs of Staff and my own, so far as I know, were practically identical." He pictured his ties with the JCS as idealistic, indeed, unrealistic: "The relationships between the Joint Chiefs of Staff and myself have been admirable. All members are personal friends of mine. I hold them individually and collectively in the greatest esteem."[38] It was a desperate endeavor to demonstrate that the basic friction lay between the civilian and the military leadership, not between him and the Pentagon, but it became a pathetic revelation of how out of touch he was with the Joint Chiefs. For want of conclusive proof as to his motivation, however, leeway must be allowed for MacArthur's wiliness, which had not altogether abandoned him: He may have been trying to exploit tensions between the State and Defense departments, with few uniformed leaders holding Acheson and his lieutenants in high regard.

Fortunately for MacArthur, Marshall and the Joint Chiefs, who had chafed over Acheson's obvious eagerness to see the proud MacArthur fall, felt an affinity with this senior professional in their field who had long commanded with distinction. They could not bring themselves to court-martial him. Further, Truman's terrible ratings in the polls—worse than Nixon's at the ebb of Watergate—and the firestorm that McCarthyism had produced for him and Acheson weakened him so politically that a court-martial of MacArthur would have been foolhardy in the extreme. During the first five days after MacArthur's relief, a White House staff count showed that Truman received almost thirteen thousand letters and telegrams on the issue, of which 67 percent opposed the President's action.[39] By the end of the Senate hearings on the general's relief, much of the public, Congress, and the press had lost interest in the inquiry, though polls indicated that a majority of those who cared enough to give an opinion now were against MacArthur. The notion that he might have touched off World War III was on its way to becoming one of the more unfortunate myths about the general.

Insubordination, or defiance of authority, was the charge most frequently leveled against MacArthur at the time and later by high-ranking officials of the Truman administration, including those in uniform. Of course, there was no doubt of his insubordination in the minds of the two chief architects of his dismissal, Truman and Acheson. On numerous occasions during his days of testimony before the Senate committees, it will be recalled, MacArthur himself said that the nation's commander in chief was empowered to appoint and dismiss his uniformed leaders for whatever reason, which surely included rank insubordination. There was no serious question about Truman's authority to relieve MacArthur, but the President and the Joint Chiefs found such great difficulty in dismissing him because there was no genuine threat to the principle of civilian supremacy over the military in this case. MacArthur was not an "American Caesar" and held very conservative views of the Constitution, the necessity of civilian control, and the traditions and history of the American military. When the President finally decided to gird his loins and dismiss MacArthur, the action was swift and Ridgway replaced him smoothly and effectively in short order. All the President had to do was issue the order to bring about the change in command, and it was clear that his power as commander in chief was secure and unchallenged. The President and his Far East commander had differed over strategic priorities and the direction of the war, but their collision had not posed a serious menace to civilian dominance over the military in America.

## BREAKDOWNS IN COMMAND AND COMMUNICATION

A significant and often overlooked reason for the termination of MacArthur's command was a breakdown in communications between him and his superiors. During the Second World War, MacArthur and the Joint Chiefs of Staff sometimes differed in ways that indicated misperceptions more than strategic differences, but the two sides and their key lieutenants had personal ties between them that were lacking between the Tokyo and Washington leaders of 1950–1951. During the Korean War, the camps of Truman and MacArthur strongly influenced each man's perception of the other. This is not to say that on their own Truman and MacArthur would have become cordial friends. But their lieutenants undoubtedly were important in molding their judgments. Their only direct contact had been a few hours at Wake Island on October 15, 1950, of which a very small portion had been spent alone. Despite the fact that they had never met before and were never to talk again, they would go to their graves implacable enemies.[40]

If the Truman-MacArthur personal relationship was limited to one brief encounter, the personal links between the Far East leader and the seven men who were the President's principal advisers on the Korean War—the Big Four and the service chiefs— were almost nil. Acheson never met him. Marshall visited him once during World War II while going to Eisenhower's headquarters numerous times. Bradley and Harriman had no personal ties with MacArthur at all prior to June of 1950, although each traveled to Tokyo to confer with him after the Korean hostilities commenced. None of the Big Four was an admirer of MacArthur's flamboyant leadership style, yet Marshall, who had been his military superior in World War II, had treated him with commendable fairness despite the Southwest Pacific commander's sometimes difficult ways. All of the Big Four were strongly committed to the security of West Europe, and all had considerable experience and friends there.

None of the service chiefs had any personal contacts with MacArthur of any importance prior to the outbreak of war in Korea, whereupon they made a number of trips to Tokyo to meet with him and his senior commanders and staff leaders. Collins was on the faculty of the United States Military Academy during MacArthur's last year as superintendent (1921–1922), and Vandenberg was a cadet for the three years (1919–1922) of his tenure. Neither of them, however, really got to know the aloof superintendent, though both knew much about him, especially his hero image from the battlefields of France and his efforts to bring reforms to the school despite faculty and alumni resistance. Collins and Vandenberg achieved their senior commands in the Second World War in the European theater; the former had seen combat first in the Solomons, which was not in MacArthur's theater. When he was on Admiral Chester W. Nimitz's staff during the war in the Pacific, Sherman conferred with MacArthur at three or more intertheater planning sessions. Sherman, who had the most significant pre-1950 personal contact with MacArthur, was his strongest supporter of the seven men on a number of his ideas and plans, notably the Inchon assault. On the other hand, Marshall, the oldest of the seven (like MacArthur, born in 1880), and the officer with seniority in the service, was the last of the group to be persuaded that MacArthur should be relieved of his commands.

Of these key advisers to the President, Acheson stands out for his vituperativeness toward the Tokyo commander. In a bitter exchange of press statements in the autumn of 1945 contradicting each other over estimated troop strength needed in occupied Japan, Acheson and MacArthur seemed to exhibit a deep and natural incompatibility. Acheson blamed MacArthur in part for trouble in getting his approval as under secretary of state passed by the Senate that fall. When he was secretary of state later, he visited Europe often but never Japan, and in 1949 he was behind the move to oust the general as head of the Allied occupation. Certainly as proud and arrogant as MacArthur, Acheson could be invidious. Writing nearly two decades after the dismissal, Acheson still harbored deep wrath: "As one looks back in calmness, it seems impossible to overestimate the damage that General MacArthur's willful insubordination and incredibly bad judgment did to the United States in the world and to the Truman Administration in the United States."[41] Acheson was the abiding voice in Truman's ear from 1945 onward urging him to dump "the Big General," and it was he who primarily continued to stoke the long-cold coals even after most of his cohorts had let the fire die as far as public statements were concerned.

The sorry spectacle of MacArthur testifying at the Senate hearings about his harmonious relations with the Joint Chiefs not only exposed his ignorance of the situation but also pointed up how poorly the JCS had communicated their doubts and anxieties, as well as their anger, to the theater commander. It was an invitation to trouble to place him in the UN command in the first place because of both his prior record of defying authority and his long career of distinction and seniority in comparison to theirs. It should have been understood from the beginning of the Korean War that his past achievements gave him no claim to special privileges in obeying orders and directives, especially in such an unprecedented limited conflict that could quickly become a third world war. Time after time, especially after the Red Chinese intervention, the Joint Chiefs retreated from the policy guidance and new directives they should have given MacArthur and should have demanded his obedience. Instead, his intimidation of the Joint Chiefs led them to appease him.

On the other hand, MacArthur discovered that he could not awe or intimidate Truman. Indeed, at the end, the President dismissed him so abruptly and crudely that the general heard of it first from a commercial radio broadcast. Speaking as a professional, MacArthur later said, "No office boy, no charwoman, no servant of any sort would have been dismissed with such callous disregard for the ordinary decencies."[42] For MacArthur, his erroneous image of Truman as a fox terrier yapping at his heels instead of a tough, decisive commander in chief was a costly failure in communication.

If the Joint Chiefs had been more responsible in keeping MacArthur on a short leash, perhaps the collision course between the President and the general might have been averted. The absurd spectacle of the Senate investigation into the general's relief, which bestowed upon Pyongyang, Peking, and Moscow an abundance of data on American strategy in the midst of war, surely could have been avoided. While MacArthur's career was terminated by the confrontation, Truman's also was cut short, the controversy mightily affecting his chances for reelection. Truman won over MacArthur, but it was a Pyrrhic victory politically.

MacArthur's relief was, in part, a legacy of World War II and the strategic priorities of that conflict. Roosevelt and his Joint Chiefs of Staff had early agreed to the British priority on the defeat of Germany because the Atlantic community of nations was vital to American national security and the threat by Japan was more distant. In the midst of another Asian war, MacArthur was sacrificed by a different President and his Defense and State advisers, who did not consider American strategic interests as menaced in East Asia as in Europe. It remains to be seen whether a century hence the Far East will loom as important to American self-interests as MacArthur predicted.

# CHAPTER
# 10

# Try for Victory or Settle for an Armistice?

## POLICY IMPACT OF THE CHINESE SPRING DEFEAT

Washington's decision in the late spring of 1951 to seek a negotiated peace rather than to try to crush the communist forces in Korea was difficult for the many American veterans of World War II then in the UN Command to accept. Beginning with the Declaration of the United Nations in January 1942, the Allies had tried to ensure that their coalition was not divided by some members' seeking separate peace terms with the Axis. A year later at the Casablanca Conference, Roosevelt set forth the principle of unconditional surrender that ultimately became a multilateral Allied policy. General Van Fleet became only the most vociferous of a number of senior American commanders who were convinced that it was a mistake not to exploit the opportunity to drive the CCF out of North Korea. He had been trained to try to win, had been highly successful as a corps commander against the German Army, and thought he had achieved a crucial turn of the tide against the communist forces in Korea.

The two stages of the Chinese Spring, or Fifth-Phase, Offensive of 1951 had been devastating setbacks for the enemy. The reconstituted North Korean Army, totaling about twenty-four divisions at the start of the spring offensive, had suffered heavily. The widespread CCF operations of April 22–30 had cost the enemy 70,000 casualties, while the thrust against the UNC-ROK lines mainly below the Soyang River, May 16–20, had resulted in 105,000 casualties, with several CCF divisions virtually wiped out. When the Eighth Army went on the counteroffensive, pushing northward to restore Lines Kansas and Wyoming, it encountered enemy troops surrendering in unprecedented numbers.

No leaders in Washington, Tokyo, or Korea were euphoric enough to believe that another easy advance to the Yalu was in the offing, as had been the illusion in October 1950. But the enormity of the enemy's costly defeat in the Spring Offensive coincided with significant reviews of policy in Washington and new directives for Ridgway and his commanders. These new orders, however, were poorly conceived. The aftermath of the Chinese Spring Offensive was a period of crucial blunders and missed opportunities for the UNC to bring the war to a decisive and successful end.

The first mistake was the decision by the JCS not to discuss an armistice. In late March 1951, their report to Secretary of Defense Marshall concluded that "an armistice arrangement of itself would not, even temporarily, constitute an acceptable solution of the Korean situation."[1] An important factor in their judgment may have been their orientation to total war from their experiences in the Second World War. By then the Eighth Army was advancing north of the 38th parallel again, and on April 5, MacArthur informed the Joint Chiefs that he and Ridgway were in agreement on Lines Kansas and Wyoming as the best defensive positions for the UNC forces if and when the anticipated Chinese Spring Offensive struck. Line Kansas ran from Munsan on the west to Kojin-ni on the coast of the Sea of Japan, above the 38th parallel but below the Iron Triangle and Punchbowl battlegrounds, while Line Wyoming was an extension to Chorwon and Kumhwa at the south base of the Iron Triangle.

Meanwhile, the State Department was working on a possible diplomatic way out of the Korean entanglement that would bring peace with honor for the United States and the UN, as well as security for South Korea. This required a strong defensible line that could be held militarily and not bargained away politically. A satisfactory resolution would not be found by military action alone, but a lucid, workable policy on the possibility of terminating hostilities needed to be formulated.

The official JCS history states, "By the time of General Mac-Arthur's removal [April 11], a tacit agreement had emerged within the Administration concerning policy toward Korea."[2] The aim was now to bring a halt to the hostilities and to achieve the status quo antebellum; the Eighth Army's mission was to cause such combat attrition among the enemy forces as to compel the communists to agree to these conditions. Although representatives of the State and Defense departments had worked together to reach this stage, the JCS had gone along reluctantly. Its primary concern was the defense of Japan against a potential Soviet incursion and the maintenance of a strong defense line to ensure the protection of South Korea. Meanwhile, Acheson's lieutenants focused on retaining the coalition against further global communist expansion and averting an enlargement of the Korean conflict. As on other occasions when the two agencies had tried to cooperate and coordinate their moves since World War II, the State Department's position prevailed.

Throughout the later phase of the occupation of Japan and the first nine months of the Korean War, MacArthur had repeatedly expressed consternation over the growing impact of State on essentially military matters. Ridgway, having become acclimated to the new system of interagency coordinating committees while serving in the postwar Pentagon, adjusted much better to the emphasis on cautious military action. "I wanted to keep always in mind the clear policy decisions communicated to me by President Truman and the Joint Chiefs of Staff, the most immediate of which was to avoid any action that might result in an extension of hostilities and thus lead to a worldwide conflagration."[3] He requested clarification of the directives and policy statements issued by the JCS, the President, and the secretary of defense during the months preceding his appointment.

He was troubled particularly by a contradiction that had plagued MacArthur, namely, reconciling his chief mission as CINCFE, to defend Japan, with his paramount aim as CINCUNC, to defend South Korea and stabilize the situation on the peninsula if possible. In the first phase of new JCS directives to him, on April 17 and 19, Ridgway met rejection in his request for authorization to withdraw UNC forces from Korea to defend Japan in case of intervention in the Korean War by the USSR; in such a situation, he was somehow to defend both until further notification.

Ridgway kept Van Fleet on a much shorter rein than MacArthur had imposed on him. On April 19, he restricted Van Fleet to Line

Wyoming and three days later instructed him to repel aggression against the territory he occupied and to establish and maintain order there. This directive was an effort by Ridgway to strike a balance between the military authority he possessed and the JCS directive. He had Van Fleet restrict his troops to a line beyond which they could not advance without the approval of CINCFE.

The first step of the Chinese Spring Offensive was defeated with heavy enemy losses by the end of April. But on May 1, Ridgway received a new JCS directive that restricted his responsibilities as CINCFE and CINCUNC. The JCS limited the advance of UN units and forbade Ridgway to allow them beyond Lines Kansas-Wyoming without prior permission. This action reflected the growing belief in Washington that military operations alone would not solve the Korean dilemma. Ridgway, as well as his superiors, began to face the military realities. These were that no large UNC reinforcements would be forthcoming, that a large number of the UN nations with forces in Korea wanted to withdraw from active involvement in the war, and that the UNC's advancement northward was increasing its logistical problems as well as its exposure to enemy air attacks and mounting casualties. "But most of all," states the Army chronicle, "both the Joint Chiefs of Staff and General Ridgway knew that the Chinese had ground forces available in North Korea and Manchuria that had not been tapped and that far outnumbered those of the United Nations Command in the area."[4] The enemy casualties for the first year of the war totaled about one million, but American planners had to remember that the Communist Chinese troops had numbered over five million at the end of the civil war in December 1949.[5]

Ridgway objected that his mission to destroy the enemy armies in North Korea and at the same time provide adequate protection for Japan was "completely beyond the capabilities of this command to accomplish with forces presently available." The Joint Chiefs responded that "the mission assigned in their directive was beyond the capabilities of CINCFE. However, it was in consonance with existing national objectives, which were currently [May 11] under review by the President and the National Security Council; when the review was completed, the mission would if necessary be amended."[6]

On May 17, President Truman approved NSC 48/5, a policy statement of far-reaching proportions which determined the future course of combat. The same day, UNC forces below the Soyang began to thwart the final step of the enemy's huge Spring Offensive, and the MacArthur Hearings continued to attract Senate and national attention in America. The battle beyond the Soyang River ended successfully on May 20 and was followed by an immediate UNC counteroffensive. But the triumph on the battlefield was not reflected in American policy reformulation, which pointed steadfastly toward a negotiated settlement of the hostilities. The NSC deliberations seemed to be based on reactions to the Senate hearings on the MacArthur period rather than on the post-MacArthur developments.

The "Policy Guide Lines for United States Action" related to Korea in NSC 48/5 stated that one Korea, free and democratic, was the ultimate aim and to be sought primarily by political rather than military means. The United States would work through the UN to achieve a settlement in Korea that would include an armistice, extension of the authority of the ROK government over all the peninsula south of a satisfactory defense line north of the 38th parallel, withdrawal of non-Korean troops from the peninsula, and strengthening of ROK military power to deter or repel future aggression. Military action would be continued until the above conditions were attained. Also, the document stated that the United States would avoid expanding the war with Communist China or engaging in a general war with the USSR, especially if "our major allies" are not in support.[7]

Regarding NSC 48/5, the official Army history maintains, "The significance of this blueprint for American action in Asia can hardly be overstated. . . . The statement implied no hope of military victory in Korea, but it did bespeak a certain confidence that Communist designs could be thwarted even though United States aims could not be fully accomplished."[8]

The State Department–dominated circle of Washington policymakers stubbornly clung to the illusion that North Korea could be liberated from communist control and reunited with South Korea. Whether this feat was to be accomplished by force, as earlier tried, or by diplomacy, as now contemplated, the means of severance would matter little in Moscow or Peking. The consequence of losing a communist satellite state would undoubtedly provoke strong reactions by the Soviet Union and Communist China.

In a meeting of the JCS with Paul H. Nitze's Policy Planning Staff of the State Department on May 29, however, it was clear that NSC 48/5 had not settled a number of practical matters. Bradley raised the question of whether Ridgway was to defend as far as the Yalu or the 38th parallel or somewhere between them. It was unclear whether Ridgway was required to obtain JCS approval before advancing above the line running through the Hwachon Reservoir or whether the line should be farther north, as Admiral Sherman desired. Dean Rusk responded saying he and his colleagues Nitze, Harriman, and Matthews were concerned over advancing too far north and provoking the Soviets.[9] No one at the State-JCS discussions took into account the change in favor of the UNC that was occurring along the Korean front line.

The JCS directive to Ridgway on May 31 remained in effect until the armistice was signed two years later. The Joint Chiefs straddled the long-standing conflict of missions by entitling the first part "Directive to CINCFE" and the second part "Directive to CINCUNC." CINCFE's missions remained to defend Japan as top priority if the USSR attacked FECOM but also to support UN operations in Korea and to keep Formosa and the Pescadores neutralized as targets of attacks or bases for assaults.

As CINCUNC, Ridgway was to "inflict the maximum personnel and materiel losses" on enemy forces in Korea "in order to create conditions favorable to a settlement of the Korean conflict." Ridgway's decision-making authority was thus carefully circumscribed so that his army's operations all pointed toward a negotiated settlement on the terms of NSC 48/5 that would be satisfactory to the U.S. government. The JCS also directed him to obtain their approval prior to advancing beyond "some line passing approximately through the Hwachon reservoir area."[10] This vague reference to a defense line referred to Lines Kansas and Wyoming, but Ridgway's staff was puzzled until this was clarified; they did not interpret a Hwachon line as synonymous with these. Ultimately, the JCS directive did not have much effect on Ridgway's mission as CINCFE, but it redefined his mission as CINCUNC. The directive shaped the objective of the Kansas and Wyoming operations. Their purpose was to lead to a negotiated peace.

On June 20, the JCS asked Ridgway's opinion about possible further advances northward, apparently based on his recent reports of the deteriorating state of the enemy forces and their logistical plight. Ridgway responded favorably on removing the Kansas-Wyoming restriction on advances, but he told the JCS he wanted to study Van Fleet's impending plan for a general movement to a line extending from Pyongyang to Wonsan. Both commanders had concluded that Line Kansas would be the most effective defense line during a cease-fire period, although Ridgway preferred an outpost line ten miles beyond Kansas and a cease-fire line twenty miles above Kansas. He felt that would allow the ten-mile withdrawal that might become necessary, and would still leave the Eighth Army in its Kansas position. He and Van Fleet both felt that in view of a potential cease-fire, they were justified in not wanting to expend lives and matériel to seize territory they might have to yield as a consequence of armistice negotiations.

Ridgway's operation options were limited so much by the mountains, shortages in men and matériel, and strong enemy entrenchments farther north that it actually was of little import whether the JCS restraint on the Eighth Army's advance was lifted. At a meeting of State and Pentagon leaders on June 28, after five days of diplomatic flurries following Malik's peace overture, Rusk and U. Alexis Johnson of the State Department presented a checklist of political and military steps suggested as lines of action "to meet present Korean situation." The revised statement was approved by Marshall and Truman; it was dispatched to Ridgway that same day. He was to be involved in announcing and arranging a meeting between the opposing military commands in Korea regarding armistice negotiations. Ridgway was informed that he would be permitted "maximum freedom of action in the conduct of military operations until such time as a satisfactory cease-fire shall have been arranged." In fact, he was told that he "should continue to be guided by his existing military directives and should not be inhibited by cease-fire negotiations in taking such action as is necessary to maintain his military position and protect his forces in relation to enemy action."[11]

On July 10, 1951, the day the truce talks began at Kaesong, the JCS informed Ridgway that Truman had removed limits on operations in order to secure the cease-fire line that the United States wanted. But Ridgway and Van Fleet had already decided not to advance beyond Kansas-Wyoming. Van Fleet believed more forces were needed for a move to the Pyongyang-Wonsan line, especially in view of intelligence reports of an impending enemy offensive. Ridgway concurred because he thought the truce talks might result in quick outcomes. Also, economy in UNC casualties seemed in order if ground gained in combat might be lost in armistice bargaining. On the day the Kaesong negotiations began, the opposing sides were about equal in ground strength, the Eighth Army having about 554,500 troops, while the Communist Chinese and North Korean soldiers numbered about 569,200.[12] Four decades later the debate is still heated over whether the UN forces should have pressured the enemy armies in Korea more vigorously before and during the armistice negotiations.

## THE DEBATE OVER CONTINUING THE UNC GROUND OFFENSIVE

Policy developments in Washington seemed to have a momentum of their own, divorced from battlefield actions. Talk of truce negotiations preceded UNC combat successes in the spring of 1951. The Truman administration seemed to be in desperate search of any way out of the war that could be attained with national honor still intact. A continuing controversy ensued over how badly the enemy was beaten in late May and early June of 1951 in evaluating whether an offensive should be authorized. In the long run, this factor was almost irrelevant, because the consensus had already been reached by Truman and his top advisers on the war that the status quo antebellum would be minimally acceptable.

Questions arose among Washington planners about the objectives of continued offensive operations and were debated in the public sphere. The MacArthur Hearings provided generous servings of valuable data that were unprecedented in their revelations in the midst of a war. The testimony at the Senate investigation publicly made clear that the United States did not want a general war with Red China or the Soviet Union, that it might be interested in future offensives not necessarily to secure all of North Korea and reunite the peninsula but to achieve a strong defensive line somewhere between the 38th parallel and the narrow waist of North Korea, and that it intended to hurt the communist forces so badly with overwhelming firepower that they would settle quickly on an armistice that was favorable to the UNC. There was uneasiness among some high-level officials in Washington, however, that the very destructive defeat of the CCF Spring Offensive was making Moscow uneasy and that a rousingly successful counteroffensive by the UNC heightened the possibility of the Soviet Union's entry into the conflict.

There were many people in 1951 who argued in favor of a continued, but well-defined, UNC offensive. Van Fleet lamented that he was not allowed to launch a major drive in late May and early June of 1951. Others argued for offensive operations continuing through that summer and perhaps longer. Some wanted the UNC to exert military pressure on the enemy throughout the truce negotiations. Few with experience or knowledge of the issues argued either for an offensive or an armistice as mutually exclusive factors.

The much-talked-about but-never-undertaken UNC offensive was envisioned not only with different time spans but also with different objectives. Some saw it as another drive to the Yalu, culminating in the reunion of the Koreas by force. Others interpreted it as an advance to the narrow waist of Korea, usually the Pyongyang-Wonsan line, with the idea of holding there until an armistice was concluded. Still others have envisioned an offensive to the narrow waist or to some other defensive position north of Lines Kansas-Wyoming with the possible goal of trading the territory in bargaining at the truce table. A considerable number favored offensive action but left the limits undefined, the aim being to exert military pressure at timely occasions during the truce talks to force the enemy to accept certain terms or to come to a satisfactory agreement sooner.

Among the contemporary leaders certainly the one who expressed his discontent with the most vehemence during and just after the war was General Van Fleet, who headed the Eighth Army during the Korean War longer than his predecessor, Ridgway, or his successor, Taylor, and who was its commander during the Chinese Spring Offensive of 1951. He knew the battlefront situation firsthand during the critical period of April-June when the decision was made to halt the UNC offensive operations. In early March 1953, Van Fleet was called to testify at Senate hearings on alleged ammunition shortages during the Korean hostilities. Like the MacArthur Hearings in 1951, this inquiry wandered off on many tangents, one of which was the alleged opportunity for decisive military action that he was prevented from undertaking.

In his three days of testimony Van Fleet reiterated to the senators his outspoken conviction, publicly repeated many times over the previous year and a half, that "the only solution is a military victory in Korea" and that "anything short of that would be a defeat." When queried by a senator, Van Fleet hedged a bit in admitting that he was not referring to "a complete victory, but in June of 1951 we had the Communist armies on the run; they were hurting badly." The general said that at the time he "was crying to turn me loose" in messages to Ridgway. Later in his testimony he maintained that he had had in mind a "counteroffensive, limited in nature" that, nevertheless, could have produced "a very great victory" over the enemy in North Korea.[13]

In May 1953, Van Fleet lashed out strongly in a two-part series in *Life*, lamenting the lost opportunity: "I cannot help but feel sad as I trace the footsteps of our policy downfall since May of 1951." This window of opportunity to crush the enemy, he claimed, existed only briefly: "The enemy recovered quickly from the beating we gave him in May and was entrenched again by June 10." Sounding much like MacArthur, he maintained that "though we could readily have followed up our successes and defeated the enemy, that was not the intention in Washington: our State Department had already let the Reds know that we were willing to settle on the 38th Parallel."[14]

Admiral Joy, the NAVFE commander and frustrated head of the UNC armistice delegation, confided to a naval friend six weeks after the Kaesong negotiations had begun: "Looking back on everything, I believe we were much too much in a hurry to get started on these negotiations."[15] Four years later Joy wrote: "The armistice effort in Korea taught this: Never weaken your pressure when the enemy sues for armistice. Increase it. In June 1951, the Communist forces were falling back steadily, suffering grievously. . . . As soon as armistice discussions began, United Nations Command ground forces slackened their offensive operations." Looking back two years after the war's end, he believed that if an all-out effort had been made to achieve military victory between July 1951 and the armistice, it would have been neither impossible nor "even unusually difficult." Moreover, such decisive action probably would have meant fewer American casualties than were actually suffered during the stalemate period.[16] Also, he noted, there was an undetermined number of UNC prisoners of war in enemy POW camps who died during that two-year period of truce talks.

General Almond, who was commander of the X Corps during the defeat and immediate aftermath of the Chinese Spring Offensive, believed the UNC could have won in Korea when the Chinese forces were massing along the Yalu in October-November

1950 and also in early June 1951 when Van Fleet was prohibited from launching a major offensive.[17] In 1969, Almond wrote the Army's chief of military history about the official history's version of the issue emphasizing that Ridgway opposed Van Fleet's plan because of the risks involved: "General Ridgway's strategic philosophy was a compromise with politics."[18]

MacArthur's shadow hung over the controversy of continuing the offensive because the Senate inquiry into his relief was presenting the American public and, indeed, the world daily revelations into the thinking of America's leaders on the strategic direction of the war. In his address to Congress upon his return to the States in April 1951, MacArthur made it clear where he would stand if he were still the FEC/UNC commander and faced the situation that occurred a few weeks hence when the enemy forces seemed shattered and near total collapse. His words are famous now because they recalled the decisive end of World War II and America at its apex of military glory and triumph: "But once war is forced upon us, there is no other alternative than to apply every available means to bring it to a swift end. War's very object is victory—not prolonged indecision. In war, indeed, there can be no substitute for victory."[19] In his memoirs of 1964, he reiterated for the last time before his death that year his firm belief that the UNC forces in Korea "could have attained victory without recourse to other than conventional warfare and with much less [casualties] than actually occurred under protracted negotiations."[20] This controversy over going for victory or negotiated peace is heavily tinged by the contemporaries' exhilarating triumphs in World War II and their chagrin over trying for less in Korea where the limitations already appeared to be excessive.

In the autumn of 1952, General Clark had expressed mixed feelings about the strategy of the war. Although he felt it would be foolish to attempt to gain a decisive triumph over a larger enemy army solidly entrenched, still he advocated a strong offensive, backed by adequate reinforcements, instead of a negotiated peace. Clark agreed with Ridgway's prevention of Van Fleet from launching attacks above battalion size without first getting CINCFE's approval. On the other hand, Clark was also in favor of "an all-out offensive to win the war, providing Washington could furnish . . . the additional infantry divisions and air and naval support required."[21]

The contemporary leader who was most in favor of going for victory instead of settling for a negotiated peace was ROK President Rhee, whose extremist position reflected the sentiments of the vast majority of his officials and people. John J. Muccio, the U.S. ambassador to South Korea, 1949–1952, warned the State Department often during the war to expect trouble from Rhee, who passionately advocated unification by force.

A number of later analysts of the war argued in favor of continuing the attack in June 1951 when the CCF appeared to be near collapse. By far, the most powerful voice raised in protest of going to the truce table prematurely was that of Bernard Brodie, one of the giants among post-1945 strategic intellectuals. He maintains that in June 1951 "the military situation could not have been better" for the UNC. The purpose of the UNC offensive "should have been to continue maximum pressure on the disintegrating Chinese armies," not to acquire more territory but "as a means of getting them not only to request but actually to conclude an armistice." Brodie believes that "the Communists were left without incentive to come to terms" because of "what I do not hesitate to call the 'blunder' of halting the June 1951 offensive."[22]

The testimonies of the administration officials at the MacArthur Hearings in May and June 1951 provide the earliest contemporary views of top military leaders who opposed a major offensive in lieu of truce talks following the defeat of the Chinese Spring Offensive. Of course, Van Fleet's charges had not been made at the time of this Senate inquiry. The key military officials of the Truman administration who testified were Secretary of Defense Marshall and the four members of the Joint Chiefs of Staff—Generals Bradley, Collins, and Vandenberg, and Admiral Sherman.

In his two memoirs, Ridgway lets loose with some subtle, as well as not so subtle, jabs at Van Fleet about the issue of a major offensive in May–June 1951. His opposition to Van Fleet's offensive plan "from the purely military standpoint" is reminiscent of arguments over the race for Berlin in April 1945, with Van Fleet appearing in a similar minority position to Lieutenant General William H. Simpson in his claim that his Ninth Army could have captured Berlin. Ridgway was on solid ground in presenting the problems of a successful advance northward: "It would have greatly lengthened our own supply routes [as well as shortening the enemy's], and widened our battlefront from 110 miles to 420 [to push to the Yalu].

Would the American people have been willing to support the great army that would have been required to hold that line?" It must be remembered that more than half a million troops were required to defend the 110-mile line, and it was not unreasonable to anticipate at least 2 million would be needed to guard a line along the Yalu and Tumen rivers, the northern border of North Korea. Ridgway observed, "It is clear to me, though, that when all the factors were taken into consideration, it was decided that the political advantage of driving the Chinese back to their lair was not worth the blood it would have cost."[23]

Secretary of State Acheson's testimony was, not surprisingly, in line with the generals who defended the administration's policy. After all, from the first week of the war through the end of the truce negotiations, he had been the principal architect of the administration's chief positions on the direction of the war, as well as on America's relations with its coalition and with the United Nations. Waxing eloquently in a later autobiography, Acheson wrote with the confidence of the military strategist and tactician that he sometimes perceived himself to be: "Experience had taught a costly lesson: to push the Chinese back upon their border—their source of reinforcement and supply—only increased their strength, as Hercules increased that of Antaeus when he threw him upon his Mother Earth, while decreasing our own as our forces attenuated their lines of supply, became separated, and lost touch with their air support as they moved north." He concluded, "The generals, among them James Van Fleet and Mark Clark, who later declared that they had been deprived of their chance for total victory, were antedating thoughts conceived in tranquility."[24] Ironically, Acheson in this passage reveals an innate kinship with his nemesis MacArthur: although both men overflowed with gall and genius, Acheson knew little about military matters and MacArthur had slight knowledge of things Japanese, but each man was amazingly lucky in the alien fields he entered.

While Rhee was a strong champion of the June 1951 offensive, Britain favored a diplomatic settlement. As Herbert S. Morrison, the British secretary of state for foreign affairs, expressed it in May 1951, "I do not think we should seek to impose a political settlement on North Korea by force if we can possibly solve the problem by negotiation and agreement."[25]

Among the postwar analysts who support the position of Ridgway and his superiors on halting large-scale offensive action in June 1951 is Rosemary Foot, an Oxford University scholar, who finds that "while U.S. capabilities remained restricted and the threat of Chinese armies loomed large, a limited war and negotiated settlement had to remain the preferred outcome."[26]

Roy E. Appleman, the foremost historian of the operational aspects of the war, comes to the cautious conclusion that since the UNC forces were never able to seize and hold the entire Iron Triangle and had experienced the utmost difficulty in capturing and retaining the Punchbowl, it was stretching the imagination a bit too much to imagine the Eighth Army, without significant reinforcements, advancing northward in a large-scale offensive to destroy or oust the CCF from North Korea. In view of the facts also that the savage seesaw fighting for Pork Chop Hill, southwest of the Iron Triangle, reached its zenith of ferocity between March and July 1953 and that in June and July that year the II Corps and other elements of the ROK Army were dealt severe setbacks by the enemy, it is difficult to disagree with Appleman on this crucial point.

The United States and its coalition in the war frankly possessed neither the will nor the available manpower to maintain a series of large-scale offensive operations over the long two years from the start to the end of the truce negotiations. If the blood of their young men had to be shed further, the American-led alliance members were agreed that it should be for higher global priorities in more strategically valuable areas. Communism had been contained on the Korean peninsula; that was accomplishment enough.

How different had been the steadfast commitment to all-out victory and the overwhelming manpower and matériel resources of the Grand Alliance in relentlessly pushing toward victory over the Axis powers in World War II. The goals had been noble and the sites of large campaigns of great strategic worth. Korea, however, did not prove so valuable strategically nor even possible to reunite without paying too high a price. On the tactical and technological dimensions, it is true, the Korean conflict would at times seem like an attempt to refight the last war, but at the strategic level it was not the occasion for either side to remove the restraints that had been so carefully emplaced.

# CHAPTER

# 11

# *From Total to Limited War*

### Limits on the Ground War

The limitations imposed on both sides were of various types, consisting of both unilateral and bilateral restrictions and covering ground, sea, and air operations, as well as a host of nonoperational factors. Most were specifically designed to avert general war, but some were forced by enemy moves or by miscellaneous obstacles, such as logistical shortages, terrain or weather difficulties, and adverse public opinion.

One of the most persistent demands of MacArthur from the summer of 1950 until his removal the next spring was to take advantage of the offers of Chiang Kai-shek to use his troops in Korea or in operations against the Chinese mainland. The State Department, along with the British and other Allied governments, strongly believed that the introduction of Nationalist Chinese forces in Korea would help to bring the Communist Chinese into the fray, or if the CCF was already engaged, would cause Peking to commit even more of its estimated 4.5 million troops into the Korean conflict. During the Chinese civil war, moreover, the United States had gradually decreased its support of Chiang's regime from the peak assistance during World War II. Following the Nationalist move to Formosa, State officials had expected the island to be overrun shortly by Mao's forces, and the American relationship to Chiang had become even more tepid. Soon after the Korean hostilities began, Truman had, in effect, set forth a policy of acknowledging two Chinas and of neutralizing Formosa by means of the Seventh Fleet patrol in the Formosa Strait. Among America's coalition members and, indeed, throughout the UN, the use of Nationalist troops in Korea would be viewed as a return by Washington to its close identification with Chiang during the war against Japan.

The JCS, in addition, did not need much persuasion to reject Chiang's offer because, as military chiefs, they were sharply critical of the low state of combat readiness of Chiang's soldiers. Collins testified at the Senate hearings in May 1951 that the Joint Chiefs "were highly skeptical that we would get anything more out of these [Nationalist] Chinese than we were getting out of the South Koreans, because these were the same people that were run off [mainland] China, in the first place."[1] They also foresaw the Nationalist troops causing a heavy drain on American logistics in Korea, which were never adequate to satisfy altogether the supply needs of all the American units and the ROK and Allied forces that were also dependent upon those stores.

Chiang, in turn, clung to several small offshore islands, mainly Quemoy, Matsu, and the Tachens, in the vain hope during the Korean War as well as in the later 1950s, that communist shellings of the islands' garrisons might draw the Seventh Fleet and ultimately more American forces into entanglements with Communist China in those areas. Formosa's strategic location complicated the war's contingencies enough without the addition of Chiang's forces in action in Korea or on the Chinese mainland. Unlike Rhee, Chiang was sufficiently isolated on his island redoubt so that, whatever his discontent about American policy, he had little chance to disrupt the armistice negotiations or to intervene by force on his own.

At Panmunjom on November 27, 1951, the UN and communist truce delegations ratified an agreement that the military demarcation line was to be the line of contact, with a demilitarized zone formed by both armies pulling back two kilometers when the armistice was signed. Combat casualties on both sides had been heavy since July when the truce talks had begun, but now Ridgway, on orders from Washington, kept the UNC ground forces on a short leash, permitting Van Fleet to launch no major ground operations after the agreement on the demarcation line. The casualty rate would reach high levels again at times when one army or the other would try to improve its outpost lines or main defensive positions by seizing certain key points of high terrain, such as the ferocious battles over Pork Chop Hill. But by and large, combat operations were kept at small-unit levels after Panmunjom.

The demarcation issue had been settled principally on terms that the communist side had pushed, with Washington leaders hoping that the UN concession would lead to an armistice soon. This proved illusory, but the UN demarcation gesture and the abandonment of large-scale offensive operations by the UN forces were efforts at restricting the war and hastening a cease-fire that the civilian leaders in Washington appreciated far more than did Van Fleet and his commanders, who felt that their forces were unnecessarily restricted in their operations after November 1951.

While the UN side's refusal to employ Nationalist Chinese forces seems to have been an ameliorating influence on Red China's further escalation of the Korean combat, the deliberate limitation on UN major assaults after the settlement of the demarcation line was not followed by a corresponding willful restriction on the enemy side. Instead, the CCF's offensive possibilities were limited usually by the tremendous artillery and air firepower the UNC could focus upon large preassault assemblies of enemy troops. But willfully or not, the CCF and UNC remained in a stalemate. On only one occasion, the CCF offensive of June 10–July 20, 1953, did the enemy gain considerable ground, and that was achieved against relatively weak ROK forces.

The refusal of the Truman administration to condone any form of American ground operations outside Korea was significant because it apparently signaled Moscow and Peking that the United States was anxious to avoid an expansion that could trigger a global holocaust. On June 27, 1950, when Truman ordered the Seventh Fleet to the Formosa Strait, he ordered more military forces and matériel to the Philippines as well, together with greater military assistance to the French forces in the Indochina war and the dispatch of an American military mission there. Truman and his lieutenants might have decided to contribute more substantial military aid to the French in Indochina, which might have turned the advantage to the French and provoked Red China to divert more aid to the North Vietnamese. In fact, however, America had no viable option of sending considerable aid to the French at the time because logistically the U.S. military establishment was already seriously overextended in meeting its global commitments. Also, upon the strong urging of Britain and others of the UN coalition fighting in Korea, America remained adamant against any ground operations in the Far East outside Korea.

An important corollary to the refusal to send troops into combat beyond Korea's borders was the administration's decision to demonstrate just how severely it was willing to keep the Korean conflict a "police action" by its negligible reinforcements of the UN Command after the first stages of the war. Washington's position was made clearer when the four divisions for which MacArthur had begged were assigned, instead, to Eisenhower's new NATO command in 1951 and no new divisions were assigned to the Korean fighting. (Two National Guard divisions were sent to Korea in the winter of 1951–1952, but in fulfillment of a pledge much earlier to MacArthur.)

Thus the United States sent an emphatic message to the communist powers that, regardless of the fighting under way in Korea, it was not interested in escalating that conflict and that its top global strategic priority remained the containment of Soviet advances in Europe. The limits on the ground war in Korea made it possible for NATO to develop a reasonably strong deterrent to Soviet expansion in West Europe. In essence, the limits on the ground operations in Korea left the United States with more options in deploying its relatively meager forces globally, especially in the security of its key European allies.

## LIMITS ON THE SEA WAR

With its sizable Far East fleet stationed at Vladivostok, the Soviet Union had the capability by loan, lease, or direct dispatch of these vessels to Korean waters of turning the naval operations into high-risk, costly ventures for the UNC. As it was, for reasons of its own, the USSR refrained, and UNC naval functions were important but not comparatively costly adjuncts of the ground fighting. If MacArthur had gotten his wish, however, the naval side of the war would have been greatly accelerated, so much so that his superiors feared a third world war would result.

MacArthur had made two proposals involving naval surface forces that he believed would be useful in pressuring Communist

China to remove its troops from the Korean peninsula: a naval blockade of Communist China and the shelling of targets along the Red Chinese coast. Neither of these was a viable alternative. The blockade was too provocative and would not have been effective without the cooperation of Britain and the USSR. America's allies would not support it. The bombardment along the coast was also deemed unfeasible because there were not enough available combat ships to make an impact. In addition, there was the problem that, though much of Communist China's heavy industry was located in port cities within range of naval guns, it was sparse and most of her military hardware came from the USSR. Moreover, her mainland military and air bases were located largely beyond the reach of naval gunfire. Shelling of the heavily populated Chinese coastal cities would cause widespread civilian casualties, produce reactions of horror in world opinion, and might well anger the Soviet Union into providing more combat aircraft and a submarine fleet to Peking, if not actually entering the war. There was little question in Washington and other Western capitals that such naval action would be widely perceived as a deliberate American step to enlarge the war with Communist China.

The refusal to allow UNC naval operations beyond the Korean combat zone, except in the Formosa Strait, and the decision to reinforce NAVFE rather adequately in the long run but only for Korean and Formosa Strait missions were the main restrictions applied by the United States and its coalition in the naval realm. Beyond that, the Seventh Fleet and the Allied sea units supported ground and air forces in a myriad of ways, ranging from carrier-based air raids to transportation of troops and war matériel. Virtually all of the war's personnel and supplies arrived by sea.

## LIMITS ON THE AIR WAR

Air operations, of course, cannot be separated from the Navy's story in the war because much of the air action was undertaken by carrier aircraft. Much of the following, however, will concern issues of strategic bombing that were mainly in the realm of the ground-based Far East Air Forces. Even at the very beginning of the Korean War, American airmen were complaining about restrictions, a practice that was to become a habit for the remainder of the conflict, though the specific focus of the complaints changed. Throughout the war a variety of aerial limits were deliberately imposed by the American-led alliance. In his diary two days after the outbreak of hostilities, Lieutenant General Earle E. Partridge, head of the Fifth Air Force, was already discontented: "FEAF handicapped in this shooting war by not being permitted to cross the 38th parallel to destroy enemy at its source of staging."[2] This restriction was lifted shortly, but as the hostilities evolved through various phases, numerous other handicaps were added while others were withdrawn. Although a number of important restrictions on UNC air operations had been removed by the end of the war, they were in effect during crucial periods when many airmen were convinced that their lifting could have been conclusive.

One of the most important restrictions which prevented a total refighting of World War II was the unwillingness to employ aerial delivery of nuclear, chemical, and biological weapons. The use of unconventional weapons was considered by the United States at various times during the Korean War, particularly during periods when the UNC forces were on the defensive. As the armistice talks dragged on, the Joint Chiefs studied the possibility of using nuclear, chemical, and biological weapons in the event that the negotiations broke down irrevocably. In December 1950, Prime Minister Attlee's hasty visit to confer with Truman after the latter's suggestion that he would not rule out consideration of any weapons in Korea, however, did not keep Pentagon planners from often mulling contingency situations where nuclear bombs might seem necessary. In the spring of 1953, President Eisenhower let it be known that he was considering the use of nuclear bombs if the communist negotiators at Panmunjom did not agree to an armistice soon, though such intimidation did not appear to figure significantly in the final outcome that summer.

The atomic bomb, or worse, the newly developed hydrogen bomb of late 1952, symbolized the total war that America had finally resorted to against Japan in the Second World War. A major reason it was not used in Korea undoubtedly was because it was such a powerful symbol of total war and thus entirely inappropriate for a limited conflict such as that in Korea. Nuclear warfare was a very sensitive issue with America's partners in the Korean struggle and with the United Nations in general, partly because of the threat of general war but also because of the symbolism and the prospect of using nuclear destruction again on Asian people.

Washington decision-makers concluded that it was questionable whether such unconventional weapons would have been decisive if dropped on the rugged Korean battlegrounds or if used in bombing Red China. Lack of suitable targets, terrain problems, and powerful negative symbolism, as well as the impetus for a Soviet atomic counterstrike, made the "doomsday" bombs only a background emergency consideration in Washington.

According to Air Force General Jack J. Catton, "Available to General MacArthur and later General Ridgway, was the atomic capability of a unit of the 43d Wing, which we put on the island of Guam. . . . We could have had atomic weapons if the President decided to use them. We could have had atomic weapons very reliably and very accurately delivered within a period of about sixteen hours."[3] Another source maintains that nonassembled nuclear weapons were placed aboard an American carrier off Korea in December 1950, and that simulated nuclear air raids were made over Pyongyang, the North Korean capital.[4] On April 6, 1951, five days before MacArthur's dismissal, Truman authorized the Atomic Energy Commission to transfer nine nuclear bombs to the Air Force for possible use in Korea.

As late as May 1953, the Joint Chiefs recommended that if the truce talks were halted and the war expanded, all necessary courses of action against Communist China and North Korea should be pursued, including "extensive strategical and tactical use of atomic bombs."[5] Surely the most important weapons limit by the UNC was its decision not to resort to nuclear warfare.

Charges of UNC aerial attacks using poison gas and germ warfare were hurled by communist negotiators at Panmunjom, as well as through propaganda leaflets and broadcasts from Peking and Pyongyang and speeches before the United Nations in 1952. No evidence of worth was ever forthcoming, however, and both the UNC and Washington vehemently denied the allegations, citing their strict orders against keeping deadly gases or germs in stock. According to the JCS official history, Ridgway, at the time, "suggested three possible motives for this unusually vitriolic propaganda program. The enemy might merely be manufacturing propaganda, either for home consumption . . . or to sway world opinion. He might be putting up a smoke screen to conceal his inability to control epidemics in his territories. . . . Most ominously of all, the enemy might be establishing justification for biological warfare when it appeared advantageous."[6]

Nevertheless, when the JCS studied the possible options for action if the armistice negotiations broke down in the spring of 1953 and hostilities escalated, one of its assumptions was that "chemical, biological, and radiological weapons would not be used except to retaliate."[7] This suggests that by that time there may have been stores of all three of those weapons in the Far East Command. It does appear that if the communists had used any of these types of unconventional warfare, the UNC had the capacity by the spring of 1953 to retaliate in kind. But, afraid of the terrible consequences, they hoped not to resort to these weapons.

Another limitation on air power was the restriction against "hot pursuit," which was chasing enemy aircraft for two or three minutes' flight across the Yalu River over Manchuria. During the autumn of 1950 particularly, many heated messages passed back and forth between Tokyo and Washington regarding such transboundary pursuit. It was an important morale issue to UNC airmen, but it is questionable how militarily significant hot pursuit might have been if allowed. The Joint Chiefs, Truman, Marshall, and Acheson all appeared to agree with MacArthur that limited pursuit of enemy planes across the Manchurian border should be permitted, but America's coalition partners were strongly opposed to it.

Even before China came into the war, the borders of Communist China and the Soviet Union were considered very sensitive by the UNC. Once the Red Chinese entered the conflict, it was very clear to everyone that the bombing of mainland Chinese targets would be a drastic expansion of the hostilities. Communist China was placed off limits for UNC aerial attacks because of fear of Soviet entry into the war; enemy bombing of vulnerable strategic targets like the ports of South Korea or even targets in Japan or Okinawa; strong opposition from America's partners; and concern that American air strength was not adequate to do much serious damage or to absorb heavy losses in attacking Red China.

No aerial campaign against mainland China was undertaken, but in its final report on recommended courses of action if the truce talks collapsed and the war accelerated, the Joint Chiefs in May 1953 proposed to include air and naval operations directly against China and Manchuria. This idea, earlier advanced by MacArthur, was only seriously considered by the JCS after two frustrating years of truce talks and continued, indecisive fighting.

There were also UNC limits on bombing targets along the Yalu River that were felt to be especially sensitive to the Chinese and

Soviets, such as urban centers, bridges, dams, and hydroelectric facilities. At first, certain cities near the Chinese or Soviet borders were forbidden to UNC bombers, notably Sinuiju, North Korea, which lay across the Yalu from Antung, Manchuria, where a complex of Chinese army and air installations was located; and Rashin, which was a port and road-rail hub in northeastern North Korea close to the Soviet border. Later restrictions on attacking both cities were removed.

One of the war's most controversial restrictions forbade UNC aircraft from attacking the north end of Yalu bridges. They had to follow set runs on their small targets without violating the border along the snaking Yalu while facing intense antiaircraft fire from gunners who could aim with confidence about their line of approach. The airmen's problems were compounded by the facts that MiG-15s often rose to intercept them from nearby Manchurian bases; many of the bridges had been sturdily built by the Japanese during their occupation; dropped spans were repaired quickly; pontoon bridges were added to assist in moving the large numbers of CCF units into North Korea; and once winter arrived, the Yalu froze over and the enemy troops could walk across the river during the night when UNC aircraft were usually absent.

Although the UNC strove to limit its aggression, there were times when all attempts at restraint broke down. After gaining the approval that Washington had denied earlier UNC commanders in chief, Clark approved Weyland's request to bomb a number of facilities in North Korea. Beginning in late June 1952, Weyland's FEAF bombers destroyed hydroelectric installations on the Yalu that supplied a considerable amount of the electrical power to North Korea and southern Manchuria. The FEAF bombers then launched a strategic bombing offensive against North Korea that summer which targeted virtually every possible industrial, transportation, or military facility of considerable size in the country, together with a number of irrigation dams that caused extensive flooding. The raids devastated countless nonmilitary structures and civilian dwellings. In the biggest bombing attack of the war, over 1,400 FEAF planes raided Pyongyang on August 29.

The heavy air assault continued on into the autumn of 1952 but without any noticeable effects on the Communist Chinese and North Korean determination to continue the war or their negotiators' wills to persist in obstructing the completion of an armistice agreement at Panmunjom. Except for not violating the Manchurian and Soviet borders and for not hurling even more aircraft into the strategic bombing campaign, the UNC land-based and carrier-based planes exercised no restraint in the summer and autumn of 1952. The massive air assault gradually wound down, largely for want of targets, leaving the North Korean cities and towns in ruins but the defensive entrenchments along the front line almost intact. Air Force leaders were dismayed and felt that further activity of this sort would weaken American air power potential in case of an emergency elsewhere. To conserve air resources, more restraints were imposed until suitable targets could be found.

The ability of the North Korean and Communist Chinese troops to operate with far fewer supplies and to move logistical matériel without great dependence on roads and rail lines was also a crucial factor in handicapping the UNC's air interdiction operations. Not only did the enemy's tactics of dispersing supplies hinder effectiveness, but his unconventional logistical techniques spelled trouble for the conventional war that the UNC ground, air, and sea forces, shaped by their World War II experiences, fought. For the UNC airman, foot soldier, and sailor, the Korean War was a very different war both in its limited and its unconventional nature.

## Other Limits

Besides the limits on ground, sea, and air operations set forth by the UN side, other restrictions did not directly involve command decisions by the UNC. Some limitations on the UNC's combat activities were imposed primarily through the diplomatic dimension. Britain and the Allies exercised great influence on Washington policy-making. The Truman administration did pay careful heed to the views of its partners, especially the British. But there were many decisions by Washington on the direction of the war, both as to its acceleration and limitation, that were unilateral and left the Allies feeling far less than equal members of the coalition. Ultimately, America acted as it wished. Britain's post–World War II dependence on America precluded serious disagreement over Korea.

Meanwhile, in Washington, diplomatic as well as military policy was being decided by the State Department in a notable change from the practices in World War II. Then, the officials at Foggy

Bottom, even Secretary of State Hull, were relegated largely to Western Hemispheric and United Nations matters. The era of the Korean conflict, however, was marked by extremely close ties between the President and his diplomatic advisers. Secretary Acheson, in particular, was given a powerful hand in the making of military strategy and the conduct of the war. There were no major military moves made without extensive consultation with and endorsement by Acheson and his lieutenants.

The enormous shift in influence of the State Department in military affairs had begun with the National Security Act of 1947 and had been strongly demonstrated in 1947–1949 in State's new impact on American programs in occupied Japan, Korea, and Germany. American command decisions in the Korean and Vietnam conflicts normally came down from policy decisions worked out jointly by the White House and the State and Defense departments. Civilian supremacy over the military took on new meaning with the State Department's key roles in the limitations enacted during both those wars. This enhanced position of the State Department in war-making should have meant more attention to political, economic, social, and psychological restraints on the war that transcended the usual realm of command decisions. In the case of the Korean War, it did produce more attention to Allied interests and to postwar consequences, though not to the extent desired by other members of the UN coalition.

President Truman and Congress made conscientious efforts to convey to the enemy, as well as to the all-important "neutral" power, the USSR, that the U.S. government regarded the Korean hostilities as a "police action" in the sense of being a combat situation that did not require a declaration of war against either North Korea or Communist China, that was not seen as a war for survival by America, and that required only partial mobilization. By limiting the war and portraying it in propaganda as a localized conflict, however, the Truman administration sometimes became enmeshed in contradictory moves. The war was alternately portrayed as localized and as the key to the survival or downfall of the Communist Chinese regime itself.

Other restrictions were imposed by the enemy and were fully as significant in averting global war as those laid down by the American-led coalition. Communist China, North Korea, and their background co-belligerent, the Soviet Union, maintained a disciplined form of restrictions and did not wage all-out war any more than the

UNC did. The United States and its coalition were fully aware that both sides were observing mutual restraints.

The Soviets did provide a considerable number of combat aircraft to the Chinese and North Koreans, most formidable of which was the MiG-15 fighter, but the enemy air forces were never large enough to wrest control of the skies over Korea from the FEAF and UNC carrier aircraft. The Soviets simply did not supply enough aircraft for that. Moreover, they never undertook strategic bombing campaigns against the highly vulnerable targets in South Korea, such as the ports of Pusan and Inchon. General Weyland commented, "The outcome of the conflict would have been vastly different had enemy domination of the air reversed the military positions of the Communists and the United Nations Command."[8] In a sobering and lengthy diary entry in October 1950, Stratemeyer reflected on the UNC's benefits from the enemy's restrictions on air warfare:

> We must keep in mind that our home bases in Japan, and even in South Korea, have not been interfered with by enemy air. . . . If there had been an enemy air force [of comparable strength], it is questionable—to my way of thinking—that the ground troops could have ever been supplied by long truck columns and trains as they were from Pusan [operating through the nights with lights on]. . . . All of us must be careful not to draw wrong conclusions from this small, "police action" war. . . . We have had no communications' jamming. . . . We have not considered in all-out night operations the fact that the enemy could well employ night intruders against our light and medium bomber activities.[9]

Besides aerial restraints, the communists did not utilize submarines or major combatant surface ships against the UNC. Such vessels, especially undersea craft, were a source of great anxiety to Joy, Struble, and other Seventh Fleet and Allied commanders— and for sound reasons: Not only was the Soviet submarine fleet large but also the antisubmarine warfare capabilities of NAVFE were unimpressive. Two of the turning points of the war were amphibious operations, Inchon and Hungnam, and both could have been greatly handicapped, if not defeated, by Soviet surface ships and submarines on loan to the North Koreans or Communist Chinese.

Like the United States and its coalition, the communist belligerents did not issue formal declarations of war, perhaps intending to signal that they, too, did not desire an expanded conflict. Indeed, Peking officially identified its troops in action in Korea as "volunteers," claiming that its regular units had not been ordered into the combat.

Like the West, the communist powers made no attempt to initiate operations beyond the borders of Korea. When the Korean War began, the Red Chinese had been busily preparing for an invasion of Formosa, but that operation was suspended once it became apparent the North Korean offensive had failed and Red Chinese intervention would be required to save the Pyongyang regime. If Communist China, with its vast manpower reserves, had obtained Soviet vessels and had gone ahead with its amphibious assault on Formosa, the Seventh Fleet patrol would have become embroiled and other UNC forces from the Korean theater of operations might have been transferred to aid Chiang, creating an unbelievably complex international situation.

Few Chinese ground forces from South and Southwest China appear to have been transferred to Manchuria and North Korea, as were the crack Third and Fourth Field armies of North and East China. It is possible that Chinese troops and war matériel in the southern regions of China, as well as shipments of military equipment and supplies from the Soviet Union, could have been sent to North Vietnam in sufficient strength to enable Ho Chi Minh's forces to turn the tide of battle against the French in 1950–1953 rather than after the Korean War.

If the West had been confronted by local wars in Korea, Formosa, and Indochina simultaneously, it is likely that even the vaunted American production capability would have been unable to maintain effective lines of resupply to all three theaters. Korea undoubtedly would have taken precedence because of the preponderance of strength already in action there, but it would have been a painful dilemma for Washington and Allied leaders to choose between Formosa and Indochina as the next-ranking priority of defense in the Far East. With additional Soviet assistance, the communists could have made the Asian situation much more complicated and menacing for the West.

After the hostilities ceased in Korea, the war gradually came to be accepted as a stalemate by all but the deeply committed on both sides. In the communist camp the faithful boasted that Communist China had emerged as one of the great powers, while in the western camp the true believers saw communist aggression contained and South Korea saved for democracy and capitalism. At a distance from the ideological and emotional aspects of the Korean conflict, the consequences were not so clear. Red China remained an isolated and backward giant but now alienated from the Soviet Union in many spheres of mutual interest; communism flooded into critical areas of Southeast Asia, especially Indochina and Indonesia; North Korea remained primitive and dictatorial, with growing ties to Peking rather than to Moscow; and South Korea learned more about making money than practicing freedom. Both Koreas underwent many years of slow recuperation from the devastation of the war, the ruination matching the worst suffered by any peoples in World War II.

While this strange and ugly limited war at times bore similarities to a microcosmic Second World War, the most remarkable phenomenon of the Korean conflict was the inexplicable communication, neither oral nor written, between implacably hostile camps who signaled restraint to each other. Without a single word of formal agreement they set up an intricate system of limitations amid the fighting of 1950–1953 that kept Korea from becoming the fiery fuse of Sarajevo in 1914 or Poland in 1939. The armed forces of the United States in Korea were supplied with commanders, troops, tactics, weapons, and equipment heavily drawn from World War II. If they had been able to conduct a war as their experience in 1941–1945 prompted them to, it would have been a war of overwhelming firepower and annihilation. Even though restricted to operations on the Korean peninsula, it is likely that in such a war the Communist Chinese and North Korean troops would have been mauled below the Yalu. But it is also probable that a decisive triumph of World War II proportions would have guaranteed the eruption of another and more terrible global war. As it was, the silent agreement on limitations worked, but it was a risk of perilous magnitude. It is astounding that only a decade later a gamble on unspoken limits would be tried again in another Asian war and that the world would be spared once more.

# Notes

## Prologue  *The Last War Revisited*

1. John E. Wiltz, "The MacArthur Inquiry, 1951," in Arthur M. Schlesinger, Jr., and Roger Bruns, eds., *Congress Investigates: A Documented History, 1792–1974* (New York: Chelsea House, 1975) 5: 3632.

## Chapter 1  *Truman: The Right Thing to Do*

1. Robert H. Ferrell, *Harry S. Truman and the Modern American Presidency* (Boston: Little, Brown, 1983), 116.
2. Harry S. Truman, *Off the Record: The Private Papers of Harry S. Truman*, ed. Robert H. Ferrell (New York: Harper and Row, 1980), 188.
3. Harry S. Truman, *Memoirs*, 2 vols. (New York: New American Library, 1965; 1st ed., 1955) 2: 524.
4. Dean G. Acheson, *Present at the Creation: My Years in the State Department* (New York: W. W. Norton, 1969), 405.
5. Truman, *Memoirs* 2: 525.
6. U.S. Joint Chiefs of Staff (JCS), Directive to Gen. of the Army Douglas MacArthur, Sept. 15, 1950, in James F. Schnabel and Robert J. Watson, *The Korean War. The History of the Joint Chiefs of Staff: The Joint Chiefs of Staff and National Policy*, vol. 3 [in 2 pts.] (Wilmington, Del.: Michael Glazier, 1979), 230.
7. Sec. of Defense George C. Marshall to MacArthur, Sept. 29, 1950, Record Group (RG) 6, MacArthur Memorial, Norfolk, Va.
8. MacArthur to Marshall, Sept. 30, 1950, RG 6, MacArthur Memorial.
9. United Nations General Assembly, Resolution on Korea, Oct. 7, 1950, in Raymond Dennett, et al., eds., *Documents on American Foreign Relations* (Princeton, N.J.: Princeton University Press, 1953) 12:459–61.
10. *New York Times*, Jan. 8, 1951.
11. Kozo Yamamura, *Economic Policy in Postwar Japan: Growth versus Economic Democracy* (Berkeley: University of California Press, 1967), 53.
12. Gen. Matthew B. Ridgway to Chief of Staff J. Lawton Collins, Sept. 26, 1951, Matthew B. Ridgway Papers, U.S. Army Military History Institute, Carlisle Barracks, Pa.
13. Quoted in Alvin J. Cottrell and James E. Dougherty, "The Lessons of Korea: War and the Power of Man," *Orbis* 2 (Spring 1958): 55.
14. U. Alexis Johnson, Interview, June 19, 1975, p. 79, Oral History Collection, Harry S. Truman Library, Independence, Mo.

15. U. Alexis Johnson, with J. O. McAllister, *The Right Hand of Power* (Englewood Cliffs, N.J.: Prentice-Hall, 1984), 130.
16. Truman, *Off the Record*, 199; Truman, *Memoirs* 2: 501.
17. Washington *Daily News*, Jan. 25, 1952; Boston *Herald*, Jan. 14, 1952.
18. Clark did not hold the post of Supreme Commander for the Allied Powers, Japan, as MacArthur and Ridgway had, because the Peace Treaty with Japan went into effect in April 1952.
19. Truman, *Memoirs* 2: 514.
20. Mark W. Clark, *From the Danube to the Yalu* (New York: Harper and Row, 1954), 1, 2.
21. Morris J. MacGregor, Jr., *Integration of the Armed Forces, 1940–1965* (Washington, D.C.: Center of Military History, Department of the Army, 1981), 292.
22. Bernard C. Nalty and Morris J. MacGregor, eds., *Blacks in the Military: Essential Documents* (Wilmington, Del.: Scholarly Resources, 1981), 239–40; *Washington Post*, Mar. 6, 1990.
23. Barton J. Bernstein, "The Ambiguous Legacy: Civil Rights," in Barton J. Bernstein, ed., *Politics and Policies of the Truman Administration* (New York: New Viewpoints, 1974; 1st ed., 1970), 297.
24. MacGregor, *Integration of the Armed Forces, 1940–1965*, 617.
25. Ibid., 433.
26. David K. Carlisle to the author, Mar. 29, 1990.
27. Jack D. Foner, *Blacks and the Military in American History: A New Perspective* (New York: Frederick A. Praeger, 1974), 190; Clay Blair, *The Forgotten War: America in Korea, 1950–1953* (New York: Times Books, 1987), 684; Bernard C. Nalty, *Strength for the Fight: A History of Black Americans in the Military* (New York: Free Press, 1986), 258–59. On blacks in the Korean War, see also Richard M. Dalfiume, *Desegregation of the U.S. Armed Forces: Fighting on Two Fronts, 1939–1953* (Columbia: University of Missouri Press, 1969), 201–19.
28. *New York Times*, May 28, 1951.
29. Doris M. Condit, *The Test of War, 1950–1953. History of the Office of the Secretary of Defense*, vol. 2 (Washington, D.C.: Historical Office, Office of the Secretary of Defense, 1988), 493.
30. Interview, author with Gov. W. Averell Harriman, June 20, 1977, Washington, D.C.
31. Quoted in Francis H. Heller, ed., *The Korean War: A 25-Year Perspective* (Lawrence: Regents Press of Kansas, 1977), 231, 235.

## Chapter 2    *MacArthur: The Flawed Military Genius*

1. Samuel E. Morison, *The Liberation of the Philippines: Luzon, Mindanao, and Visaya, 1944–1945. History of the United States Naval Operations in World War II*, vol. 13 (Boston: Little, Brown, 1959), 214.
2. Interview, author with Maj. Gen. John H. Chiles, July 27, 1977, Independence, Mo.

3. Interview, author with Amb. William J. Sebald, July 30, 1971, Naples, Fla.

4. Douglas MacArthur, *A Soldier Speaks: Public Papers and Speeches of General of the Army Douglas MacArthur* (New York: Frederick A. Praeger, 1965), 266–67.

5. MacArthur to Gen. of the Army Dwight D. Eisenhower, Jan. 25, 1946, in U.S. Department of State, *Foreign Relations of the United States [FRUS], 1946* 8: 397.

6. United Nations Security Council, Resolution, July 7, 1950, in *FRUS, 1950* 7: 329.

7. Schnabel and Watson, *Korean War,* 135.

8. MacArthur to Truman, July 11, 1950, RG 7, MacArthur Memorial.

9. Truman to MacArthur, July 12, 1950, RG 7, MacArthur Memorial.

10. *New York Times,* July 9, 1950.

11. Interview, author with Kimpei Shiba, Aug. 19, 1977, Tokyo.

12. Philip LaFollette, *Adventure in Politics: The Memoirs of Philip La Follette,* ed. Donald Young (New York: Holt, Rinehart and Winston, 1970), 891.

13. Daniel E. Barbey, *MacArthur's Amphibious Navy: Seventh Amphibious Force Operations, 1943–1945* (Annapolis, Md.: U.S. Naval Institute, 1969), 232.

14. Interview, author with Turner Catledge, Mar. 25, 1971, Starkville, Miss.; Turner Catledge, *My Life and The Times* (New York: Harper and Row, 1971), 155–56.

15. Gen. of the Army Omar N. Bradley, "Substance of Statements Made at Wake Island Conference on 15 October 1950, Compiled from Notes Kept by the Conferees from Washington," 10–12, Omar N. Bradley File, RG 218, National Archives, Washington, D.C.

16. MacArthur, Far East Command Communiqué No. 12, Nov. 24, 1950, RG 9, MacArthur Memorial; *New York Times,* Nov. 24, 1950.

17. Omar N. Bradley and Clay Blair, *A General's Life: An Autobiography,* (New York: Simon and Schuster, 1983), 526.

18. Joseph C. Goulden, *Korea: The Untold Story of the War* (New York: Times Books, 1982), viii–ix, xxii–xxiii.

19. Lt. Gen. Pedro A. del Valle to Miles Duval, Apr. 30, 1969; del Valle to MacArthur, Dec. 14, 1950, and Feb. 10, 1951, RG 10, MacArthur Memorial.

20. JCS to MacArthur, July 12, 28, 1950, quoted in Schnabel and Watson, *Korean War,* 137–40.

21. U.S. Senate, *Military Situation in the Far East: Hearings . . . to Conduct an Inquiry into the Military Situation in the Far East and the Facts Surrounding the Relief of General of the Army Douglas MacArthur from His Assignments in that Area,* 82nd Cong., 1st Sess., 5 pts. in 2 vols. (Washington, D.C.: U.S. Senate, 1951), 10.

22. Lt. Gen. Matthew B. Ridgway, Memorandum of Conference with Gen. MacArthur, Dec. 26, 1950, Ridgway Papers.

23. U.S. Senate, *Military Situation in the Far East: Hearings,* 41–45, 135–37, 211–12.

24. MacArthur, Address to Joint Meeting of Congress, Apr. 19, 1951, President's Secretary's File, Harry S. Truman Papers, Harry S. Truman Library, Independence, Mo.
25. MacArthur to Maj. Henry A. Grace, June 15, 1956, RG 21, MacArthur Memorial.

## Chapter 3  *Ridgway: From Wolfhound to Koje-do*

1. Matthew B. Ridgway, Interview, Jan. 6, 1972, p. 77, Ridgway Papers. Later Ridgway said he was "an Instructor and Graduate Manager of Athletics" at West Point during MacArthur's superintendency. Gen. Matthew B. Ridgway to author, Apr. 6, 1977.
2. Clay Blair, *Ridgway's Paratroopers: The American Airborne in World War II* (Garden City, N.Y.: Dial Press, 1985), 4.
3. Ridgway, "Troop Leadership at the Operational Level: The Eighth Army in Korea," address, May 9, 1984, U.S. Army Command and Staff College, Ridgway Papers.
4. David Halberstam, *The Best and the Brightest* (Greenwich, Conn.: Fawcett Crest, 1972; 1st ed., 1969), 402.
5. Ridgway, Memorandum for the Record, Aug. 15, 1950, Ridgway Papers.
6. Ridgway, Memorandum for the Record, Aug. 16, 1950, Ridgway Papers.
7. Interview, author with Harriman.
8. Gen. J. Lawton Collins to Ridgway, Dec. 23, 1950, Ridgway Papers.
9. Interview, author with Brig. Gen. Walter F. Winton, Jr., May 31, 1977, Clearwater, Fla.
10. Interview, author with Gen. Frank T. Mildren, May 24, 1977, Beaufort, S.C.
11. Interview, author with Brig. Gen. James H. Lynch, May 25, 1977, Augusta, Ga.
12. Interview, author with Maj. Gen. Ned D. Moore, June 21, 1977, Falls Church, Va.
13. Interview, author with Sec. of the Army Frank Pace, Jr., July 12, 1977, New York, N.Y.
14. Matthew B. Ridgway, with Harold H. Martin, *Soldier: The Memoirs of Matthew B. Ridgway* (New York: Harper, 1956), 204–5.
15. Interview, author with Maj. Gen. James G. Christiansen, Aug. 4, 1971, Columbus, Ga.
16. Gen. J. Lawton Collins, Interview, 1972, p. 336, U.S. Army Military History Institute.
17. Interview, author with Maj. Gen. Gines Perez, May 25, 1977, Columbia, S.C.
18. Interview, author with Lt. Gen. Edward A. Craig, Sept. 3, 1971, El Cajon, Calif.
19. Ridgway, Interview, Aug. 29, 1969, p. 27, Ridgway Papers.
20. Ridgway to Collins, Jan. 8, 1951, Ridgway Papers.
21. Ibid.
22. Interview, author with Gen. John H. Michaelis, June 1, 1977, St. Petersburg, Fla.
23. James F. Schnabel, *Policy and Direction: The First Year. United States Army*

*in the Korean War* (Washington, D.C.: Office of the Chief of Military History, U.S. Army, 1972), 326.

24. J. Lawton Collins, *War in Peacetime: The History and Lessons of Korea* (Boston: Houghton Mifflin, 1969), 253.

25. *New York Times*, Jan. 17, 1950.

26. Matthew B. Ridgway, *The Korean War* (Garden City, N.Y.: Doubleday, 1967), 107.

27. Lt. Gen. Edward M. Almond to Collins, Feb. 28, 1951, Edward M. Almond Papers, U.S. Army Military History Institute.

28. Ridgway, *Soldier*, 223.

29. Ridgway, Memorandum for the Record, Aug. 15, 1950; Gen. James A. Van Fleet, Testimony, Sept. 29, 1954, in U.S. Senate, Committee on the Judiciary, *Interlocking Subversion in Government Departments: Hearings Before the Subcommittee to Investigate the Administration of the Internal Security Act and Other International Security Laws*, 83rd Cong., 2nd Sess. (Washington, D.C.: U.S. Senate, 1954–1955), 2026–27.

30. Interview, author with Lt. Gen. Joseph M. Swing, Aug. 26, 1971, San Francisco, Calif.

31. Ridgway, Interview, Jan. 6, 1972, p. 85.

32. Ridgway, Interview, Mar. 24, 1972, pp. 1–2, Ridgway Papers.

33. Ibid., p. 14.

34. Ridgway, *Korean War*, 203.

35. Ridgway, Interview, Aug. 29, 1969, p. 26.

36. Lt. Gen. George E. Stratemeyer, Diary, entry of May 11, 1951, Office of Air Force History, Washington, D.C.

37. Gen. Otto P. Weyland, Interview, Nov. 19, 1974, pp. 107, 112–13, Air Force Historical Research Center, Maxwell Air Force Base, Montgomery, Ala.

38. Vice Adm. C. Turner Joy to R. D. Markham, Oct. 31, 1951, C. Turner Joy Papers, Naval Historical Center, Washington, D.C.

39. Joy to Vice Adm. Arthur D. Struble, May 19, 1951, Joy Papers.

40. Ridgway, Foreword, in C. Turner Joy, *Negotiating While Fighting: The Diary of Admiral C. Turner Joy at the Korean Armistice Conference*, ed. Allan E. Goodman (Stanford, Calif.: Hoover Institution Press, 1978), vii.

41. Interview, author with Maj. Gen. Edwin K. Wright, Aug. 28, 1971, Monterey, Calif.

42. Maj. Gen. William F. Marquat to MacArthur, Dec. 14, 1951, RG 10, MacArthur Memorial.

43. Ridgway, Interview, Aug. 29, 1969, p. 1.

44. Interview, author with Sebald.

45. Amb. William J. Sebald, Reminiscences, 1977, p. 732, Naval Historical Center.

46. Ridgway, Interview, Apr. 18–19, 1984, p. 9, Ridgway Papers.

47. Schnabel and Watson, *Korean War*, 477.

48. Ibid., 482.

49. Ridgway, *Korean War*, 166.

50. Interview, author with Gen. James A. Van Fleet, May 30, 1977, Polk City, Fla.

51. Billy C. Mossman, *Ebb and Flow, November 1950–July 1951. United States Army in the Korean War* (Washington, D.C.: Center of Military History, 1990), 506.
52. Ridgway, *Korean War*, 183.
53. Walter G. Hermes, *Truce Tent and Fighting Front. United States Army in the Korean War* (Washington, D.C.: Office of the Chief of Military History, United States Army, 1966), 77, 513; Mossman, *Ebb and Flow*, 502.
54. Ridgway, *Korean War*, 204.
55. Schnabel and Watson, *Korean War*, 619.
56. Ridgway, Interview, Apr. 18–19, 1984, p. 21.
57. Interview, author with Maj. Gen. George W. Hickman, Jr., Sept. 4, 1971, Solana Beach, Calif.
58. Edwin O. Reischauer, *Japan: The Story of a Nation* (New York: Alfred A. Knopf, 1970), 239.
59. Collins to Ridgway, May 24, 1951, Ridgway Papers.
60. Ridgway, *Korean War*, 193.
61. Ridgway, Interview, Aug. 29, 1969, p. 70.
62. Sec. of the Army Frank Pace, Jr., to Ridgway, Apr. 23, 1951, Ridgway Papers.
63. Ridgway, Interview, Apr. 18–19, 1984, p. 22.
64. Ibid., p. 20.

## Chapter 4    *Admiral Joy: Commander and Negotiator*

1. U.S. Navy, Office of Information, Biography of Adm. C. Turner Joy, Nov. 20, 1964, Biographical File, Naval Historical Center.
2. Washington *Star*, Aug. 24, 1952.
3. Interview, author with Vice Adm. Felix L. Johnson, July 7, 1971, Leonardtown, Md.
4. Vice Adm. Felix L. Johnson, Reminiscences, 1971–1972, p. 73, Naval Historical Center.
5. Interview, author with Wright.
6. Interview, author with Craig.
7. Ernest J. King and Walter M. Whitehill, *Fleet Admiral Ernest J. King: A Naval Record* (New York: W. W. Norton, 1952), 413.
8. Interview, author with Adm. Arthur D. Struble, June 22, 1971, Chevy Chase, Md.
9. Struble's successors as head of the Seventh Fleet were Vice Adm. Harold M. Martin (March 1951–March 1952), Robert P. Briscoe (March–May 1952), and J. J. (Jocko) Clark (May 1952–July 1953).
10. Vice Adm. C. Turner Joy to Rear Adm. James H. Doyle, Aug. 14, 1951, Joy Papers.
11. Joy to Adm. Forrest P. Sherman, Feb. 22, 1951, Joy Papers.
12. Joy to Horatio W. Turner, Sept. 1, 1950, Joy Papers.
13. James A. Field, Jr., *History of United States Naval Operations: Korea* (Washington, D.C.: Naval History Division, Navy Department, 1962), 341.

14. Malcolm W. Cagle and Frank A. Manson, *The Sea War in Korea* (Annapolis, Md.: U.S. Naval Institute, 1957), 331.
15. Stratemeyer, Diary, entry of July 5, 1950.
16. Field, *United States Naval Operations: Korea*, 388.
17. Stratemeyer, Diary, entry of Aug. 27, 1950.
18. Ibid., entry of Aug. 14, 1950.
19. Joy to Stratemeyer, Sept. 1, Oct. 7, 1950; Stratemeyer to Joy, Aug. 26, 1950; Joy to NAVFE Unit Commanders, Sept. 9, 1950, Joy Papers.
20. Joy to Vice Adm. Felix L. Johnson, Nov. 9, 1950, Joy Papers.
21. Joy to Lt. Gen. O. P. Weyland, May 22, 1952, Joy Papers.
22. Cagle and Manson, *Sea War in Korea*, 73.
23. Richard P. Hallion, *The Naval Air War in Korea* (New York: Zebra Books, 1988; 1st ed., 1986), 139.
24. Cagle and Manson, *Sea War in Korea*, 349.
25. Robert F. Futrell, *The United States Air Force in Korea, 1950–1953* (New York: Duell, Sloan and Pearce, 1961), 52.
26. JCS to MacArthur, Feb. 13, Mar. 27, 1951; MacArthur to JCS, Mar. 25, 1951, RG 9, MacArthur Memorial.
27. Cagle and Manson, *Sea War in Korea*, 70.
28. Joy to Douglas Turner, May 16, 1951, Joy Papers.
29. Joy to Rear Adm. B. W. Decker, Dec. 3, 1950, Joy Papers.
30. "People of the Week," *U.S. News and World Report* 29 (Aug. 4, 1950): 40.
31. Cagle and Manson, *Sea War in Korea*, 151.
32. Field, *United States Naval Operations: Korea*, 367.
33. Joy to Cmdr. Walter Karig, June 19, 1951, Joy Papers.
34. Cagle and Manson, *Sea War in Korea*, 493.
35. Joy to Capt. W. E. Gentner, Dec. 5, 1951, Joy Papers.
36. Ridgway, Memorandum for the File, July 10, 1951, Ridgway Papers.
37. Joy to Rear Adm. A. K. Morehouse, Aug. 9, 1951, Joy Papers.
38. Entry of Oct. 29, 1951, in Joy, *Negotiating While Fighting*, 66.
39. Joy to MacArthur, Jan. 16, 1952, Joy Papers.
40. Joy to Cmdr. O. O. Kessing, Jan. 20, Feb. 24, 1952, Joy Papers.
41. Entry of Dec. 7, 1951, in Joy, *Negotiating While Fighting*, 113.
42. Truman, *Memoirs* 2: 520–21.
43. Joy to Maj. Gen. Laurence C. Craigie, Feb. 26, 1952, Joy Papers.
44. Adm. Arleigh A. Burke, Reminiscences, 1979, vol. 2, p. 96, Naval Historical Center.
45. Hermes, *Truce Tent and Fighting Front*, 117–18.
46. Entry of Nov. 14, 1951, in Joy, *Negotiating While Fighting*, 82–83.
47. Joy to Capt. W. H. Benson, Feb. 27, 1952, Joy Papers.
48. Collins, *War in Peacetime*, 332.
49. Memorandum on State-JCS Meeting, May 21, 1952, in *FRUS, 1952–1954* 15: 214. The principal State representatives at this particular meeting, as well as at most other State-JCS sessions on Korean truce matters, were H. Freeman Matthews, deputy undersecretary of state; John D. Hickerson, assistant secretary of state for United Nations affairs; Paul H. Nitze, director of the Policy

Planning Staff; Howland H. Sargeant, assistant secretary of state for public affairs; U. Alexis Johnson, deputy assistant secretary of state for Far Eastern affairs; and Charles E. Bohlen, counselor of the Department of State. Matthews headed the State Department contingent at the above meeting.

50. Entry of Nov. 10, 1951, in Joy, *Negotiating While Fighting*, 77.
51. Entries of Feb. 16, 18, 1952, in ibid., 257, 260.
52. Joy to Adm. Arthur W. Radford, Dec. 9, 1951, Joy Papers.
53. Entry of Dec. 11, 1951, in Joy, *Negotiating While Fighting*, 117.
54. Schnabel and Watson, *Korean War*, 585–87.
55. Ibid., 595–96.
56. Truman, *Memoirs* 2: 521.
57. C. Turner Joy, *How Communists Negotiate* (New York: Macmillan, 1955), 152.
58. Entry of Feb. 14, 1952, in Joy, *Negotiating While Fighting*, 251.
59. Ibid., 253.
60. Entry of Apr. 29, 1952, in ibid., 388.
61. Joy, *How Communists Negotiate*, 160.
62. Ibid., 177.
63. Joy to Gen. Mark W. Clark, May 19, 1952, in *FRUS, 1952–1954* 15: 209.
64. Entry of May 22, 1952, in Joy, *Negotiating While Fighting*, 437.

## Chapter 5    *Clark: The Fading of Glory*

1. Martin Blumenson, *Mark Clark* (New York: Congdon and Weed, 1984), 261.
2. Ibid., 285.
3. Collins to Ridgway, May 24, 1951, Ridgway Papers.
4. Clark, *From the Danube to the Yalu*, 143–44.
5. Ibid., 144.
6. Rutherford M. Poats, *Decision in Korea* (New York: McBride, 1954), 228.
7. Blumenson, *Mark Clark*, 283, 284.
8. Interview, author with Maj. Gen. Frank H. Britton, July 28, 1971, Largo, Fla.
9. Gen. Mark W. Clark, Interview, 1972, pp. 79, 106, U.S. Army Military History Institute.
10. Lt. Gen. Glenn O. Barcus, Interview, Aug. 10–13, 1976, p. 141, Air Force Historical Research Center.
11. Clark, Interview, 1972, pp. 98, 99.
12. T. R. Fehrenbach, *This Kind of War: A Study in Unpreparedness* (New York: Macmillan, 1963), 576.
13. Clark, *From the Danube to the Yalu*, 33.
14. Schnabel and Watson, *Korean War*, 768–69.
15. Interview, author with Brig. Gen. Edwin A. Zundel, May 29, 1977, Sarasota, Fla.
16. Hermes, *Truce Tent and Fighting Front*, 243, 253, 254.
17. Donald Knox, *The Korean War: An Oral History*, vol. 2: *Uncertain Victory* (San Diego: Harcourt Brace Jovanovich, 1988), 426.

18. Robert Murphy, *Diplomat Among Warriors* (New York: Doubleday, 1964), 348.
19. Clark, *From the Danube to the Yalu*, 93–94.
20. Hermes, *Truce Tent and Fighting Front*, 333.
21. Murphy, *Diplomat Among Warriors*, 354.
22. Schnabel and Watson, *Korean War*, 901, 902.
23. Hermes, *Truce Tent and Fighting Front*, 276.
24. Maxwell D. Taylor, *Swords and Plowshares* (New York: W. W. Norton, 1972), 135–36.
25. Hermes, *Truce Tent and Fighting Front*, 431–32.
26. Clark, Interview, 1973, pp. 5, 17, U.S. Army Military History Institute.
27. Hermes, *Truce Tent and Fighting Front*, 456.
28. Ibid., 458.
29. Blumenson, *Mark Clark*, 268.
30. Murphy, *Diplomat Among Warriors*, 359–60.
31. Fehrenbach, *This Kind of War*, 651–52.
32. Clark, Interview, 1972, p. 12.
33. Clark, *From the Danube to the Yalu*, 233.
34. Richard Whelan, *Drawing the Line: The Korean War, 1950–1953* (Boston: Little, Brown, 1990), 358.
35. Schnabel and Watson, *Korean War*, 937.
36. Clark, *From the Danube to the Yalu*, 90, 91.
37. Weyland, Interview, 1974, pp. 124–25.
38. Clark, Interview, 1972, p. 113.
39. Callum A. MacDonald, *Korea: The War Before Vietnam* (New York: Free Press, 1986), 224–25.
40. Hermes, *Truce Tent and Fighting Front*, 389.
41. Taylor, *Swords and Plowshares*, 140.
42. Ibid., 137.
43. Clark, *From the Danube to the Yalu*, 91, 92.
44. William Reitzel, *United States Foreign Policy, 1945–1955* (Washington, D.C.: Brookings Institution, 1956), 260.
45. Clark, Interview, 1972, pp. 12, 13.
46. Quoted in Harry J. Middleton, *Compact History of the Korean War* (New York: Hawthorn Books, 1965), 223.
47. Clark, Interview, 1972, p. 103.
48. Burton I. Kaufman, *The Korean War: Challenges in Crisis, Credibility, and Command* (New York: Alfred A. Knopf, 1986), 355.
49. Clark, Interview, 1972, p. 106.
50. Ibid., p. 104.
51. Rosemary Foot, *A Substitute for Victory: The Politics of Peacemaking at the Korean Armistice Talks* (Ithaca, N.Y.: Cornell University Press), 211.
52. Schnabel and Watson, *Korean War*, 881.
53. Hermes, *Truce Tent and Fighting Front*, 321.
54. MacDonald, *Korea*, 240.
55. Weyland, Interview, 1971, Air Force Historical Research Center.
56. Clark, *From the Danube to the Yalu*, 73.

57. Max Hastings, *The Korean War* (New York: Simon and Schuster, 1987), 269.
58. Schnabel and Watson, *Korean War,* 926.
59. Clark, *From the Danube to the Yalu,* 71.
60. Clark, Interview, 1972, p. 100.
61. Clark, *From the Danube to the Yalu,* 100–101.
62. Harry G. Summers, Jr., *Korean War Almanac* (New York: Facts on File, 1990), 208.
63. Clark, *From the Danube to the Yalu,* 79.
64. Taylor, *Swords and Plowshares,* 141–42.
65. Whelan, *Drawing the Line,* 367.
66. Taylor, *Swords and Plowshares,* 146.
67. Quoted in Hermes, *Truce Tent and Fighting Front,* 477.
68. Robert Leckie, *Conflict: The History of the Korean War, 1950–1953* (New York: G. P. Putnam, 1962), 385.
69. Blumenson, *Mark Clark,* 271.
70. Clark, *From the Danube to the Yalu,* 317.

## Chapter 6   *Sending Americans to Fight in Korea*

1. Amb. John J. Muccio, Interview, Dec. 27, 1973, pp. 14–15, Oral History Collection, Truman Library.
2. Schnabel and Watson, *Korean War,* 13.
3. Ibid., 17.
4. Schnabel, *Policy and Direction,* 50.
5. *New York Times,* Mar. 2, 1949.
6. Quoted in D. Clayton James, *The Years of MacArthur,* 3 vols. (Boston: Houghton Mifflin, 1970–1985) 3: 402.
7. Bradley and Blair, *General's Life,* 526.
8. James, *Years of MacArthur* 3: 69, 412–13; Schnabel, *Policy and Direction,* 52–60; Schnabel and Watson, *Korean War,* 41–46; James A. Huston, *The Sinews of War: Army Logistics, 1771–1953* (Washington, D.C.: Office of the Chief of Military History, U.S. Army, 1966), 615–19; Walter S. Poole, *The History of the Joint Chiefs of Staff: The Joint Chiefs of Staff and National Policy,* vol. 4, *1950–1952* (Washington, D.C.: Historical Division, Joint Chiefs of Staff, 1979), 120, 133.
9. Collins, *War in Peacetime,* 4.
10. Bradley and Blair, *General's Life,* 529.
11. James, *Years of MacArthur* 3: 412.
12. Richard H. Rovere, *Senator Joe McCarthy* (New York: John Wiley, 1959), 134.
13. Charles E. Bohlen, *Witness to History, 1929–1969* (New York: W. W. Norton, 1973), 300, 302.
14. Glenn D. Paige, *1950: Truman's Decision: The United States Enters the Korean War* (New York: Chelsea House, 1970), 73.
15. Collins, *War in Peacetime,* 22.
16. Roy K. Flint, "The Tragic Flaw: MacArthur, The Joint Chiefs, and the Korean War" (Ph.D. dissertation, Duke University, 1975), 85.

17. Collins, *War in Peacetime*, 22.

18. Truman, *Memoirs* 2: 390.

19. Ibid., 391.

20. JCS to MacArthur, June 30, 1950, RG 6, MacArthur Memorial.

21. Sen. Kenneth S. Wherry, Senate Speech, June 30, 1950, in Paige, *1950: Truman's Decision*, 164.

22. Heller, *Korean War*, 105, 107.

23. Truman, Press Statement, June 30, 1950, in Harry S. Truman, *Public Papers of the Presidents of the United States: Harry S. Truman, 1950* (Washington, D.C.: U.S. Government Printing Office, 1965), 513.

24. JCS to MacArthur, June 30, 1950, RG 6, MacArthur Memorial.

25. See especially the six options cited in Richard E. Neustadt and Ernest R. May, *Thinking in Time: The Uses of History for Decision-Makers* (New York: Free Press, 1986).

26. Clay Blair, "Remembering the Forgotten War," MS paper presented to Carnegie Council on Ethics and International Affairs, New York, N.Y., June 22, 1988. Original in possession of the author.

27. George, "American Policy-Making and the North Korean Aggression," 210–17.

28. A provocative study of the ethnocentric and racial aspects of the Korean War needs to be undertaken; its model might well be John W. Dower, *War Without Mercy: Race and Power in the Pacific War* (New York: Pantheon Books, 1986).

29. See Edward J. Marolda, "Invasion Patrol: The Seventh Fleet in Chinese Waters," in Edward J. Marolda, ed., *A New Equation: Chinese Intervention into the Korean War* (Washington, D.C.: Naval Historical Center, 1991), 13–27.

30. James M. Burns, *Roosevelt: The Soldier of Freedom* (New York: Harcourt, Brace, Jovanovich, 1970), 366, 427–29.

## Chapter 7   *MacArthur's Grand Obsession: Inchon*

1. James L. Stokesbury, *A Short History of the Korean War* (New York: William Morrow, 1988), 61.

2. Robert D. Heinl, *Victory at High Tide: The Inchon-Seoul Campaign* (Philadelphia: J. B. Lippincott, 1968), 3.

3. Gen. Lemuel C. Shepherd, Jr., Oral Reminiscences, 1967, p. 147, Marine Corps Historical Center, Washington, D.C.

4. Lt. Gen. Edward M. Almond, Testimony, Nov. 23, 1954, in U.S. Senate, Committee on the Judiciary, *Interlocking Subversion in Government Departments: Hearings . . .* , pp. 2060–61.

5. Douglas MacArthur, *Reminiscences* (New York: McGraw-Hill, 1964), 333, 334.

6. MacArthur to JCS, June 30, 1950, RG 7, MacArthur Memorial.

7. Beverly Smith, "The White House Story: Why We Went to War in Korea," *Saturday Evening Post* 224 (Nov. 10, 1951): 88; JCS to MacArthur, June 30, 1950, RG 6, MacArthur Memorial; Joint Chiefs of Staff, "Record of Actions

Taken by the Joint Chiefs of Staff Relative to the United Nations Operations in Korea from 25 June to 11 April 1951," CCS 013.36 (4-20-51), RG 218, National Archives, Washington, D.C.

8. Acheson, *Present at the Creation*, 413.
9. Collins, *War in Peacetime*, 81.
10. MacArthur to JCS, July 23, 1950, RG 9, MacArthur Memorial.
11. Maj. Gen. Edward M. Almond, "Notes on the Commander-in-Chief's Conference on Military Operations in Korea and Formosa [Aug. 8, 1950]," RG 6, MacArthur Memorial.
12. Ridgway, Memorandum on Tokyo Conference, 8 August 1950, Ridgway Papers.
13. Interview, author with Harriman.
14. Almond, "Notes on the Commander-in-Chief's Conference on Military Operations in Korea [Aug. 21, 1950]," RG 6, MacArthur Memorial.
15. Lynn Montross, et al., *U.S. Marine Operations in Korea, 1950–1953*, 5 vols. (Washington, D.C.: Historical Branch, U.S. Marine Corps, 1954–1972) 2: 39; Schnabel, *Policy and Direction*, 148; Andrew C. Geer, *The New Breed: The Story of the U.S. Marines in Korea* (New York: Harper, 1952), 110–13.
16. Interview, author with Lt. Gen. Edward M. Almond, Aug. 4, 1971, Anniston, Ala.; Lt. Gen. Edward M. Almond, Oral Reminiscences, Mar. 28, 1975, pt. 4, pp. 38–41, Almond Papers; Maj. Gen. Edward M. Almond, "Notes on the Commander-in-Chief Conference [Aug. 23, 1950]," RG 6, MacArthur Memorial; James, *Years of MacArthur* 3: 466–71; Collins, *War in Peacetime*, 123–27; H. Pat Tomlinson, "Inchon: The General's Decision" *Military Review* 47 (Apr. 1967): 30–32; Walter Karig, Malcolm C. Cagle, and Frank A. Manson, *Battle Report: The War in Korea; Prepared from Official Sources* (New York: Farrar and Rinehart, 1952), 166–69; Arthur W. Radford, *From Pearl Harbor to Vietnam: The Memoirs of Admiral Arthur W. Radford*, ed. Stephen Jurika, Jr. (Stanford, Calif.: Hoover Institution Press, 1980), 230–37.
17. MacArthur, *Reminiscences*, 349–50.
18. Heinl, *Victory at High Tide*, 42.
19. MacArthur, *Reminiscences*, 350.
20. JCS to MacArthur, Aug. 29, 1950, RG 6, MacArthur Memorial.
21. MacArthur to JCS, Sept. 5, 1950, RG 6, MacArthur Memorial.
22. JCS to MacArthur, Sept. 7, 1950, RG 6, MacArthur Memorial.
23. MacArthur, *Reminiscences*, 351.
24. MacArthur to JCS, Sept. 8, 1950, RG 6, MacArthur Memorial.
25. MacArthur, *Reminiscences*, 352; JCS to MacArthur, Sept. 8, 1950, RG 6, MacArthur Memorial.
26. MacArthur to Cmdr. Malcolm W. Cagle, Mar. 19, 1956, Naval Historical Center; Radford, *From Pearl Harbor to Vietnam*, 238; MacArthur, *Reminiscences*, 352.
27. Lynn D. Smith, "A Nickel After a Dollar," *Army* 20 (Sept. 1970): 25, 32–34.
28. Pres. Harry S. Truman to MacArthur, Sept. 29, 1950, in U.S. Senate, Committees on Armed Services and Foreign Relations, *Military Situation in the Far East: Hearings*, p. 3482.
29. JCS to MacArthur, Sept. 29, 1950, quoted in Roy E. Appleman, *South to the*

*Naktong, North to the Yalu. United States Army in the Korean War* (Washington, D.C.: Office of the Chief of Military History, Department of the Army, 1961), 538.

30. Collins, *War in Peacetime*, 485.
31. Ridgway, *Korean War*, 62.
32. Karig, Cagle, and Manson, *Battle Report*, 298.
33. Bradley and Blair, *General's Life*, 568.
34. Ibid., 567, 568.

## Chapter 8    *The Liberation of North Korea*

1. John M. Allison to Asst. Sec. of State Dean Rusk, July 1, 1950, in *FRUS, 1950* 7: 272.
2. United Nations Security Council, Resolution, June 27, 1950, in ibid., 211.
3. Quoted in E. Lloyd Murphy, *The U.S./UN Decision to Cross the 38th Parallel, October 1950: A Case Study of Changing Objectives in Limited War* (Montgomery, Ala.: Air War College, 1968), 28.
4. Truman, Broadcast to the Nation, Sept. 1, 1950, in Truman, *Public Papers, 1950*, 231–32.
5. NSC 81/1, United States Courses of Action with Respect to Korea, Sept. 9, 1950, in *FRUS, 1950* 7: 712–21.
6. JCS to MacArthur, Sept. 27, 1950, in ibid., 781–82.
7. Marshall to MacArthur, Sept. 29, 1950, in ibid., 826.
8. MacArthur to Marshall, Sept. 30, 1950, RG 6, MacArthur Memorial.
9. Charles A. Willoughby and John Chamberlain, *MacArthur: 1941–1951* (New York: McGraw-Hill, 1954), 352; Schnabel, *Policy and Direction*, 63–64.
10. Willoughby and Chamberlain, *MacArthur*, 386.
11. Allen S. Whiting, *China Crosses the Yalu: The Decision to Enter the Korean War* (New York: Macmillan, 1960), 62–63.
12. Ibid., 108.
13. *FRUS, 1950* 7: 839, 848–52, 858–59, 864–77; K. M. Panikkar, *In Two Chinas: Memoirs of a Diplomat* (London: Allen and Unwin, 1955), 109–13.
14. Bradley, "Substance of Statements Made at Wake Island Conference on 15 October 1950," 10–11.
15. United Nations General Assembly, Resolution on Korea, Oct. 7, 1950, in *FRUS, 1950* 7: 904.
16. JCS, "Record of Actions," 46.
17. Schnabel and Watson, *Korean War*, 262.
18. Willoughby and Chamberlain, *MacArthur*, 386.
19. JCS, "Record of Actions," 48, 49.
20. Quoted in Robert J. Donovan, *Tumultuous Years: The Presidency of Harry S. Truman, 1949–1953* (New York: W. W. Norton, 1982), 284.
21. Robert Sherrod, "The General Rose at Dawn," *Time* 56 (Oct. 23, 1950): 20.
22. Acheson, *Present at the Creation*, 456.
23. MacArthur to Maj. Gen. E. W. Snedeker, Feb. 24, 1956, RG 21, MacArthur Memorial.
24. Truman, *Off the Record*, 196, 199.

25. Acheson to Amb. John J. Muccio, Oct. 21, 1950, in *FRUS, 1950* 7: 987.
26. MacArthur to JCS, Oct. 22, 1950, in ibid., 991–92; JCS, "Record of Actions," 50.
27. Lt. Gen. Walton H. Walker to MacArthur, Nov. 6, 1950, RG 9, MacArthur Memorial.

## Chapter 9    *MacArthur's Dare Is Called*

1. Collins, *War in Peacetime*, 177.
2. MacArthur to JCS, Oct. 24, 1950, RG 9, MacArthur Memorial.
3. JCS to MacArthur, Oct. 24, 1950, ibid.
4. MacArthur to JCS, Oct. 25, 1950, ibid.
5. Schnabel and Watson, *Korean War*, 276.
6. U.S. Senate, *Military Situation in the Far East: Hearings*, 1300.
7. Collins, *War in Peacetime*, 180.
8. JCS to MacArthur, Nov. 8, 1950, in *FRUS, 1950* 7: 1098; MacArthur to JCS, Nov. 9, 1950, in ibid., 1108.
9. Dean G. Acheson, *The Korean War* (New York: W. W. Norton, 1969), 68.
10. Bradley and Blair, *General's Life*, 597.
11. Richard E. Neustadt, *Presidential Power: The Politics of Leadership* (New York: John Wiley, 1960), 128.
12. JCS to MacArthur, Nov. 24, 1950, in *FRUS, 1950* 7: 1223–24.
13. MacArthur to JCS, Nov. 25, 1950, in ibid, 1231, 1233.
14. *New York Times*, Nov. 24, 25, 1950; MacArthur, Communiqué No. 12, Nov. 24, 1950, RG 9, MacArthur Memorial.
15. MacArthur to JCS, Nov. 28, 1950, ibid.
16. MacArthur to JCS, Nov. 7, 1950, ibid.
17. MacArthur to JCS, Dec. 30, 1950, Ridgway Papers.
18. MacArthur, Memorandum on Formosa, June 14, 1950, John Foster Dulles Papers, Seeley G. Mudd Library, Princeton University, Princeton, N.J.
19. Truman, *Memoirs* 2: 405.
20. JCS to MacArthur, Dec. 6, 1950, Official Files, Harry S. Truman Papers, Truman Library.
21. Truman, *Memoirs* 2: 492.
22. MacArthur, Memorandum on Ending the Korean War, Dec. 14, 1952, Ann Whitman Files, Dwight D. Eisenhower Papers, Dwight D. Eisenhower Library, Abilene, Kan.
23. Truman, Press Conference, Nov. 30, 1950, in Truman, *Public Papers, 1950*, 726–27.
24. Quoted in Goulden, *Korea*, xxv.
25. Morison, *The Liberation of the Philippines*, 214.
26. Truman, *Memoirs* 1: 520–21.
27. Marshall, Testimony, May 7, 1951, in U.S. Senate, *Military Situation in the Far East: Hearings*, 325.
28. MacArthur, Public Statement to the CCF Commander in Chief, Mar. 24, 1951, David D. Lloyd Files, Truman Papers.

29. Truman to George M. Elsey, Apr. 16, 1951, George M. Elsey Papers, Truman Library.
30. Acheson, *Korean War*, 102.
31. MacArthur to Rep. Joseph W. Martin, Jr., Mar. 20, 1951, Official Files, Truman Papers.
32. MacArthur, Testimony, May 4, 1951, in U.S. Senate, *Military Situation in the Far East: Hearings*, 113.
33. Truman, *Off the Record*, 210.
34. Acheson, *Korean War*, 103.
35. Gen. of the Army Omar N. Bradley, Memorandum for the Record, Apr. 24, 1951, Omar N. Bradley Papers, U.S. Army Military History Institute.
36. U.S. Senate, *Military Situation in the Far East: Hearings*, 26, 27, 282, 283, 289.
37. Ibid., 30, 39, 45, 68.
38. Ibid., 13, 166, 283.
39. For a revealing study of White House mail about MacArthur's dismissal, covering April 11–May 8, 1951, see Merne A. Harris, "The MacArthur Dismissal: A Study in Political Mail" (Ph.D. dissertation, University of Iowa, 1966). The mail favored Truman by early May.
40. This section is based heavily on the author's interviews with the following: Lt. Gen. Edward M. Almond, Aug. 4, 1971, Anniston, Ala.; Lt. Gen. Alpha L. Bowser, Sept. 3, 1971, San Diego, Calif.; Col. Laurence E. Bunker, July 12, 1971, Wellesley Hills, Mass.; Maj. Gen. John H. Chiles, July 27, 1977, Independence, Mo.; Gen. J. Lawton Collins, Aug. 30, 1967, and June 15, 1971, Washington, D.C.; Lt. Gen. Edward A. Craig, Sept. 3, 1971, El Cajon, Calif.; Gen. of the Army Dwight D. Eisenhower, Aug. 29, 1967, Gettysburg, Pa.; Gov. W. Averell Harriman, June 20, 1977, Washington, D.C.; Amb. Philip C. Jessup, July 14, 1977, Norfolk, Conn.; Under Sec. of State U. Alexis Johnson, June 24, 1971, Washington, D.C.; Deputy Under Sec. of State H. Freeman Matthews, June 15, 1977, Washington, D.C.; Sec. of the Army Frank Pace, Jr., July 12, 1977, New York; Amb. William J. Sebald, July 30, 1971, Naples, Fla.; Gen. Oliver P. Smith, Aug. 25, 1971, Los Altos, Calif.; Mrs. George E. Stratemeyer, July 27, 1971, Winter Park, Fla.; Adm. Arthur D. Struble, June 22, 1971, Chevy Chase, Md.; Gen. James A. Van Fleet, May 30, 1977, Polk City, Fla.; Gen. Albert C. Wedemeyer, July 6, 1971, Boyds, Md.; Maj. Gen. Courtney Whitney, Aug. 28–29, 1967, Washington, D.C.; Maj. Gen. Charles A. Willoughby, Aug. 28, 1967, Washington, D.C., and July 30, 1971, Naples, Fla.; Maj. Gen. Edwin K. Wright, Aug. 28, 1971, Monterey, Calif.
41. Acheson, *Korean War*, 111.
42. MacArthur, *Reminiscences*, 395.

## Chapter 10 *Try for Victory or Settle for an Armistice?*

1. JCS to Marshall, Mar. 27, 1951, in *FRUS, 1951* 7: 286.
2. Schnabel and Watson, *Korean War*, 477.

3. Ridgway, *Korean War*, 162.
4. Schnabel, *Policy and Direction*, 384–85.
5. Edgar O'Ballance, *The Red Army of China: A Short History* (London: Faber and Faber, 1962), 199–200.
6. Schnabel and Watson, *Korean War*, 491, 492.
7. Memorandum Containing the Sections Dealing with Korea from NSC 48/5, May 17, 1951, in *FRUS, 1951* 7: 440.
8. Schnabel, *Policy and Direction*, 393.
9. Memorandum on State-JCS Meeting, May 29, 1951, in *FRUS, 1951* 7: 471–72.
10. JCS to Ridgway, May 31, 1951, in *FRUS, 1951* 7: 489–90.
11. Memorandum on State-JCS Meeting Regarding a Korean Armistice, June 28, 1951, in *FRUS, 1951* 7: 571.
12. Mossman, *Ebb and Flow*, 502.
13. Gen. James A. Van Fleet, Testimony, Mar. 5, 6, 10, 1953, in U.S. Senate, Committee on Armed Services, 83rd Cong., 1st Sess., *Ammunition Supplies in the Far East: Hearings* . . . , 11, 31, 46, 108. Actually the earliest recorded protest by a senior American leader was that of Gen. Vandenberg, the Air Force chief of staff, in a joint meeting of high-ranking Pentagon and State officials on June 28, 1951. He said that he was "unalterably opposed" to a recommendation for Ridgway to send a message to the enemy command proposing a meeting regarding an armistice.
14. James A. Van Fleet, "The Truth About Korea: From a Man Now Free to Speak," *Life* 34 (May 11, 1953): 127, 132.
15. Joy to Capt. C. D. Smith, Sept. 21, 1951, Joy Papers.
16. Joy, *How Communists Negotiate*, 166, 176, 177.
17. Almond to Van Fleet, Sept. 30, 1954, Almond Papers.
18. Almond, "Review of the Manuscript 'Policy and Direction: The First Year,'" Feb. 20, 1969, Almond Papers.
19. MacArthur, Address to Congress, Apr. 19, 1951, RG 10, MacArthur Memorial.
20. MacArthur, *Reminiscences*, 390.
21. Clark, *From the Danube to the Yalu*, 80.
22. Bernard Brodie, *War and Society* (New York: Macmillan, 1973), 93–94, 95, 105.
23. Ridgway, *Soldier*, 219–20.
24. Acheson, *Korean War*, 116.
25. Herbert S. Morrison to Acheson, May 10, 1951, in *FRUS, 1951* 7: 427.
26. Foot, *Substitute for Victory*, 39–40.

## Chapter 11  *From Total to Limited War*

1. Collins, Testimony, May 26, 1951, in U.S. Senate, Committees on Armed Services and Foreign Relations, 82nd Cong., 1st Sess., "Hearings on the Military Situation in the Far East: Transcript Deletions of Classified Testimony," 3217, copy in Special Collections Department, Mitchell Memorial Library, Mississippi State University, Mississippi State, Miss.
2. Lt. Gen. Earle E. Partridge, Diary, entry of June 27, 1950, Office of Air Force History.

3. Quoted in Richard H. Kohn and Joseph P. Harahan, eds., *Strategic Air Warfare: An Interview with Generals Curtis E. LeMay, Leon W. Johnson, David A. Burchinal, and Jack J. Catton* (Washington, D.C.: Office of Air Force History, 1988), 91.
4. Goulden, *Korea*, xxv. No source is given by Goulden.
5. Schnabel and Watson, *Korean War*, 961.
6. Ibid., 810–11.
7. Ibid., 950.
8. Quoted in Futrell, *United States Air Force in Korea*, 647.
9. Stratemeyer, Diary, entry of Oct. 2, 1950.

# Index

Chinese Nationalist troop
involvement, possible, 49,
105, 110, 124, 144, 202–4,
232–34
Formosa Patrol Force (Task
Force 72) interdiction of, 84,
87, 142, 154, 184, 203, 233,
234, 236, 244
invasion of Formosa, possible,
143, 244
MacArthur's visit to, 163,
204
strategic value of Formosa, 87,
203–4
Forrestal, James V., 13
Fox, Alonzo P. (Pat), 69–70
France, Korean War and, 122.
*See also individual military
units*
liberation of North Korea and,
182

Gavin, James M., 57
Great Britain, Korean War and,
5, 120, 122, 235–37, 241.
*See also individual military
units*
Chinese intervention and,
201, 203, 232
contributions to the war effort,
17, 147, 150–51, 186, 190
liberation of North Korea and,
181, 182, 186, 199–200
nuclear weapons, possible use
of, 206
truce talks and, 230
Great Debate, 19, 205
Greece, Korean War and,
64
Gruenther, Alfred M. 55,
77

Haislip, Wade H., 67, 77
Halsey, William F., 40
Harriman, W. Averell, 192
decision to involve U.S., 144,
145
Inchon landing and, 163, 164
influence on Truman, 18, 20,
23, 28
MacArthur and, 23, 163, 164,
210–12, 215
Ridgway and, 55–56, 223
Harrison, William K., Jr., 93
truce talks and, 97, 110, 114,
115, 121
Heartbreak Ridge, 74
Herren, Thomas W., 124
Hickerson, John D., 142, 253
Hickey, Doyle O., 66, 70, 94,
100, 170
Clark and, 108
Inchon landing and, 166, 167,
173
MacArthur and, 166, 167,
173
Hickman, George W., Jr., 76–
77
Hill 440, 63
Hirohito, emperor of Japan, 36
Hitler, Adolf, 11, 16, 146, 149,
150
Ho Chi Minh, 244
Hodes, Henry I., 92–93, 96
Hoover, Herbert C., 34
Hopkins, Harry L., 135–36
Hull, Cordell, 136, 242
Hull, John E., 99–100
Hungnam, 82, 87, 89, 243
Hwachon Reservoir, 223

Inchon landing (Operation
Bluehearts, Operation